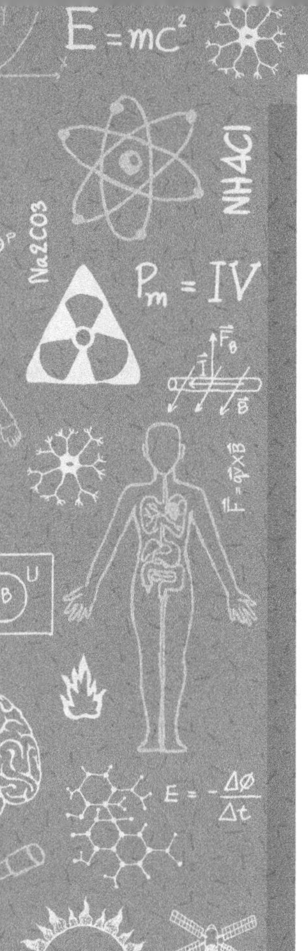
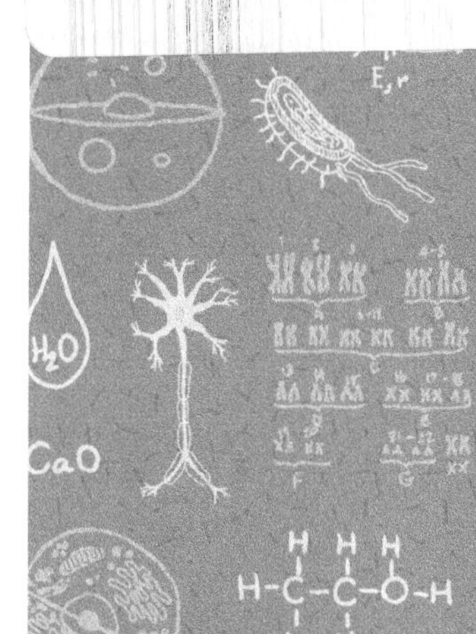
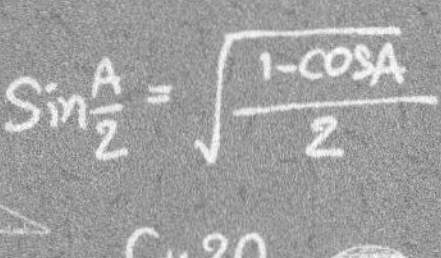

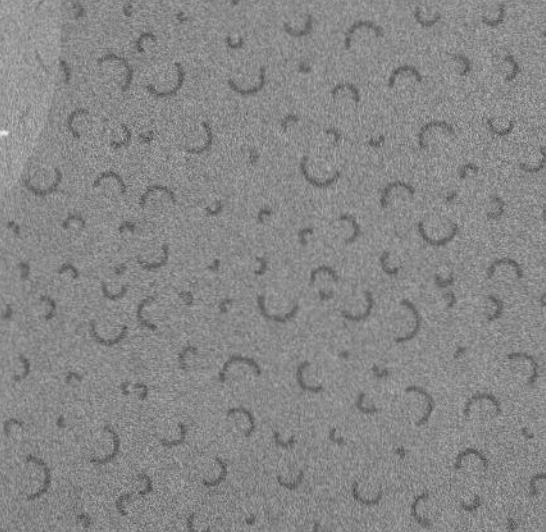
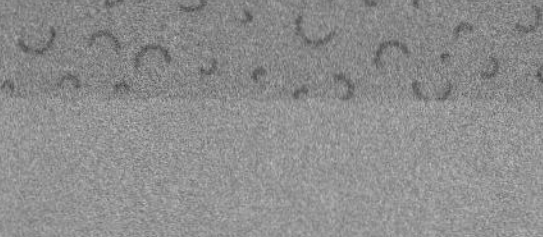

OSWAL – GURUKUL

CBSE CLASS XII

SAMPLE
QUESTION PAPERS

2021 EXAMINATION

MATHEMATICS

New Sample Question Paper
Released by CBSE in Sept 2021
(Fully Solved)

BY
PANEL OF AUTHORS

DISCLAIMER

With the ambition of providing standard academic resources, we have exercised extreme care in publishing the content. In case of any discrepancies in the matter, we request readers to excuse the unintentional lapse and not hold us liable for the same. Suggestions are always welcome.

EDITION : 2021

ISBN : 978-93-91184-89-6

PRICE : ₹ 225.00

PRINTED AT : Upkar Printing Unit, Agra

PUBLISHED BY

OSWAL PUBLISHERS

Head Office: 1/12, Sahitya Kunj, M.G. Road, Agra - 282002

Phone : (0562) 2527771-4, +91 7534077222

E-mail : info@oswalpublishers.in

Website : www.oswalpublishers.com

The cover of this book has been designed using resources from Freepik.com

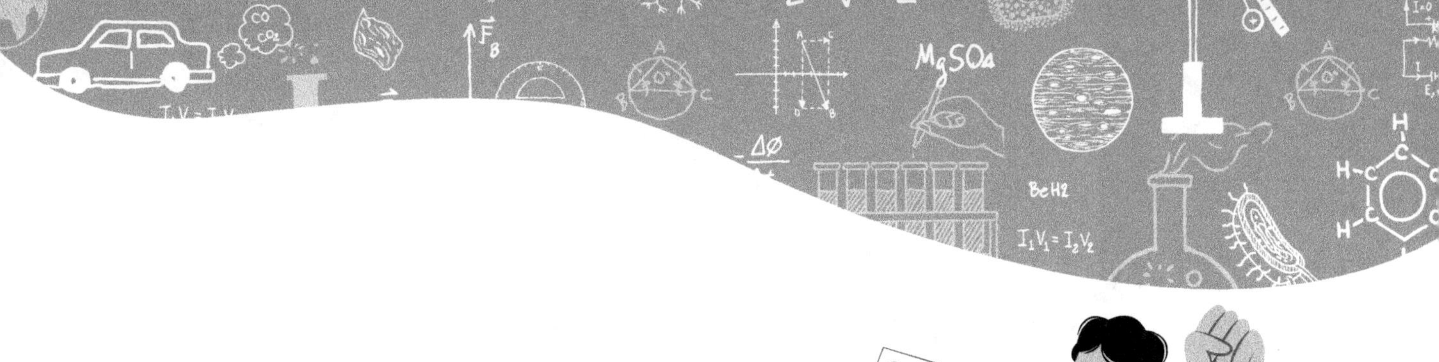

Preface

Based on the [CBSE/DIR (ACAD)/2021] Circular No. Acad-75/2021, issued by the Board.

We at Oswal-Gurukul believe that preparation in the right direction is the key to avoid stress, and perform well in one's board exams. Therefore, in order to excel in exams we have compiled CBSE 36 Sample Question Papers for TERM I Examination of class XII. To provide best matter to students, subject-matter experts and the experienced teachers from across the country have collaborated to bring together this book.

This book comprises detailed solved Sample Question Paper by CBSE according to the new SQP, explained in detail for better understanding of the concepts. We have made every attempt to cover as much ground as possible from the entire syllabus and to keep the language of the book lucid and crisp for easy grasping.

We sincerely hope that this book will prove to be a tool for effective time-management, as well as enable smart-study practices.

—The Publisher

⊛oswal.io

create your own exam sample papers in 2 mins

Prepare a chapter, take practice test & get —— evaluated to perform better ——

Create unlimited tests based on the latest board paper pattern once you are done practicing the book questions

Scan the QR code and get instant access to oswal.io for free. Just register & get started!

A winning effort begins with daily practice of tests

Easy steps to follow :

Step 1 - In a few clicks, you can completely customize your test

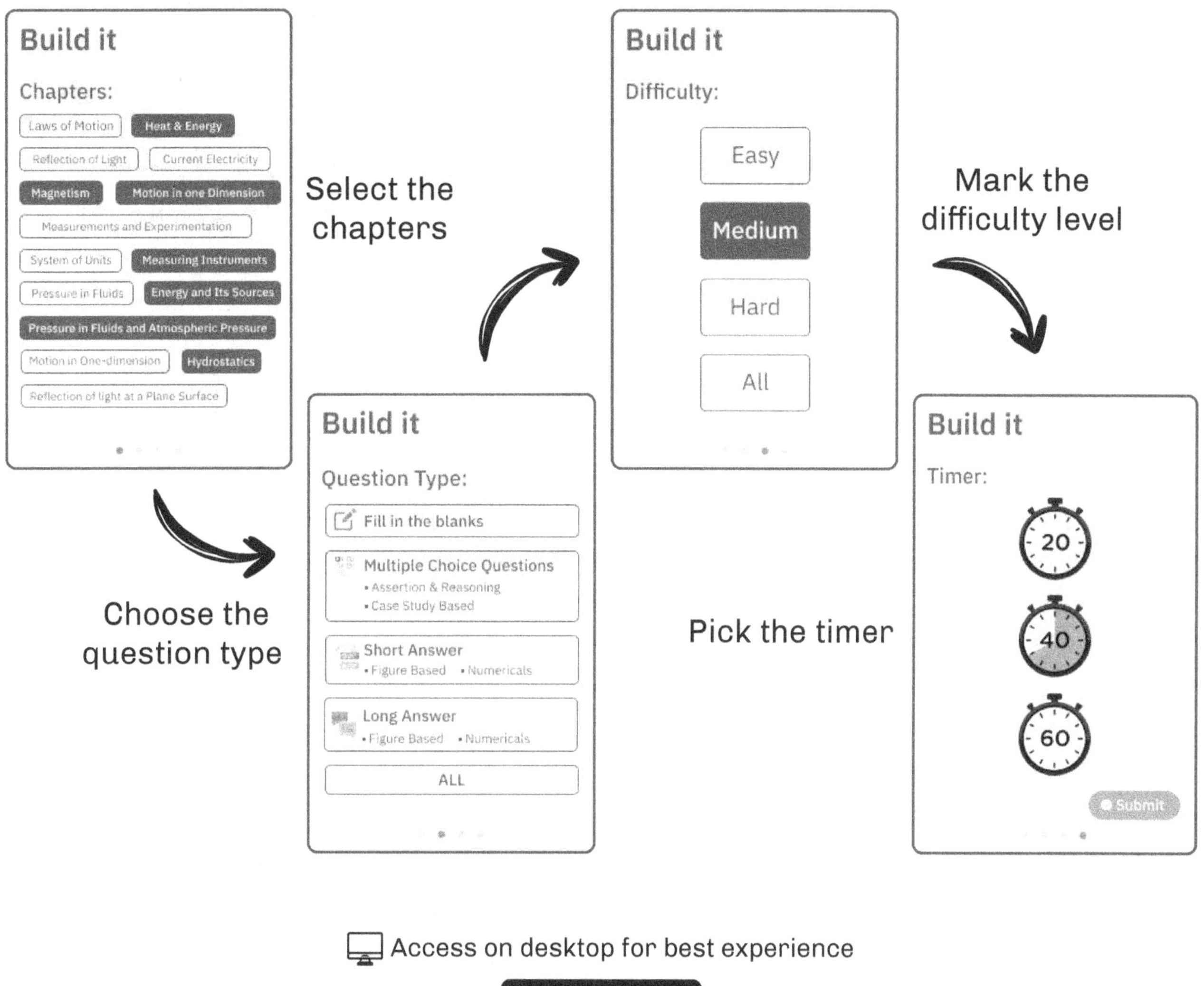

Access on desktop for best experience

www.oswal.io

Step 2 - Test is based on the selected question type, chapters, difficulty, time

Step 3 - Click on start and type your answers in the given space

Step 4 - Use insert $\TeX$ equation editor to quickly & accurately insert the difficult math/physics/chem formulas

Step 5 - Skip any question if not sure, proceed to next & submit

Step 6 - You will get your result emailed right away

Contents

केन्द्रीय माध्यमिक शिक्षा बोर्ड
(शिक्षा मंत्रालय, भारत सरकार के अधीन एक स्वायत्त संगठन)
CENTRAL BOARD OF SECONDARY EDUCATION
(An Autonomous Organisation under the Ministry of Education, Govt. of India)

CBSE/DIR (ACAD)/2021

Date: 02-09-2021
Circular No. Acad-75/2021

All the Heads of Schools Affiliated to CBSE

**Subject: Sample Question Papers of Classes X and XII
for Term 1 Exams 2021-22**

Dear Principal,

The Sample Question Papers for classes X and XII Term 1 Exams 2021-22 are now available at CBSE website www.cbseacademic.nic.in at the link given below:

Sample Papers Class X:
http://cbseacademic.nic.in/SQP_CLASSX_2021-22.html

Sample Papers Class XII:
http://cbseacademic.nic.in/SQP_CLASSXII_2021-22.html

**Dr. Joseph Emmanuel
Director (Academics)**

'शिक्षा सदन' ,17 राऊज़ एवेन्यू ,इंस्टीट्शनल एरिया, नई दिल्ली—110002
'Shiksha Sadan', 17, Rouse Avenue, Institutional Area, New Delhi - 110002 

फ़ोन/Telephone: 011-23212603,23233227 वेबसाइट/Website :http://www.cbseacademic.nic.in ई-मेल/e-mail: mailto:directoracad.cbse@nic.in.

<u>NOTICE</u>

Important Points for Sample Question Papers

The following points are to be noted while studying/referring to the Sample Papers for Classes X & XII Term 1 for the academic session 2021-22:

1. The Multiple Choice Questions given in the sample papers are not of one mark each for all papers.

2. In the SQPs of Mathematics and all languages except English, each question carries one mark.

3. For other subjects, each question carries equal marks viz.-a-viz. the total marks given i.e. 40 or 35 or 25 or 15 and the weight age of marks per question will be as follows:-

Max. Marks	No. of Questions to be attempted	Marks per Question
40	50	0.80
35	50	0.70
40	45	0.88
35	45	0.77
25	40	0.625
15	25	0.60

4. If total marks scored by a candidate is in fraction, then the same will be rounded off to the next higher numerical number, for example, if the child gets 16.1marks then the total marks will be rounded off to 17 and so on.

Sample Question Paper

Mathematics [Code (041)]

Term - I

Time : 90 Minutes

Max. Marks : 40

General Instructions :

1. This question paper contains three section – A, B and C. Each part is compulsory.
2. Section A has 20 MCQs, attempt any 16 out of 20.
3. Section B has 20 MCQs, attempt any 16 out of 20.
4. Section C has 10 MCQs, attempt any 8 out of 10.
5. There is no negative marking.
6. All questions carry equal marks.

Section - A

In this section, attempt any 16 questions out of Questions 1 – 20.

Each Question is of 1 mark weightage.

1. $\sin\left[\dfrac{\pi}{3} - \sin^{-1}\left(-\dfrac{1}{2}\right)\right]$ is equal to :   1

(a) $\dfrac{1}{2}$ (b) $\dfrac{1}{3}$ (c) -1 (d) 1

Sol. (d) 1

    Explanation: We have

$$\sin\left[\frac{\pi}{3} - \sin^{-1}\left(-\frac{1}{2}\right)\right]$$

$$\sin\left[\frac{\pi}{3} + \sin^{-1}\left(\frac{1}{2}\right)\right] \qquad [\because \sin^{-1}(-x) = -\sin^{-1}x]$$

$$\sin\left[\frac{\pi}{3} + \frac{\pi}{6}\right] = \sin\left(\frac{\pi}{2}\right) = 1$$

2. The value of $k(k < 0)$ for which the function f defined as

$$f(x) = \begin{cases} \dfrac{1-\cos kx}{x\sin x}, & x \neq 0 \\ \dfrac{1}{2}, & x = 0 \end{cases}$$

    is continuous at $x = 0$ is :   1

(a) ± 1 (b) -1 (c) $\pm\dfrac{1}{2}$ (d) $\dfrac{1}{2}$

Sol. (a) $+1$

    Explanation: The given function is continuous at $x = 0$

So,
$$\lim_{x\to 0}\left(\frac{1-\cos kx}{x\sin x}\right)=f(0)$$

$$\lim_{x\to 0}\left(\frac{1-\cos kx}{x^2}\times\frac{x}{\sin x}\right)=\frac{1}{2}$$

$$\Rightarrow\quad\lim_{x\to 0}\left(\frac{1-\cos kx}{x^2}\right)\times\lim_{x\to 0}\left(\frac{\sin x}{x}\right)=\frac{1}{2}$$

$$\lim_{x\to 0}\left(\frac{2\sin^2\frac{kx}{2}}{x^2}\right)\times 1=\frac{1}{2}\qquad\left[\because\lim_{x\to 0}\left(\frac{\sin x}{x}\right)=1\right]$$

$$2\lim_{x\to 0}\left(\frac{\sin\frac{kx}{2}}{x}\right)^2=\frac{1}{2}$$

$$\Rightarrow\quad 2\lim_{x\to 0}\left(\frac{\frac{k}{2}\sin\frac{kx}{2}}{\frac{kx}{2}}\right)^2=\frac{1}{2}$$

$$\Rightarrow\quad 2\times\frac{k^2}{4}=\frac{1}{2}$$

$$\Rightarrow\quad k^2=1$$

$$\Rightarrow\quad k=\pm 1$$

3. If $A=\{a_{ij}\}$ is a square matrix of order 2 such that $a_{ij}=\begin{cases}1,\text{ when }i\neq j\\0,\text{ when }i=j\end{cases}$, then A^2 is: 1

(a) $\begin{bmatrix}1&0\\1&0\end{bmatrix}$ (b) $\begin{bmatrix}1&1\\0&0\end{bmatrix}$ (c) $\begin{bmatrix}1&1\\1&0\end{bmatrix}$ (d) $\begin{bmatrix}1&0\\0&1\end{bmatrix}$

Sol. (d) $\begin{bmatrix}1&0\\0&1\end{bmatrix}$

Explanation: According to question we have to construct a 2×2 matrix

So,
$$A=\begin{bmatrix}a_{11}&a_{12}\\a_{21}&a_{22}\end{bmatrix}$$

So,
$$a_{11}=0;\ a_{12}=1;\ a_{21}=1;\ a_{22}=0\qquad\left[\because a_{ij}=\begin{cases}1,&\text{when }i\neq j\\0,&\text{when }i=j\end{cases}\right]$$

$$A=\begin{bmatrix}0&1\\1&0\end{bmatrix}\text{ so }A^2=\begin{bmatrix}0&1\\1&0\end{bmatrix}\begin{bmatrix}0&1\\1&0\end{bmatrix}=\begin{bmatrix}1&0\\0&1\end{bmatrix}$$

4. Value of k, for which $A=\begin{bmatrix}k&8\\4&2k\end{bmatrix}$ is a singular matrix is :   1

(a) 4   (b) -4 (c) ± 4 (d) 0

Sol. (c) ± 4

Explanation: We know for singular matrix $|A|=0$

$$\begin{vmatrix}k&8\\4&2k\end{vmatrix}=0$$

$$\Rightarrow\quad (2k^2-32)=0$$

$$\Rightarrow\quad k^2=16\Rightarrow k=\pm 4$$

5. Find the intervals in which the function f given by $f(x) = x^2 - 4x + 6$ is strictly increasing : **1**

    (a) $(-\infty, 2) \cup (2, \infty)$ (b) $(2, \infty)$

    (c) $(-\infty, 2)$ (d) $(-\infty, 2) \cup (2, \infty)$

Sol. (b) $(2, \infty)$

    Explanation: For strictly increasing function $f'(x) > 0$

    Here, $\qquad\qquad\qquad\qquad\qquad f(x) = x^2 - 4x + 6$

    So $\qquad\qquad\qquad\qquad\qquad\quad f'(x) = 2x - 4$

    For strictly increasing function $2x - 4 > 0$

$$x > 2$$

    So, $\qquad\qquad\qquad\qquad\qquad\quad x \in (2, \infty)$

6. Given that A is a square matrix of order 3 and $|A| = -4$, then $|adj\ A|$ is equal to : **1**

    (a) -4 (b) 4 (c) -16 (d) 16

Sol. (d) 16

    Explanation: We know $|adj\ A| = |A|^{n-1}$ where n is the order of the matrix

    So, $\qquad\qquad\qquad\qquad |adj\ A| = (-4)^{3-1} = (-4)^2 = 16$

7. A relation R in set $A = \{1, 2, 3\}$ is defined as $R = \{(1, 1), (1, 2), (2, 2), (3, 3)\}$. Which of the following ordered pair in R shall be removed to make it an equivalence reation in A? **1**

    (a) $(1, 1)$ (b) $(1, 2)$ (c) $(2, 2)$ (d) $(3, 3)$

Sol. (b) $(1, 2)$

    Explanation: It is clear if we removed (1, 2) from the given relation then it makes identify relation. We know identity relation is an equivalence relation.

8. If $\begin{bmatrix} 2a+b & a-2b \\ 5c-d & 4c+3d \end{bmatrix} = \begin{bmatrix} 4 & -3 \\ 11 & 24 \end{bmatrix}$, then value of $a + b - c + 2d$ is : **1**

    (a) 8 (b) 10 (c) 4 (d) -8

Sol. (a) 8

    Explanation: By equality of two matrix

$$2a + b = 4 \qquad\qquad\text{...(i)}$$

    and $\qquad\qquad\qquad\qquad a - 2b = -3 \qquad\qquad\text{...(ii)}$

$$5c - d = 11 \qquad\qquad\text{...(iii)}$$

    and $\qquad\qquad\qquad\qquad 4c + 3d = 24 \qquad\qquad\text{...(iv)}$

    On solving (i) and (ii), we get $a = 1$ and $b = 2$

    On solving (iii) and (iv), we get $c = 3$ and $d = 4$

    So, $\qquad\qquad a + b - c + 2d = (1) + (2) - (3) + 2(4) = 8$

9. The point at which the normal to the curve $y = x + \dfrac{1}{x}$, $x > 0$ is perpendicular to the line $3x - 4y - 7 = 0$ is : **1**

    (a) $(2, 5/2)$ (b) $(\pm 2, 5/2)$ (c) $(-1/2, 5/2)$ (d) $(1/2, 5/2)$

Sol. (a) $(2, 5/2)$

    Explanation: Given curve $\qquad\qquad y = x + \dfrac{1}{x}, x > 0 \qquad\qquad\text{...(i)}$

    Let coordinate of the required point be (h, k)

    This point lies on curve

$$k = h + \frac{1}{h}, h > 0 \qquad\qquad\text{...(ii)}$$

    Differentiate equation (i), w.r.t. x

$$\frac{dy}{dx} = 1 - \frac{1}{x^2}$$

$$\left.\frac{dy}{dx}\right|_{(h,k)} = 1 - \frac{1}{h^2} = \frac{h^2 - 1}{h^2} = \text{slope of tangent}$$

$$\text{Slope of normal} = \frac{h^2}{1 - h^2} = -\frac{4}{3}$$

$$3h^2 = -4 + 4h^2$$

$$h^2 = 4$$

$$\Rightarrow \qquad h = \pm 2$$

ATQ $\qquad\qquad\qquad h > 0$

So, $\qquad\qquad\qquad h = 2$

From equation (ii) $\qquad k = 2 + \frac{1}{2} = \frac{5}{2}$

So required point be $\left(2, \dfrac{5}{2}\right)$

10. $\sin(\tan^{-1} x)$, where $|x| < 1$, is equal to: **1**

(a) $\dfrac{x}{\sqrt{1 - x^2}}$
(b) $\dfrac{1}{\sqrt{1 - x^2}}$
(c) $\dfrac{1}{\sqrt{1 + x^2}}$
(d) $\dfrac{x}{\sqrt{1 + x^2}}$

Sol. (d) $\dfrac{x}{\sqrt{1 + x^2}}$

Explanation: $\sin(\tan^{-1} x)$

Let $\qquad\qquad\qquad \tan^{-1} x = \theta$

$$\Rightarrow \qquad\qquad \frac{x}{1} = \tan\theta \Rightarrow \sin\theta = \frac{x}{\sqrt{1 + x^2}}$$

$$\Rightarrow \qquad\qquad \theta = \sin^{-1}\frac{x}{\sqrt{1 + x^2}}$$

$$\sin\left(\sin^{-1}\frac{x}{\sqrt{1 + x^2}}\right) = \frac{x}{\sqrt{1 + x^2}}$$

11. Let the relation R in the set $A = \{x \in Z : 0 \le x \le 12\}$, given by $R = \{(a, b) : |a - b|$ is a multiple of 4\}. Then [1], the equivalence class containing 1, is : **1**

(a) $\{1, 5, 9\}$
(b) $\{0, 1, 2, 5\}$
(c) ϕ
(d) A

Sol. (a) $\{1, 5, 9\}$

Explanation: Given relation define on set $A = \{0, 1, 2, 3, 4, 5, 6, 7, 8, 9, 10, 11, 12\}$

Let element x be the equivalence class of 1

So, by relation $|1 - x|$ is multiple of 4

It is possible only for $x = 1, 5, 9$

So, $\qquad\qquad\qquad [1] = \{1, 5, 9\}$

12. If $e^x + e^y = e^{x+y}$, then $\dfrac{dy}{dx}$ is : **1**

(a) e^{y-x}
(b) e^{x+y}
(c) $-e^{y-x}$
(d) $2e^{x-y}$

Sol. (c) $-e^{y-x}$

Explanation: $\qquad\qquad\qquad e^x + e^y = e^{x+y}$ $\qquad\qquad$ ...(i)

Differentiate (i), w.r.t. x

$$e^x + e^y \frac{dy}{dx} = e^{x+y}\left\{1 + \frac{dy}{dx}\right\}$$

$$e^x + e^y \frac{dy}{dx} = e^{x+y} + e^{x+y} \frac{dy}{dx}$$

$$(e^x - e^{x+y}) = \frac{dy}{dx}(e^{x+y} - e^y)$$

$$\frac{(e^x - e^{x+y})}{(e^{x+y} - e^y)} = \frac{dy}{dx}$$

From equation (i)

$$\frac{(e^x - e^x - e^y)}{(e^x + e^y - e^y)} = \frac{dy}{dx}$$

$$\Rightarrow \qquad \frac{(-e^y)}{(e^x)} = \frac{dy}{dx}$$

$$\Rightarrow \qquad \frac{dy}{dx} = -e^{y-x}$$

13. Given that matrices A and B are of order $3 \times n$ and $m \times 5$ respectively, then the order of matrix $C = 5A + 3B$ is : 1

(a) 3×5 and $m = n$ (b) 3×5 (c) 3×3 (d) 5×5

Sol. (b) 3×5

Explanation: ATQ order of matrix A is $3 \times n$

$\Rightarrow$ Order of matrix $5A$ is $3 \times n$

ATQ order of matrix B is $m \times 5$

$\Rightarrow$ order of matrix $3B$ is $m \times 5$

Two matrices can be added if their order are same so by observation $n = 5$ and $m = 3$

So order of matrix $C = 5A + 3B$ is 3×5

14. If $y = 5 \cos x - 3 \sin x$, $\dfrac{d^2 y}{dx^2}$ is equal to : 1

(a) $-y$ (b) y (c) $25y$ (d) $9y$

Sol. (a) $-y$

Explanation: $\qquad\qquad y = 5 \cos x - 3 \sin x$

Differentiate w.r.t. x

$$\frac{dy}{dx} = -5 \sin x - 3 \cos x$$

Again differentiate w.r.t. x

$$\frac{d^2 y}{dx^2} = -5 \cos x + 3 \sin x$$

$$\frac{d^2 y}{dx^2} = -(5 \cos x - 3 \sin x)$$

$$\frac{d^2 y}{dx^2} = -y$$

15. For matrix $A = \begin{bmatrix} 2 & 5 \\ -11 & 7 \end{bmatrix}$, $(adj\ A)'$ is equal to : 1

(a) $\begin{bmatrix} -2 & -5 \\ 11 & -7 \end{bmatrix}$ (b) $\begin{bmatrix} 7 & 5 \\ 11 & 2 \end{bmatrix}$ (c) $\begin{bmatrix} 7 & -5 \\ 11 & 2 \end{bmatrix}$ (d) $\begin{bmatrix} 7 & -5 \\ 11 & 2 \end{bmatrix}$

Sol. (d) $\begin{bmatrix} 7 & -5 \\ 11 & 2 \end{bmatrix}$

Explanation: Given matrix $\quad A = \begin{bmatrix} 2 & 5 \\ -11 & 7 \end{bmatrix}$

Than $\quad adj\, A = \begin{bmatrix} 7 & 11 \\ -5 & 2 \end{bmatrix}$

and $\quad (adj\, A)' = \begin{bmatrix} 7 & -5 \\ 11 & 2 \end{bmatrix}$

16. The points on the curve $\dfrac{x^2}{9}+\dfrac{y^2}{16}=1$ at which the tangents are parallel to y-axis are : 1

(a) $(0, \pm 4)$ (b) $(\pm 4, 0)$ (c) $(\pm 3, 0)$ (d) $(0, \pm 3)$

Sol. (c) $(\pm 3, 0)$

Explanation: Given curve

$$\frac{x^2}{9}+\frac{y^2}{16}=1 \qquad\qquad \text{...(i)}$$

Let coordinate of the required point be (h, k)

This point lies on the curve

$$\frac{h^2}{9}+\frac{k^2}{16}=1 \qquad\qquad \text{...(ii)}$$

Differentiate equation (i), w.r.t. x

$$\frac{2x}{9}+\frac{2y}{16}\frac{dy}{dx}=0$$

$$\Rightarrow \qquad \frac{2y}{16}\frac{dy}{dx}=-\frac{2x}{9}$$

$$\Rightarrow \qquad \frac{dy}{dx}=-\frac{2x}{9}\times\frac{16}{2y}$$

$$\Rightarrow \qquad \frac{dy}{dx}=-\frac{16}{9}\times\frac{x}{y}$$

$$\Rightarrow \qquad \frac{dy}{dx}\bigg|_{(h,k)}=-\frac{16}{9}\times\frac{h}{k} \qquad\qquad \text{...(iii)}$$

ATQ tangent at (h, k) parellel to Y-axis.

So, $\qquad \dfrac{dx}{dy}=0$

$$-\frac{9k}{16h}=0$$

$$\Rightarrow \qquad k=0$$

From equation(ii) if $k = 0$ then $h^2 = 9$ and $h = \pm 3$

Coordinate of required point be $(\pm 3, 0)$

17. Given that $A = [a_{ij}]$ is a square matrix of order 3×3 and $|A| = -7$, then the value of $\sum_{i=1}^{3} a_{i2}A_{i2}$, where A_{ij} denotes the cofactor of element a_{ij} is : 1

(a) 7 (b) -7 (c) 0 (d) 49

Sol. (b) -7

Explanation: We have to find

$$\sum_{i=1}^{3} a_{i2}A_{i2} = a_{12}A_{12} + a_{22}A_{22} + a_{32}A_{32}$$

$$= |A| = -7$$

18. If $y = \log(\cos e^x)$, then $\dfrac{dy}{dx}$ is : **1**

(a) $\cos e^{x-1}$ (b) $e^{-x} \cos e^x$ (c) $e^x \sin e^x$ (d) $-e^x \tan e^x$

Sol. (d) $-e^x \tan e^x$

    Explanation: Given function $\qquad y = \log(\cos e^x)$

$$\frac{dy}{dx} = \frac{1}{\cos e^x} \times (-\sin e^x) \times e^x$$

$$= -e^x \tan e^x \qquad\qquad \text{[By chain rule]}$$

19. Based on the given shaded region as the feasible region in the graph, at which point(s) is the objective function $Z = 3x + 9y$ maximum? **1**

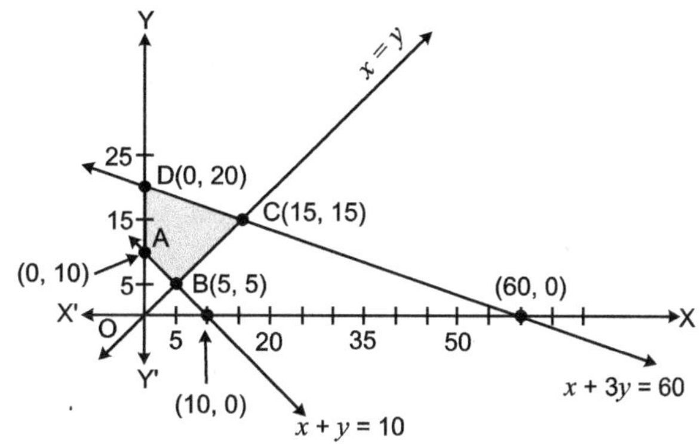

(a) Point B   (b) Point C

(c) Point D   (d) Every point on the line segment CD

Sol. (d) Every point on the line segment CD

    Explanation:

Point	Value of objective function $Z = 3x + 9y$
At point $A(0, 10)$	$Z_A = 3(0) + 9(10) = 0 + 90 = 90$
At point $B(5, 5)$	$Z_B = 3(5) + 9(5) = 15 + 45 = 60$
At point $C(15, 15)$	$Z_C = 3(15) + 9(15) = 45 + 135 = 180$ (Max)
At point $D(0, 20)$	$Z_D = 3(0) + 9(20) = 0 + 180 = 180$ (Max)

    Z is maximum at C and D

    Therefore Z is maximum every point on the line segment CD.

20. The least value of the function $f(x) = 2\cos x + x$ in the closed interval $\left[0, \dfrac{\pi}{2}\right]$ is : **1**

(a) 2   (b) $\dfrac{\pi}{6} + \sqrt{3}$

(c) $\dfrac{\pi}{2}$ (d) The least value does not exist.

Sol. (c) $\dfrac{\pi}{2}$

    Explanation: Given function $\qquad f(x) = 2\cos x + x$

    So, $\qquad\qquad\qquad\qquad\quad f'(x) = -2\sin x + 1$

For critical points $f'(x) = 0$

$$f'(x) = -2\sin x + 1 = 0$$
$$\sin x = \frac{1}{2}$$
$$x = \frac{\pi}{6}$$
$$f(0) = 2\cos(0) + 0 = 2$$
$$f\left(\frac{\pi}{6}\right) = 2\cos\left(\frac{\pi}{6}\right) + \frac{\pi}{6}$$
$$= 2\times\frac{\sqrt{3}}{2} + \frac{\pi}{6}$$
$$= \sqrt{3} + \frac{22}{42}$$
$$= \sqrt{3} + \frac{11}{21}$$
$$= 1.732 + 0.523 = 2.255$$
$$f\left(\frac{\pi}{2}\right) = 2\cos\frac{\pi}{2} + \frac{\pi}{2} = \frac{\pi}{2}$$

Therefore least value of the function in $\left[0, \dfrac{\pi}{2}\right]$ is $\dfrac{\pi}{2}$

Section - B

In this section, attempt any 16 questions out of the Questions 21 – 40.

Each Question is of 1 mark weightage.

21. The function $f : R \to R$ defined as $f(x) = x^3$ is :   1

  (a)   One-on but not onto   (b)   Not one-one but onto

  (c)   Neither one-one nor onto   (d)   One-one and onto

Sol. (d)   One-one and onto

    Explanation: Checking for one-one

    Take two arbitrary elements $x_1, x_2 \in R$ [Domain]

    Such that
$$f(x_1) = f(x_2)$$
$$x_1^3 = x_2^3$$
$$\Rightarrow \qquad x_1 = x_2$$

    $\Rightarrow f$ is one-one.

    Checking for onto :

    Let $y = f(x)$ and $y \in R$ [Co-domain]
$$y = x^3$$
$$x = (y)^{1/3}$$

    Here, it is clear for every real value of y, x is also real.

    So,   Range = Co-domain

    So given function in onto.

22. If $x = a\sec\theta$, $y = b\tan\theta$, then $\dfrac{d^2y}{dx^2}$ at $\theta = \dfrac{\pi}{6}$ is :   1

  (a) $\dfrac{-3\sqrt{3}b}{a^2}$ (b) $\dfrac{-2\sqrt{3}b}{a}$ (c) $\dfrac{-3\sqrt{3}b}{a}$ (d) $\dfrac{-b}{3\sqrt{3}a^2}$

Sol. (a) $\dfrac{-3\sqrt{3}b}{a^2}$

Explanation:

$$x = a \sec \theta$$

$$\Rightarrow \qquad \dfrac{dx}{d\theta} = a \sec \theta \tan \theta$$

$$y = b \tan \theta$$

$$\Rightarrow \qquad \dfrac{dy}{d\theta} = b \sec^2 \theta$$

$$\dfrac{\dfrac{dy}{d\theta}}{\dfrac{dx}{d\theta}} = \dfrac{dy}{dx} = \dfrac{b \sec^2 \theta}{a \sec \theta \tan \theta}$$

$$= \dfrac{b \sec \theta}{a \tan \theta} = \dfrac{b}{a} \operatorname{cosec} \theta$$

$$\dfrac{dy}{dx} = \dfrac{b}{a} \operatorname{cosec} \theta$$

Now differentiate w.r.t. x

$$\dfrac{d^2y}{dx^2} = -\dfrac{b}{a} \operatorname{cosec} \theta \cot \theta \times \dfrac{d\theta}{dx}$$

$$\dfrac{d^2y}{dx^2} = -\dfrac{b}{a} \operatorname{cosec} \theta \cot \theta \times \dfrac{1}{a \sec \theta \tan \theta}$$

$$\dfrac{d^2y}{dx^2} = -\dfrac{b}{a^2} \cot^3 \theta$$

$$\left.\dfrac{d^2y}{dx^2}\right|_{\theta=\frac{\pi}{6}} = -\dfrac{b}{a^2} \cot^3 \dfrac{\pi}{6}$$

$$= -\dfrac{b}{a^2}(\sqrt{3})^3 = -\dfrac{b}{a^2} 3\sqrt{3} = -\dfrac{3\sqrt{3}b}{a^2}$$

23. In the given graph, the feasible region for a LPP is shaded.

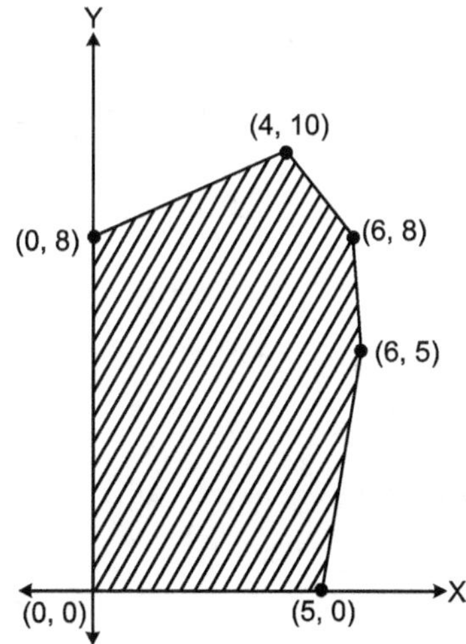

The objective function $Z = 2x - 3y$, will be minimum at : 1

(a) (4, 10)   (b) (6, 8)   (c) (0, 8)   (d) (6, 5)

Sol. (c) (0, 8)

   Explanation:

Point	Value of objective function $Z = 2x - 3y$
At point (0, 0)	$Z = 2(0) - 3(0) = 0 - 0 = 0$
At point (5, 0)	$Z = 2(5) - 3(0) = 10 - 0 = 10$
At point (6, 5)	$Z = 2(6) - 3(5) = 12 - 15 = -3$
At point (6, 8)	$Z = 2(6) - 3(8) = 12 - 24 = -12$
At point (4, 10)	$Z = 2(4) - 3(10) = 8 - 30 = -22$
At point (0, 8)	$Z = 2(0) - 3(8) = -24$

   So by table minimum value is -24 at (0, 8).

24. The derivative of $\sin^{-1}(2x\sqrt{1-x^2})$ w.r.t. $\sin^{-1} x,\ \dfrac{1}{\sqrt{2}} < x < 1$, is : **1**

(a) 2 (b) $\dfrac{\pi}{2} - 2$ (c) $\dfrac{\pi}{2}$ (d) -2

Sol. (d) -2

   Explanation: Let $\quad u = \sin^{-1}(2x\sqrt{1-x^2})$

   and $\qquad v = \sin^{-1} x$

   $\qquad u = \sin^{-1}(2x\sqrt{1-x^2})$

   put $\qquad x = \sin\theta$

   $\Rightarrow \qquad \theta = \sin^{-1} x$

   $$u = \sin^{-1}(2\sin\theta\sqrt{1-\sin^2\theta}),\ \frac{1}{\sqrt{2}} < \sin\theta < 1$$

   $$u = \sin^{-1}(2\sin\theta\sqrt{\cos^2\theta}),\ \frac{\pi}{4} < \theta < \frac{\pi}{2}$$

   $$u = \sin^{-1}(2\sin\theta|\cos\theta|),\ \frac{\pi}{4} < \theta < \frac{\pi}{2}\ \left[\because |\cos\theta| = \cos\theta, \frac{\pi}{4} < \theta < \frac{\pi}{2}\right]$$

   $$u = \sin^{-1}(2\sin\theta\cos\theta)$$
   $$u = \sin^{-1}(\sin 2\theta)$$

   $$\left[\frac{\pi}{4} < \theta < \frac{\pi}{2} \Rightarrow \frac{\pi}{2} < 2\theta < \pi \Rightarrow -\pi < -2\theta < -\frac{\pi}{2} \Rightarrow 0 < \pi - 2\theta < \frac{\pi}{2}\right]$$

   $$u = \sin^{-1}[\sin(\pi - 2\theta)]$$
   $$u = \pi - 2\theta$$
   $$u = \pi - 2\sin^{-1} x$$
   $$\frac{du}{dx} = -\frac{2}{\sqrt{1-x^2}} \qquad\qquad ...(i)$$

   $$v = \sin^{-1} x$$
   $$\frac{dv}{dx} = \frac{1}{\sqrt{1-x^2}} \qquad\qquad ...(ii)$$

   Equ (i) ÷ Equ (ii)

   $$\frac{du}{dv} = -2$$

25. If $A = \begin{bmatrix} 1 & -1 & 0 \\ 2 & 3 & 4 \\ 0 & 1 & 2 \end{bmatrix}$ and $B = \begin{bmatrix} 2 & 2 & -4 \\ -4 & 2 & -4 \\ 2 & -1 & 5 \end{bmatrix}$, then : **1**

(a) $A^{-1} = B$ (b) $A^{-1} = 6B$ (c) $B^{-1} = B$ (d) $B^{-1} = \dfrac{1}{6}A$

Sol. (d) $B^{-1} = \dfrac{1}{6}A$

Explanation:

$$AB = \begin{bmatrix} 1 & -1 & 0 \\ 2 & 3 & 4 \\ 0 & 1 & 2 \end{bmatrix}\begin{bmatrix} 2 & 2 & -4 \\ -4 & 2 & -4 \\ 2 & -1 & 5 \end{bmatrix} = \begin{bmatrix} 6 & 0 & 0 \\ 0 & 6 & 0 \\ 0 & 0 & 6 \end{bmatrix}$$

$$AB = 6I$$

$$\frac{1}{6}AB = I$$

This can be written as

$$\left(\frac{1}{6}A\right)B = I$$

$$\Rightarrow \qquad B^{-1} = \frac{1}{6}A$$

So option (d) is correct.

26. The real function $f(x) = 2x^3 - 3x^2 - 36x + 7$ is : **1**

(a) Strictly increasing in $(-\infty, -2)$ and strictly decreasing in $(-2, \infty)$

(b) Strictly decreasing in $(-2, 3)$

(c) Strictly decreasing in $(-\infty, 3)$ and strictly increasing in $(3, \infty)$

(d) Strictly decreasing in $(-\infty, -2) \cup (3, \infty)$

Sol. (b) Strictly decreasing in $(-2, 3)$

Explanation:

$$f(x) = 2x^3 - 3x^2 - 36x + 7$$
$$f'(x) = 6x^2 - 6x - 36$$
$$f'(x) = 6(x^2 - x - 6)$$
$$f'(x) = 6(x^2 - 3x + 2x - 6)$$
$$f'(x) = 6(x - 3)(x + 2)$$

For critical points

$$f'(x) = 0$$
$$f'(x) = 6(x - 3)(x + 2) = 0$$
$$x = 3$$

and

$$x = -2$$

Sub interval	Sign of $f'(x)$	Conclusion
$(-\infty, -2)$	(+)	Strictly increasing
$(-2, 3)$	(+)	Strictly decreasing
$(3, \infty)$	(+)	Strictly increasing

27. Simplest form of $\tan^{-1}\left(\dfrac{\sqrt{1+\cos x} + \sqrt{1-\cos x}}{\sqrt{1+\cos x} - \sqrt{1-\cos x}}\right)$, $\pi < x < \dfrac{3\pi}{2}$ is : **1**

(a) $\dfrac{\pi}{4} - \dfrac{x}{2}$ (b) $\dfrac{3\pi}{2} - \dfrac{x}{2}$ (c) $-\dfrac{x}{2}$ (d) $-\pi - \dfrac{x}{2}$

Sol. (a) $-\pi - \dfrac{x}{2}$

Explanation:

$$y = \tan^{-1}\left\{\frac{\sqrt{1+\cos x}+\sqrt{1-\cos x}}{\sqrt{1+\cos x}-\sqrt{1-\cos x}}\right\} \quad \pi < x < \frac{3\pi}{2}$$

$$y = \tan^{-1}\left\{\frac{\sqrt{2\cos^2\dfrac{x}{2}}+\sqrt{2\sin^2\dfrac{x}{2}}}{\sqrt{2\cos^2\dfrac{x}{2}}-\sqrt{2\sin^2\dfrac{x}{2}}}\right\} \quad \frac{\pi}{2} < \frac{x}{2} < \frac{3\pi}{4}$$

$$y = \tan^{-1}\left\{\frac{\sqrt{\cos^2\dfrac{x}{2}}+\sqrt{\sin^2\dfrac{x}{2}}}{\sqrt{\cos^2\dfrac{x}{2}}-\sqrt{\sin^2\dfrac{x}{2}}}\right\} \quad \frac{\pi}{2} < \frac{x}{2} < \frac{3\pi}{4}$$

$$y = \tan^{-1}\left\{\frac{\left|\cos\dfrac{x}{2}\right|+\left|\sin\dfrac{x}{2}\right|}{\left|\cos\dfrac{x}{2}\right|-\left|\sin\dfrac{x}{2}\right|}\right\} \quad \frac{\pi}{2} < \frac{x}{2} < \frac{3\pi}{4}$$

$$y = \tan^{-1}\left\{\frac{-\cos\dfrac{x}{2}+\sin\dfrac{x}{2}}{-\cos\dfrac{x}{2}-\sin\dfrac{x}{2}}\right\} \quad \frac{\pi}{2} < \frac{x}{2} < \frac{3\pi}{4}$$

$$y = \tan^{-1}\left\{\frac{\cos\dfrac{x}{2}-\sin\dfrac{x}{2}}{\cos\dfrac{x}{2}+\sin\dfrac{x}{2}}\right\} \quad \frac{\pi}{2} < \frac{x}{2} < \frac{3\pi}{4}$$

$$y = \tan^{-1}\left\{\frac{1-\tan\dfrac{x}{2}}{1+\tan\dfrac{x}{2}}\right\} \quad \frac{\pi}{2} < \frac{x}{2} < \frac{3\pi}{4}$$

$$y = \tan^{-1}\left\{\tan\left(\frac{\pi}{4}-\frac{x}{2}\right)\right\} \quad -\frac{\pi}{2} > -\frac{x}{2} > -\frac{3\pi}{4}$$

$$y = \tan^{-1}\left\{\tan\left(\frac{\pi}{4}-\frac{x}{2}\right)\right\} \quad -\frac{\pi}{4} > \frac{\pi}{4}-\frac{x}{2} > -\frac{\pi}{2}$$

$$y = \tan^{-1}\left\{\tan\left(\frac{\pi}{4}-\frac{x}{2}\right)\right\} \quad -\frac{\pi}{2} < \frac{\pi}{4}-\frac{x}{2} < -\frac{\pi}{4}$$

$$y = \left(\frac{\pi}{4}-\frac{x}{2}\right)$$

28. Given that A is a non-singular matrix of order 3 such that $A^2 = 2A$, then value of $|2A|$ is :   1

    (a) 4   (b) 8   (c) 64   (d) 16

Sol. (c) 64

    Explanation: Given that

$$A^2 = 2A$$
$$|A^2| = |2A|$$
$$|A|^2 = 2^3|A|$$
$$|A| = 8$$

ATQ we have to find $\quad |2A| = 2^3|A| = 8 \times 8 = 64$

$\because \quad\quad\quad\quad\quad\quad\quad |kA| = k^n|A|$

29. The value of b for which the function $f(x) = x + \cos x + b$ is strictly decreasing over R is : **1**

    (a) $b < 1$ (b) No value of b exists

    (c) $b \leq 1$ (d) $b \geq 1$

Sol. (b) No value of b exists

    Explanation: Given function $f(x) = x + \cos x + b$ is strictly decreasing over R

    So, $f'(x) < 0$

$$1 - \sin x < 0$$
$$1 < \sin x$$
$$\sin x > 1$$

    It is impossible

    So given function is increasing over R

    So, no value of b exist.

30. Let R be the relation in the set N given by $R = \{(a, b) : a = b - 2, b > 6\}$, then : **1**

    (a) $(2, 4) \in R$ (b) $(3, 8) \in R$ (c) $(6, 8) \in R$ (d) $(8, 7) \in R$

Sol. (c) $(6, 8) \in R$

    Explanation: Given relation define on the set of Natural number N

    and $R = \{(a, b) : a = b - 2, b > 6\}$

$$R = \{(5, 7), (6, 8), (7, 9) \ldots\ldots\}$$

31. The point(s), at which the function f given by $f(x) = \begin{cases} \dfrac{x}{|x|}, & x < 0 \\ -1, & x \geq 0 \end{cases}$ is continuous, is/are : **1**

    (a) $x \in R$ (b) $x = 0$ (c) $x \in R - \{0\}$ (d) $x = -1$ and 1

Sol. (a) $x \in R$

    Explanation: Here given function is $f(x) = \begin{cases} \dfrac{x}{|x|}, & x < 0 \\ -1, & x \geq 0 \end{cases}$

    We know if $x < 0$ then $|x| = -x$

    Now $f(x) = \begin{cases} -1, & x < 0 \\ -1, & x \geq 0 \end{cases}$

    Now $f(x) = -1$

    Which is a constant function

    We know a constant function is everywhere continuous.

32. If $A = \begin{bmatrix} 0 & 2 \\ 3 & -4 \end{bmatrix}$ and $kA = \begin{bmatrix} 0 & 3a \\ 2b & 24 \end{bmatrix}$, then the values of k, a and b respectively are : **1**

    (a) $-6, -12, -18$ (b) $-6, -4, -9$

    (c) $-6, 4, 9$ (d) $-6, 12, 18$

Sol. (b) $-6, -4, -9$

    Explanation: We have $kA = \begin{bmatrix} 0 & 3a \\ 2b & 24 \end{bmatrix}$

$$k\begin{bmatrix} 0 & 2 \\ 3 & -4 \end{bmatrix} = \begin{bmatrix} 0 & 3a \\ 2b & 24 \end{bmatrix}$$

$$\begin{bmatrix} 0 & 2k \\ 3k & -4k \end{bmatrix} = \begin{bmatrix} 0 & 3a \\ 2b & 24 \end{bmatrix}$$

On comparing

$$-4k = 24$$
$$\Rightarrow \qquad k = -6$$
$$3k = 2b$$
$$\Rightarrow \qquad b = \frac{3k}{2} = \frac{3\times(-6)}{2} = -9$$
$$2k = 3a$$
$$\Rightarrow \qquad a = \frac{2k}{3}$$
$$\Rightarrow \qquad a = \frac{2\times(-6)}{3} = -4$$

33. A linear programming problem is as follows : $\qquad$ 1

Minimize $\qquad Z = 30x + 50y$

subject to the constraints,

$$3x + 5y \geq 15$$
$$2x + 3y \leq 18$$
$$x \geq 0, y \geq 0$$

In the feasible region, the minimum value of Z occurs at

(a) a unique point $\qquad\qquad$ (b) no point

(c) infinitely many points $\qquad\qquad$ (d) two points only

Sol. (c) Infinitely many points

Explanation: Draw the graph of given constraints

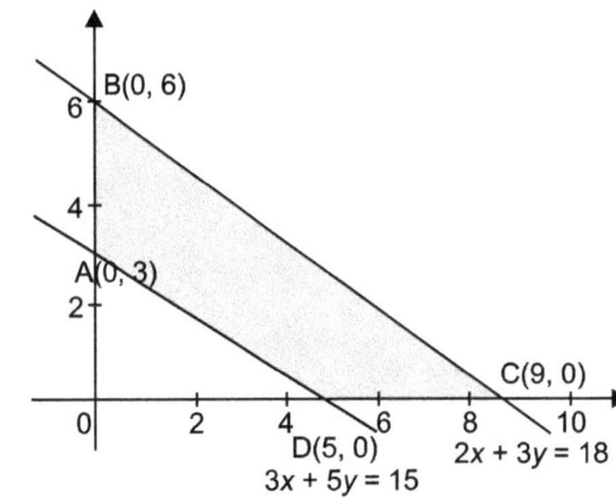

Point	Value of objective function $Z = 30x + 50y$
At point $A(0, 3)$	$Z = 0 + 50(3) = 150$
At point $B(0, 6)$	$Z = 0 + 6(50) = 300$
At point $C(9, 0)$	$Z = 30(9) + 0 = 270$
At point $D(5, 0)$	$Z = 30(5) + 0 = 150$

So by observation Z is minimum at A and D

So its also minimum at every point on line segment AD

34. The area of a trapezium is defined by function f and given by $f(x) = (10 + x)\sqrt{100 - x^2}$, then the area when

it is maximised is : $\qquad$ 1

(a) $75\ \text{cm}^2$ $\qquad$ (b) $7\sqrt{3}\ \text{cm}^2$ $\qquad$ (c) $75\sqrt{3}\ \text{cm}^2$ $\qquad$ (d) $5\ \text{cm}^2$

Sol. (c) $75\sqrt{3}\ \text{cm}^2$

Explanation: Here $\qquad f(x) = (10 + x)\sqrt{100 - x^2}$

Consider a function

$$u = [f(x)]^2$$

$$u = [(10+x)\sqrt{100-x^2}]^2$$

$$= (10+x)^2(100-x^2)$$

$$= (10+x)^3(10-x)$$

$$\frac{du}{dx} = (10+x)^3(-1) + 3(10-x)(10+x)^2$$

$$\frac{du}{dx} = (10+x)^2[-10-x+30-3x]$$

$$\frac{du}{dx} = (10+x)^2[20-4x]$$

$$\frac{du}{dx} = 4(10+x)^2[5-x]$$

$$\frac{d^2u}{dx^2} = 4[(10+x)^2(-1) + (5-x)\,2(10+x)]$$

$$\frac{d^2u}{dx^2} = 4[-(10+x)^2 + 2(5-x)(10+x)]$$

For critical points

$$\frac{du}{dx} = 0$$

$$\frac{du}{dx} = (10+x)^2[20-4x] = 0$$

$x = -10$ and $x = 5$ here $x = -10$ is not possible

Now we find

$$\left.\frac{d^2u}{dx^2}\right|_{x=5} = 4[-(10+5)^2 + 2(5-5)(10+5)]$$

$$\left.\frac{d^2u}{dx^2}\right|_{x=5} = 4[-(10+5)^2 + 0] = -900 \qquad \text{which is negative}$$

So $u = [f(x)]^2$ will be maximum at $x = 5$

$$\text{Maximum area} = f(x) = (10+5)\sqrt{100-25}$$

$$= 15\sqrt{75} = 15 \times 5\sqrt{3} = 75\sqrt{3}\ \text{cm}^2$$

35. If A is square matrix such that $A^2 = A$, then $(I+A)^3 - 7A$ is equal to :   1

   (a) A (b) $I+A$ (c) $I-A$ (d) I

Sol. (d) I

     Explanation: We have to find the value of

$$(I+A)^3 - 7A$$

$$I^3 + 3I^2A + 3IA^2 + A^3 - 7A$$

$$\text{[Applying } (A+B)^3 = A^3 + 3A^2B + 3AB^2 + B^3 \because A \text{ and } B \text{ are commute]}$$

$$I + 3IA + 3IA + A^2.A - 7A \qquad [\because I^2 = I;\ A^2 = A]$$

$$I + 3A + 3A + A - 7A = I$$

36. If $\tan^{-1} x = y$, then :   1

   (a) $-1 < y < 1$ (b) $\dfrac{-\pi}{2} \le y \le \dfrac{\pi}{2}$ (c) $\dfrac{-\pi}{2} < y < \dfrac{\pi}{2}$ (d) $y \in \left[\dfrac{-\pi}{2}, \dfrac{\pi}{2}\right]$

Sol. (c) $\dfrac{-\pi}{2} < y < \dfrac{\pi}{2}$

Explanation: We know range of $\tan^{-1} x = y$ is $\left(\dfrac{-\pi}{2}, \dfrac{\pi}{2} \right)$

37. Let $A = \{1, 2, 3\}$, $B = \{4, 5, 6, 7\}$ and let $f = \{(1, 4), (2, 5), (3, 6)\}$ be a function from A to B. Based on the given information, f is best defined as :   1
    (a) Surjective function
    (b) Injective function
    (c) Bijective function
    (d) function

Sol. (b) Injective function

Explanation: Here domain of a function is not equal to range so given function is not surjective but different elements of domain have different image. So given function is injective.

38. For $A = \begin{bmatrix} 3 & 1 \\ -1 & 2 \end{bmatrix}$, then $14A^{-1}$ is given by :   1

    (a) $14\begin{bmatrix} 2 & -1 \\ 1 & 3 \end{bmatrix}$
    (b) $\begin{bmatrix} 4 & -2 \\ 2 & 6 \end{bmatrix}$
    (c) $2\begin{bmatrix} 2 & -1 \\ 1 & -3 \end{bmatrix}$
    (d) $2\begin{bmatrix} -3 & -1 \\ 1 & -2 \end{bmatrix}$

Sol.(b) $\begin{bmatrix} 4 & -2 \\ 2 & 6 \end{bmatrix}$

Explanation: We know
$$A^{-1} = \frac{1}{|A|}(adj\, A)$$
$$|A| = (6 + 1) = 7$$
$$adj\, A = \begin{bmatrix} 2 & -1 \\ 1 & 3 \end{bmatrix}$$
$$A^{-1} = \frac{1}{7}\begin{bmatrix} 2 & -1 \\ 1 & 3 \end{bmatrix}$$
$$14A^{-1} = 14 \times \frac{1}{7}\begin{bmatrix} 2 & -1 \\ 1 & 3 \end{bmatrix}$$
$$= 2\begin{bmatrix} 2 & -1 \\ 1 & 3 \end{bmatrix} = \begin{bmatrix} 4 & -2 \\ 2 & 6 \end{bmatrix}$$

39. The point(s) on the curve $y = x^3 - 11x + 5$ at which the tangent is $y = x - 11$ is/are :   1
    (a) $(-2, 19)$
    (b) $(2, -9)$
    (c) $(\pm 2, 19)$
    (d) $(-2, 19)$ and $(2, -9)$

Sol. (b) $(2, -9)$

Explanation: Given curve is $\qquad y = x^3 - 11x + 5 \qquad$ ...(i)

Let coordinate of required point be (h, k)

This point lie on the curve so it satisfy the equation of the curve

So, $\qquad\qquad k = h^3 - 11h + 5 \qquad$ ...(ii)

Differentiate equation (i), w.r.t. x
$$\frac{dy}{dx} = 3x^2 - 11$$
$$\left.\frac{dy}{dx}\right|_{(h,k)} = 3h^2 - 11 = 1$$
$$h^2 = 4$$

$\Rightarrow$ $\qquad\qquad h = \pm 2$

If $h = 2$ then $\qquad\qquad k = 8 - 22 + 5 = 13 - 22 = -9$

So point be $(2, -9)$

And if $h = -2$ then $\qquad\qquad k = -8 + 22 + 5$

$$= -8 + 27 = 19$$

So point be $(-2, 19)$

But this point does not satisfy the equaiton $y = x - 11$

40. Given that $A = \begin{bmatrix} \alpha & \beta \\ \gamma & -\alpha \end{bmatrix}$ and $A^2 = 3I$, then : $\qquad\qquad$ 1

(a) $1 + \alpha^2 + \beta\gamma = 0$ $\qquad$ (b) $1 - \alpha^2 - \beta\gamma = 0$ $\qquad$ (c) $3 - \alpha^2 - \beta\gamma = 0$ $\qquad$ (d) $3 + \alpha^2 + \beta\gamma = 0$

Sol. (c) $3 - \alpha^2 - \beta\gamma = 0$

Explanation: We have $\qquad\qquad A^2 = 3I$

$$\begin{bmatrix} \alpha & \beta \\ \gamma & -\alpha \end{bmatrix}\begin{bmatrix} \alpha & \beta \\ \gamma & -\alpha \end{bmatrix} = \begin{bmatrix} 3 & 0 \\ 0 & 3 \end{bmatrix}$$

$$\begin{bmatrix} \alpha^2 + \beta\gamma & \alpha\beta - \alpha\beta \\ \alpha\gamma - \alpha\gamma & \beta\gamma + \alpha^2 \end{bmatrix} = \begin{bmatrix} 3 & 0 \\ 0 & 3 \end{bmatrix}$$

$$\begin{bmatrix} \alpha^2 + \beta\gamma & 0 \\ 0 & \alpha^2 + \beta\gamma \end{bmatrix} = \begin{bmatrix} 3 & 0 \\ 0 & 3 \end{bmatrix}$$

On comparing $\qquad\qquad \alpha^2 + \beta\gamma = 3$

$$3 - \alpha^2 - \beta\gamma = 0$$

Section - C

In this section, attempt any 8 questions. Each question is of 1-mark weightage.

Questions 46-50 are based on a Case-Study.

41. For an objecitve function $Z = ax + by$, where $a, b > 0$; the corner points of the feasible region determined by a set of constraints (linear inequalities) are $(0, 20)$, $(10, 10)$, $(30, 30)$ and $(0, 40)$. The condition on a and b such that the maximum Z occurs at both the poitns $(30, 30)$ and $(0, 40)$ is : $\qquad$ 1

(a) $b - 3a = 0$ $\qquad$ (b) $a = 3b$ $\qquad$ (c) $a + 2b = 0$ $\qquad$ (d) $2a - b = 0$

Sol. (a) $b - 3a = 0$

Explanation: Z is maximum at $(30, 30)$ and $(0, 40)$

$$30a + 30b = 40b$$
$$30a = 10b$$
$$3a = b$$
$$b - 3a = 0$$

42. For which value of m is the line $y = mx + 1$ a tangent to the curve $y^2 = 4x$? $\qquad$ 1

(a) $\dfrac{1}{2}$ $\qquad$ (b) 1 $\qquad$ (c) 2 $\qquad$ (d) 3

Sol.(b) 1

Explanation: We know if a line $y = mx + c$ touch a parabola $y^2 = 4ax$ then $c = \dfrac{a}{m}$

Here, $c = 1$, $m = m$ and $a = 1$

$$1 = \dfrac{1}{m}$$

$\Rightarrow$ $\qquad\qquad m = 1$

43. The maximum value of $[x(x-1)+1]^{\frac{1}{3}}, 0 \le x \le 1$ is :   **1**

   (a)   0   (b) $\dfrac{1}{2}$ (c)   1   (d) $\sqrt[3]{\dfrac{1}{3}}$

Sol. (c)   1

Explanation: Here,

$$f(x) = [x(x-1)+1]^{1/3} = [x^2 - x + 1]^{1/3}$$

$$f'(x) = \frac{1}{3}[x^2 - x + 1]^{-2/3}(2x-1) = \frac{2x-1}{3(x^2-x+1)^{2/3}}$$

For critical point

$$f'(x) = 0$$

$$\frac{2x-1}{3(x^2-x+1)^{2/3}} = 0$$

$$x = \frac{1}{2}$$

$$f(0) = [0(0-1)+1]^{1/3} = 1$$

$$f\left(\frac{1}{2}\right) = \left[\frac{1}{2}\left(\frac{1}{2}-1\right)+1\right]^{1/3} = \left[-\frac{1}{4}+1\right]^{1/3} = \left(\frac{3}{4}\right)^{1/3}$$

$$f(1) = [1(1-1)+1]^{1/3} = 1$$

So maximum value is 1.

44. In a linear programming problem, the constraints on the decision variables x and y are $x - 3y \ge 0$, $y \ge 0$, $0 \le x \le 3$. The feasible region: **1**

  (a)   is not in the first quadrant   (b)   is bounded in the first quadrant

  (c)   is unbounded in the first quadrant   (d)   does not exist

Sol. (b)   is bounded in the first quadrant

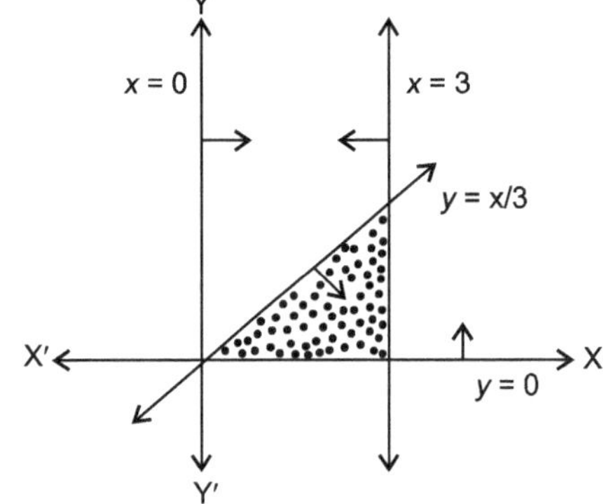

Explanation: So, it is bounded in the first quadrant.

45. Let $A = \begin{bmatrix} 1 & \sin\alpha & 1 \\ -\sin\alpha & 1 & \sin\alpha \\ -1 & -\sin\alpha & 1 \end{bmatrix}$, where $0 \le \alpha \le 2\pi$, then :   **1**

  (a) $|A| = 0$ (b) $|A| \in (2, \infty)$ (c) $|A| \in (2, 4)$ (d) $|A| \in [2, 4]$

Sol. (d) $|A| \in [2, 4]$

Explanation:

$$|A| = 1\{1 + \sin^2\alpha\} - \sin\alpha\{-\sin\alpha + \sin\alpha\} + 1\{\sin^2\alpha + 1\}$$
$$|A| = 2(1 + \sin^2\alpha)$$

We know

$$0 \le \sin^2\alpha \le 1$$
$$1 \le 1 + \sin^2\alpha \le 2$$
$$2 \le 2(1 + \sin^2\alpha) \le 4$$
$$2 \le |A| \le 4$$
$$|A| \in [2, 4]$$

The fuel cost per hour for running a train is proportional to the square of the speed it generates in km per hour. If the fuel costs ₹ 48 per hour at speed 16 km per hour and the fixed charges to run the train amount to ₹ 1200 per hour. Assume the speed of the train as v km/h.

Based on the given information, answer the following questions.

46. Given that the fuel cost per hour is k times the suqare of the speed the train generates in km/h, the value of k is : **1**

(a) $\dfrac{16}{3}$ (b) $\dfrac{1}{3}$ (c) 3   (d) $\dfrac{3}{16}$

Sol. (d) $\dfrac{3}{16}$

Explanation: ATQ

$$\text{Fuel cost/hr} \propto (\text{speed})^2$$
$$\Rightarrow \qquad \text{Fuel cost/hr} = k(\text{speed})^2$$

ATQ, fuel cost ₹ 48 per hour at speed 16 km per hour

$$48 = k(16)^2$$

So,
$$k = \frac{48}{16 \times 16} = \frac{3}{16}$$

47. If the train has travelled a distance of 500 km, then the total cost of running the train is given by function : **1**

(a) $\dfrac{15}{16}v + \dfrac{600000}{v}$ (b) $\dfrac{375}{4}v + \dfrac{600000}{v}$ (c) $\dfrac{5}{16}v + \dfrac{150000}{v}$ (d) $\dfrac{3}{16}v + \dfrac{6000}{v}$

Sol. (b) $\dfrac{375}{4}v + \dfrac{600000}{v}$

Explanation: Total cost of running the train in 1 hr = Fixed cost + Fuel cost

Total cost of running the train in 1 hr = ₹ $1200/\text{hr} + \dfrac{3}{16}v^2 / hr$

Let train takes t hour to cover 500 km

So,
$$v = \frac{500}{t}$$

Total cost of running the train in t hr = ₹ $1200t + \dfrac{3}{16}v^2 t$

Distance covered = 500 km

$$\text{Time} = \frac{500}{v} \text{ hours}$$

Total cost of running the train if train travelled distance 500 km

$$= 1200 \times \frac{500}{v} + \frac{3}{16}v^2 \times \frac{500}{v} = \frac{600000}{v} + \frac{375}{4}v$$

48. The most economical speed to run the train is : **1**

(a) 18 km/h   (b) 5 km/h   (c) 80 km/h   (d) 40 km/h

Sol. (c) 80 km/h

Explanation: For the most economical speed to run the train we have to minimize cost

$$C = \frac{600000}{v} + \frac{375}{4}v$$

Differentiate with respect to v

$$\frac{dC}{dv} = -\frac{600000}{v^2} + \frac{375}{4}$$

$$\frac{d^2C}{dv^2} = +\frac{1200000}{v^3}$$

For critical points

$$\frac{600000}{v^2} = \frac{375}{4}$$

$$\frac{600000 \times 4}{375} = v^2$$

$$v^2 = 6400$$

$$\Rightarrow \qquad v = \pm\, 80$$

At $v = 80$

$$\frac{d^2C}{dv^2} = +\text{ve}$$

So, C will be minimum

So, economical speed 80 km/hr.

49. The fuel cost for the train to travel 500 km at the most economical speed is :   1

   (a) ₹ 3750   (b) ₹ 750   (c) ₹ 7500   (d) ₹ 75000

Sol. (c) ₹ 7500

Explanation: Fuel cost for the train to travel 500 km at the most economical speed

$$= \frac{375}{4} \times 80 = 375 \times 20 = 7500$$

50. The total cost of the train to travel 500 km at the most economical speed is :   1

   (a) ₹ 3750   (b) ₹ 75000   (c) ₹ 7500   (d) ₹ 15000

Sol. (d) ₹ 15000

Explanation: Total cost of the train to travel 500 km at the most economical speed is

$$\frac{600000}{v} + \frac{375v}{4} = \frac{600000}{80} + \frac{375 \times 80}{4}$$

$$= 7500 + 7500 = 15000$$

❑❑

Sample Paper 1

Mathematics

Section - A

In this section, attempt any 16 questions out of Questions 1 – 20.

Each Question is of 1 mark weightage.

1. What is the value of $\tan^{-1}\sqrt{3} - \cot^{-1}(-\sqrt{3})$.

   (a) $\dfrac{\pi}{2}$
   (b) $-\dfrac{\pi}{2}$
   (c) 0
   (d) 1

2. What is the domain of the function $y = \sin^{-1}(-x^2)$.

   (a) $-1 \le x \le 1$
   (b) $-\infty \le x < \infty$
   (c) $x \le 1$
   (d) $x \ge 0$

3. If $A = \begin{bmatrix} 2 & 3 \\ 1 & 0 \end{bmatrix} = P + Q$, where P is symmetric matrix and Q is skew-symmetric matrix then find the matrix P.

   (a) $\begin{bmatrix} 5 & 5 \\ 1 & 5 \end{bmatrix}$
   (b) $\begin{bmatrix} 2 & 2 \\ 2 & 0 \end{bmatrix}$
   (c) $\begin{bmatrix} -1 & 0 \\ 1 & 2 \end{bmatrix}$
   (d) $\begin{bmatrix} 1 & 0 \\ 0 & 1 \end{bmatrix}$

4. If $A = [a_{ij}]_{2 \times 2}$, where $a_{ij} = \dfrac{(j + 2j)^2}{2}$, then A is equal to :

   (a) $\begin{bmatrix} 9 & 25 \\ 8 & 18 \end{bmatrix}$
   (b) $\begin{bmatrix} 9/2 & 25/2 \\ 8 & 18 \end{bmatrix}$
   (c) $\begin{bmatrix} 9 & 25 \\ 4 & 9 \end{bmatrix}$
   (d) $\begin{bmatrix} 9/2 & 15/2 \\ 4 & 9 \end{bmatrix}$

5. If $A = [a_{ij}]$ is a matrix of order 2×2, such that $|A| = -15$ and c_{ij} represents the cofactor of a_{ij}, then $a_{21}c_{21} + a_{22}c_{22}$ is equal to :

   (a) -15
   (b) 15
   (c) 0
   (d) 1

6. If $A = \begin{bmatrix} \alpha & \beta \\ \gamma & -\alpha \end{bmatrix}$ is such that $A^2 = I$, then the value of $1 - \alpha^2 - \beta\gamma$ is :

   (a) -1
   (b) 0
   (c) 1
   (d) Can't be calculated

7. Evaluate $\dfrac{dy}{dx}$, if $y = \dfrac{8^x}{x^8}$.

   (a) $\dfrac{8x^7}{8^x \log 8}$
   (b) $\dfrac{8^x \log 8}{8x^7}$
   (c) $\dfrac{8^x}{x^8}\left[\log 8 - \dfrac{8}{x}\right]$
   (d) None of these

8. What is the slope of the tangent to the curve $y = 4x^3 - 5x$ at $x = 3$.

   (a) 109
   (b) 71
   (c) 103
   (d) 98

9. If $R = \{(x, y) : x, y \in I, x^2 + y^2 \le 4\}$ is a relation in I, then domain of R is:

   (a) $\{0, 1, 2\}$
   (b) $\{-2, -1, 0\}$
   (c) $\{-2, -1, 0, 1, 2\}$
   (d) None of these

10. If the function $f(x) = \begin{cases} kx^2, & if\ x \leq 2 \\ 3, & if\ x > 2 \end{cases}$ is continuous at $x = 2$, then find the value of k.

    (a) $\dfrac{3}{4}$ (b) $\dfrac{2}{3}$ (c) $\dfrac{1}{2}$ (d) $\dfrac{1}{3}$

11. If $f(x) = \begin{cases} \dfrac{1-\cos 4x}{x^2}, & x < 0 \\ a, & x = 0 \\ \dfrac{\sqrt{x}}{\sqrt{16+x}-4}, & x > 0 \end{cases}$

    is continuous at $x = 0$, then $a =$

    (a) 4   (b) 6   (c) 8   (d) 5

12. Find the value of $\tan^{-1}\left[2\sin\left(2\cos^{-1}\dfrac{\sqrt{3}}{2}\right)\right]$.

    (a) $\dfrac{\pi}{6}$ (b) $\dfrac{\pi}{3}$ (c) $\dfrac{2\pi}{3}$ (d) $\dfrac{\pi}{2}$

13. The function $f(x) = \tan x - 4x$ is strictly decreasing on:

    (a) $\left(-\dfrac{\pi}{3}, \dfrac{\pi}{3}\right)$ (b) $\left(-\dfrac{\pi}{2}, \dfrac{\pi}{2}\right)$ (c) $(-\pi, \pi)$ (d) None of these

14. The relation R = {$(a, a), (a, b), (a, c), (b, b), (b, c), (c, a), (c, b), (c, c)$} on the set A = {$a, b, c$} is :

    (a) Reflexive   (b) Transitive   (c) Symmetric   (d) All of these

15. What is the principal value of $\sin^{-1}\left(\sin\dfrac{2\pi}{3}\right)$?

    (a) $\dfrac{\pi}{6}$ (b) $\dfrac{2\pi}{3}$ (c) $\dfrac{\pi}{2}$ (d) $\dfrac{\pi}{3}$

16. The number of all possible matrices of order 3×3 with each entry 0 or 1 is :

    (a) 264   (b) 308   (c) 512   (d) 500

17. Evaluate the determinant $\Delta = \begin{vmatrix} \log_3 512 & \log_4 3 \\ \log_3 8 & \log_4 9 \end{vmatrix}$

    (a) $\dfrac{15}{2}$ (b) 12   (c) $\dfrac{14}{3}$ (d) 6

18. Find $\dfrac{dy}{dx}$ if $y = 3x^3 - 4x^2$.

    (a) $\dfrac{3}{4}x^4 - \dfrac{4}{3}x^3$ (b) $12x^2 - 8x$ (c) $9x^2 - 8x$ (d) $16x^2 - 8x$

19. The function $f(x) = \log(\cos x)$ is :

    (a) Increasing in $[0, \pi]$ (b) Decreasing in $\left[0, \dfrac{\pi}{2}\right]$

    (c) Decreasing in $[0, \pi]$ (d) Increasing in $\left[0, \dfrac{\pi}{2}\right]$

20. Find $\dfrac{dy}{dx}\Big|_{x=\frac{\pi}{2}}$ where $y = e^{\sin x}$.

    (a) 1   (b) -1 (c) 2   (d) 0

Section - B

In this section, attempt any 16 questions out of the Questions 21 – 40.

Each Question is of 1 mark weightage.

21. If $x = a \sin^3 t$ and $y = a \cos^3 t$, then what is the value of $\dfrac{dy}{dx}$?

    (a) $\tan t$ (b) $-\cot t$ (c) $-\tan t$ (d) $\cot t$

22. The domain of R is:

    (a) $\{2, 4, 8\}$ (b) $\{2, 4, 6, 8\}$ (c) $\{2, 4, 6\}$ (d) $\{1, 2, 3, 4\}$

23. Let R be a relation on the set N be defined by $\{(x, y) : x, y \in N, 2x + y = 41\}$. Then, R is:

    (a) Reflexive   (b) Symmetric   (c) Transitive   (d) None of these

24. Range of $f(x) = \sin^{-1} x + \tan^{-1} x + \sec^{-1} x$ is:

    (a) $\left(\dfrac{\pi}{4}, \dfrac{3\pi}{4} \right)$ (b) $\left[\dfrac{\pi}{4}, \dfrac{3\pi}{4} \right]$ (c) $\left\{ \dfrac{\pi}{4}, \dfrac{3\pi}{4} \right\}$ (d) None of these

25. The value of $\sin^2 \left(\cos^{-1} \dfrac{1}{2} \right) + \cos^2 \left(\sin^{-1} \dfrac{1}{3} \right)$ is:

    (a) $\dfrac{17}{36}$ (b) $\dfrac{59}{36}$ (c) $\dfrac{36}{59}$ (d) None of these

26. If $A = \begin{bmatrix} 0 & -1 & 2 \\ 1 & 0 & 3 \\ -2 & -3 & 0 \end{bmatrix}$, then $A + 2A^T$ equals:

    (a) A (b) $-A^T$ (c) A^T (d) $2A^T$

27. If $x^y \cdot y^x = 16$, then $\dfrac{dy}{dx}$ at $(2, 2)$ is:

    (a) 1 (b) -1 (c) 0 (d) None of these

28. The value of k which makes the function defined by $f(x) = \begin{cases} \sin \dfrac{1}{x}, & \text{if } x \neq 0 \\ k, & \text{if } x = 0 \end{cases}$, continous at $x = 0$ is:

    (a) 8 (b) 1 (c) -1 (d) None of these

29. The area of a triangle with vertices $(-3, 0)$, $(3, 0)$ and $(0, k)$ is 9 sq. units. The value of k will be:

    (a) 9 (b) 3 (c) -9 (d) 6

30. A corner point of a feasible region is a point in the region, which is the .... of two boundary lines.

    (a) Union   (b) Difference   (c) Intersection   (d) None of these

31. The graphical solution of linear inequalities $x + y \geq 5$ and $x - y \leq 3$, where $L_1 \equiv x + y = 5$ and $L_2 \equiv x - y = 3$, is:

(a) 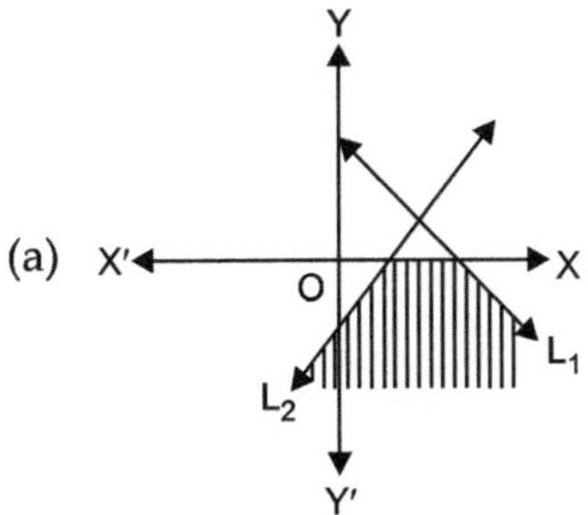

(b) 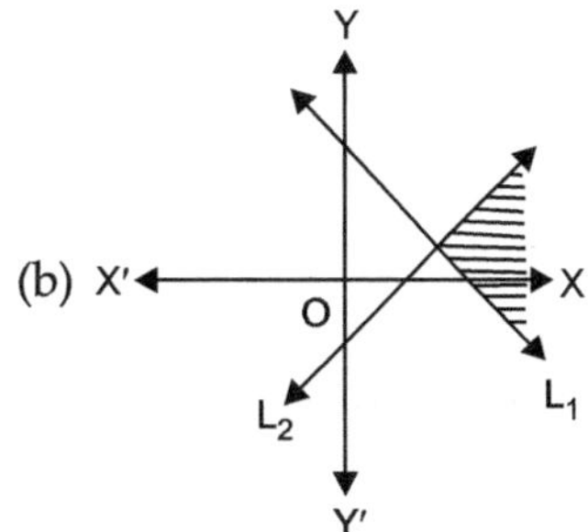

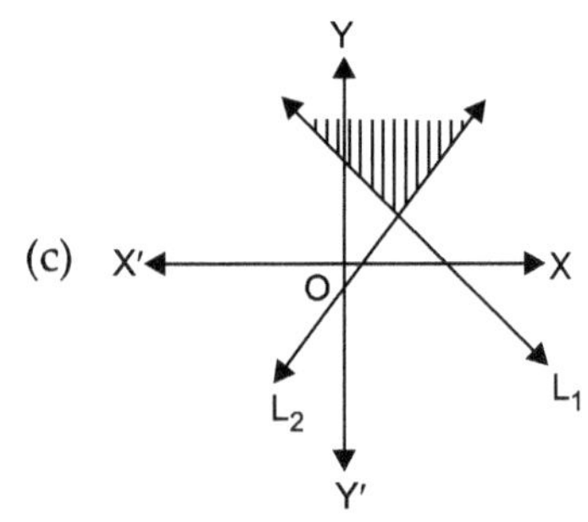

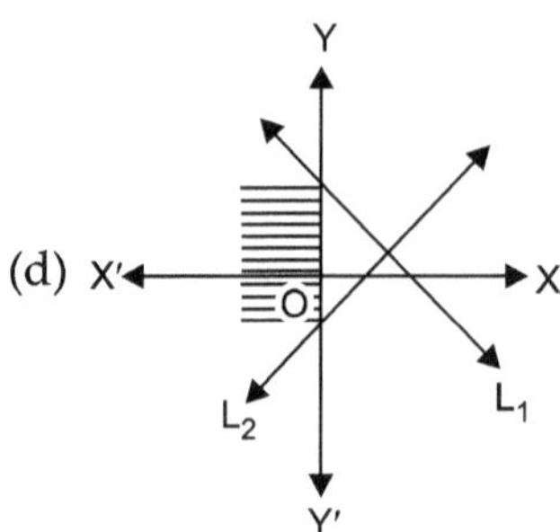

(c)

(d)

32. If $A = \begin{bmatrix} 1 & 2 \\ 2 & 1 \end{bmatrix}$ and $f(x) = (1 + x)(1 - x)$, then $f(A)$ is:

(a) $-4 \begin{bmatrix} 1 & 1 \\ 1 & 1 \end{bmatrix}$ (b) $-8 \begin{bmatrix} 1 & 1 \\ 1 & 1 \end{bmatrix}$ (c) $4 \begin{bmatrix} 1 & 1 \\ 1 & 1 \end{bmatrix}$ (d) None of these

33. If $\begin{vmatrix} 6i & -3i & 1 \\ 4 & 3i & -1 \\ 40 & 3 & i \end{vmatrix} = x + iy$, then:

(a) $x = 3, y = 1$ (b) $x = 1, y = 3$ (c) $x = 0, y = 3$ (d) $x = 0, y = 0$

34. The tangent to the curve given by $x = e^t \cdot \cos t$, $y = e^t \cdot \sin t$ at $t = \dfrac{\pi}{4}$ makes with X-axis an angle:

(a) 0 (b) $\dfrac{\pi}{4}$ (c) $\dfrac{\pi}{3}$ (d) $\dfrac{\pi}{2}$

35. If $A = \begin{bmatrix} 3 & 1 \\ -1 & 2 \end{bmatrix}$, find A^{-1}.

(a) $\dfrac{1}{7}\begin{bmatrix} 2 & -1 \\ 1 & 3 \end{bmatrix}$ (b) $\dfrac{1}{7}\begin{bmatrix} 3 & 1 \\ -1 & 2 \end{bmatrix}$ (c) $\dfrac{1}{7}\begin{bmatrix} -2 & 1 \\ -1 & -3 \end{bmatrix}$ (d) $\dfrac{1}{7}\begin{bmatrix} 2 & 1 \\ 1 & -3 \end{bmatrix}$

36. If $x = a \cos^3 \theta$ and $y = a \sin^3 \theta$, then $1 + \left(\dfrac{dy}{dx}\right)^2$ is equal to:

(a) $\tan \theta$ (b) $\tan^2 \theta$ (c) 1 (d) $\sec^2 \theta$

37. If given constraints are $5x + 4y \geq 2$, $x \leq 6$ and $y \leq 7$, then the maximum value of the function $Z = x + 2y$, is:

(a) 13 (b) 14 (c) 15 (d) 20

38. If $A = \begin{bmatrix} a & b \\ b & a \end{bmatrix}$ and $A^2 = \begin{bmatrix} \alpha & \beta \\ \beta & \alpha \end{bmatrix}$, then:

(a) $\alpha = a^2 + b^2, \beta = ab$ (b) $\alpha = a^2 + b^2, \beta = 2ab$ (c) $\alpha = a^2 + b^2, \beta = a^2 - b^2$ (d) $\alpha = 2ab, \beta = a^2 + b^2$

39. Derivative of $\cos x^3 \sin^2 (x^5)$ with respect to x is:

(a) $10x^4 (\sin x^5)(\cos x^5)(\cos x^3) - 3x^2 \sin x^3 \sin^2 x^5$
(b) $5x^3 (\sin x^5)(\cos x^5)(\cos x^3) - 3x^2 \sin x^3 \sin^2 x^5$
(c) $5x^3 (\sin x^5)(\cos x^5)(\cos x^3) - 6x^2 \sin x^3 \sin^2 x^5$
(d) None of the above

40. In a LPP, the maxium value of the objective function $z = ax + by$ is always:

(a) infinite   (b) finite   (c) 0 (d) None of these

Section – C

In this section, attempt any 8 questions. Each question is of 1–mark weightage.

Questions 46–50 are based on a Case-Study.

41. The corner points of the feasible region determined by the following system of linear inequalities:

$2x + y \leq 10$, $x + 3y \leq 15$, $x, y \geq 0$ are $(0, 0)$, $(5, 0)$, $(3, 4)$ and $(0, 5)$. Let $Z = px + qy$, where $p, q > 0$. Condition on p and q so that the maximum of Z occurs at both $(3, 4)$ and $(0, 5)$ is:

(a) $p = q$ (b) $p = 2q$ (c) $p = 3q$ (d) $q = 3p$

42. If $y = (1 + x^{1/4})(1 + x^{1/2})(1 - x^{1/4})$, then $\dfrac{dy}{dx}$ is equal to :

   (a) 1   (b) – 1   (c) x (d) $\sqrt{x}$

43. If the points $(3, -2)$, $(x, 2)$, $(8, 8)$ are collinear, then find the value of x:

   (a) 2   (b) 3   (c) 4   (d) 5

44. If $A = \begin{bmatrix} 0 & 2 & -3 \\ -2 & 0 & -1 \\ 3 & 1 & 0 \end{bmatrix}$, then A is a:

   (a) Symmetric matrix   (b) Skew-symmetric matrix
   (c) Diagonal matrix   (d) None of these

45. If $f(x) = \begin{cases} ax^2 + b, & 0 \le x < 1 \\ 4, & x = 1 \\ x + 3, & 1 < x \le 2 \end{cases}$, then the value of (a, b) for which $f(x)$ cannot be continuos at $a = 1$, is:

   (a) $(2, 2)$ (b) $(3, 1)$ (c) $(4, 0)$ (d) $(5, 2)$

In a stadium a running track of 440 m is to be laid out enclosing a football field. The shape of track is a rectangle with a semi-circle at each end. They want to keep maximum area of rectangular portion.

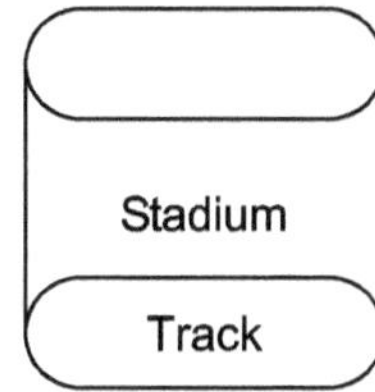

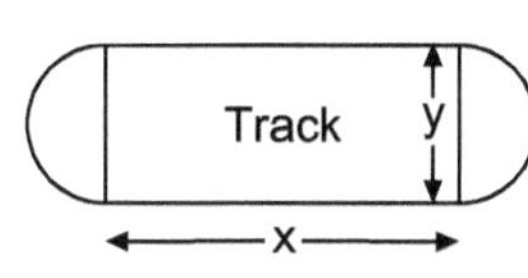

Give answers of the following questions :

46. Show the relationship of y in terms of x if $x + y$ represents the length and breadth of rectangular field :

   (a) $\dfrac{440 - 2x}{\pi}$ (b) $\dfrac{2x - 440}{\pi}$ (c) $\dfrac{440 - x}{\pi}$ (d) $\dfrac{x - 440}{\pi}$

47. If A shows area of field (rectangular portion), the function of A in terms of x will be :

   (a) $x\left(\dfrac{440 - x}{\pi}\right)$ (b) $\dfrac{1}{\pi}(440 - x^2)$ (c) $\dfrac{220 - 2x^2}{\pi}$ (d) $\dfrac{1}{\pi}(440x - 2x^2)$

48. At what value of x area will be maximum ?

   (a) 120   (b) 110   (c) 100   (d) 220

49. What is the maximum area of rectangular field ?

   (a) 7700π m^2 (b) 24200 m^2 (c) 7700 m^2 (d) $24200\,\pi$ m^2

50. The value of y will be :

   (a) 70 m   (b) $70\,\pi$ (c) $\dfrac{70}{\pi}$ (d) 110

Sample Paper 2

Mathematics

Section - A

In this section, attempt any 16 questions out of Questions 1 – 20.

Each Question is of 1 mark weightage.

1. Set A has 3 elements and set B has 4 elements. Then what are the number of injective mappings that can be defined from A to B ?

   (a) 20   (b) 24   (c) 18   (d) 16

2. The principal value of the expression $\cos^{-1}[\cos(-680°)]$ is :

   (a) $\dfrac{\pi}{4}$ (b) $\dfrac{\pi}{2}$ (c) $\dfrac{3\pi}{4}$ (d) $\dfrac{2\pi}{9}$

3. If $\begin{bmatrix} x+y & 4 \\ -5 & 3y \end{bmatrix} = \begin{bmatrix} 3 & 4 \\ -5 & 6 \end{bmatrix}$, then the value of x.

   (a) 1   (b) 5   (c) -2 (d) 0

4. Which among the following is the equation of the tangent to the curve $y = -5x^2 + 6x + 7$ at the points $\left(\dfrac{1}{2}, \dfrac{35}{4}\right)$.

   (a) $2x = 2y + 51$ (b) $x = y + 5$ (c) $4y = 4x + 33$ (d) $x - y = 10$

5. Find $\dfrac{dy}{dx}\Big|_{x=\frac{\pi}{2}}$, where $y = e^{\sin x}$.

   (a) 0   (b) 1   (c) -1 (d) 2

6. If $\begin{bmatrix} \cos\alpha & -\sin\alpha \\ \sin\alpha & \cos\alpha \end{bmatrix}$ is identity matrix then what is the value of α ?

   (a) 0   (b) $\dfrac{\pi}{2}$ (c) $\dfrac{\pi}{4}$ (d) $\dfrac{3\pi}{2}$

7. If A is a matrix of order 2×3 and B is the matrix of order 3×5, then what is the order of matrix $(AB)^T$?

   (a) 2×5 (b) 5×2 (c) 3×3 (d) 5×3

8. If $R = \{(x, y) : x + 2y = 8\}$ is a relation on N, then find the range of R is :

   (a) (2, 4, 6)   (b) (1, 3, 5)   (c) (1, 2, 3)   (d) (3, 5, 7)

9. If $\begin{bmatrix} 3-2x & x+1 \\ 2 & 4 \end{bmatrix}$ is singular, then find the value of x is :

   (a) 1   (b) 0   (c) 3   (d) $\dfrac{5}{2}$

10. Evaluate $\dfrac{dy}{dx}$ if $y = e^{\sin x^2}$.

    (a) $2x \cos x^2\, e^{\sin x^2}$ (b) $2x \sin x^2\, e^{\cos x^2}$ (c) $2x^2\, e^{\cos x^2}$ (d) $x^2 \cos x^2\, e^{\sin x^2}$

11. What is the principal value of $\tan^{-1}(-1)$?

   (a) $\dfrac{\pi}{4}$ (b) $\dfrac{\pi}{2}$ (c) $\dfrac{-\pi}{2}$ (d) $\dfrac{-\pi}{4}$

12. If $[1 \quad x]\begin{bmatrix} 2 & -1 \\ 1 & 2 \end{bmatrix}\begin{bmatrix} 1 \\ 3 \end{bmatrix} = [0]$, then $x =$

   (a) $\dfrac{2}{7}$ (b) $\dfrac{1}{7}$ (c) $\dfrac{5}{7}$ (d) $\dfrac{3}{7}$

13. What is the principal value of $\cos^{-1}\left(\cos\dfrac{2\pi}{3}\right) + \sin^{-1}\left(\sin\dfrac{2\pi}{3}\right)$?

   (a) π (b) $\dfrac{\pi}{2}$ (c) $\dfrac{\pi}{4}$ (d) $\dfrac{2\pi}{3}$

14. If $y = \tan^{-1}\left(\dfrac{\sqrt{x} - x}{1 + x^{3/2}}\right)$, then $y'(1)$ is equal to:

   (a) 0 (b) $\dfrac{1}{2}$ (c) -1 (d) $-\dfrac{1}{4}$

15. If $y = \cot^{-1}\left(\dfrac{a+x}{1-ax}\right)$; then $\dfrac{dy}{dx}$:

   (a) $\dfrac{1}{1+x^2}$ (b) $\dfrac{-1}{1+x^2}$ (c) $\dfrac{x^2}{1+x}$ (d) $\dfrac{1+x}{x^2}$

16. $[x \quad 1]\begin{bmatrix} 1 & 0 \\ -2 & 0 \end{bmatrix} = 0$, then x equals:

   (a) 0 (b) -2 (c) -1 (d) 2

17. If matrix $A = \begin{bmatrix} 3 & -3 \\ -3 & 3 \end{bmatrix}$ and $A^2 = \lambda A$, then find the value of λ.

   (a) -4 (b) 5 (c) 6 (d) 2

18. If $f(x) = \left(\dfrac{x^a}{x^b}\right)^{a+b}\left(\dfrac{x^b}{x^c}\right)^{b+c}\left(\dfrac{x^c}{x^a}\right)^{c+a}$ then $f'(x)$ is equal to:

   (a) 1 (b) 0 (c) x^{a+b+c} (d) None of these

19. What is the point on the curve $y^2 = x$, where the tangent makes an angle of $\dfrac{\pi}{4}$ with X-axis ?

   (a) $4, -2$ (b) $4, 2$

   (c) $1, -1$ (d) $\dfrac{1}{4}, \dfrac{1}{2}$

20. Let $f(x) = \begin{cases} \dfrac{\sin(a+1)x + \sin x}{x}, & x < 0 \\[2mm] c, & x = 0 \\[2mm] \dfrac{\sqrt{x + bx^2} - \sqrt{x}}{bx^{3/2}}, & x > 0 \end{cases}$

if $f(x)$ is continuous at $x = 0$, then:

   (a) $a + c = 0, b = 1$ (b) $a + c = 1, b \in R$

   (c) $a + c = -1, b \in R$ (d) $a - c = -1, b = -1$

Section - B

In this section, attempt any 16 questions out of the Questions 21 – 40.

Each Question is of 1 mark weightage.

21. Find x, if $\begin{bmatrix} 1 & 2 & x \\ 1 & 1 & 1 \\ 2 & 1 & -1 \end{bmatrix}$ is singular :

    (a) 1 (b) 2 (c) 3 (d) 4

22. Let L denotes the set of all straight lines in a plane. Let a relation R be defined by $\alpha R\beta \Leftrightarrow \alpha \perp \beta$, $\alpha, \beta \in L$. Then, R is:

    (a) Reflexive only (b) Symmetric only (c) Transitive only (d) None of these

23. The relation R is defined on the set of natural numbers as $\{(a, b) : a = 2b\}$. Then, R^{-1} is given by:

    (a) $\{(2, 1), (4, 2), (6, 3), ...\}$ (b) $\{(1, 2), (2, 4), (3, 6), ...\}$

    (c) R^{-1} is not defined (d) None of the above

24. $\sec^{-1}\left(\dfrac{-2}{\sqrt{3}}\right) =$

    (a) $\dfrac{\pi}{6}$ (b) $\dfrac{\pi}{3}$ (c) $\dfrac{5\pi}{6}$ (d) $\dfrac{2\pi}{3}$

25. If $\cos^{-1} x + \cos^{-1} y + \cos^{-1} z = 3\pi$, then $xy + yz + zx$ is equal to:

    (a) -3 (b) 0 (c) 3 (d) -1

26. A new room is to be constructed in a house to increase the living area into it. A window is to be opened on one of the walls of the room in shape of rectangle surmounted by an equilateral triangle. If the perimeter of window is 12 m and they want to bring maximum light from the window.

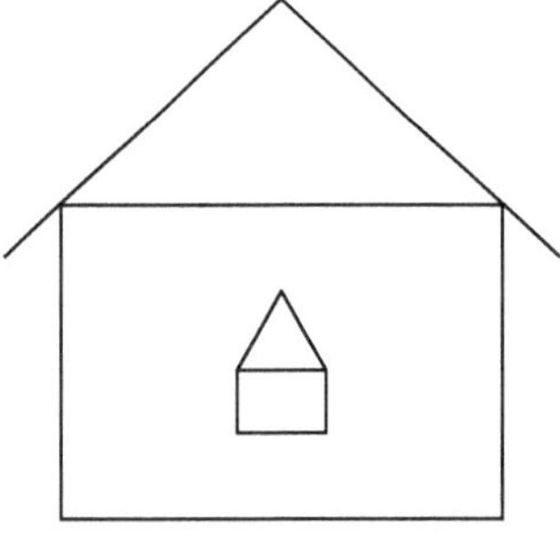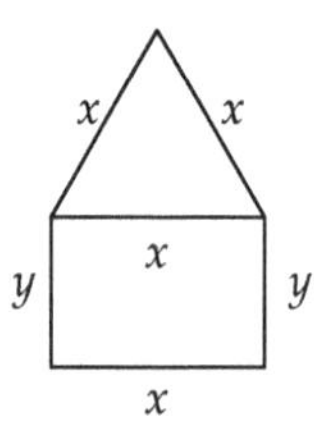

    For what value of x, the area will be maximum ?

    (a) $\dfrac{12}{6+\sqrt{3}}$ (b) $\dfrac{12}{6-\sqrt{3}}$ (c) $\dfrac{18-6\sqrt{3}}{6-\sqrt{3}}$ (d) $\dfrac{6-\sqrt{3}}{12}$

27. Which one of the following represent the shaded region in the figure?

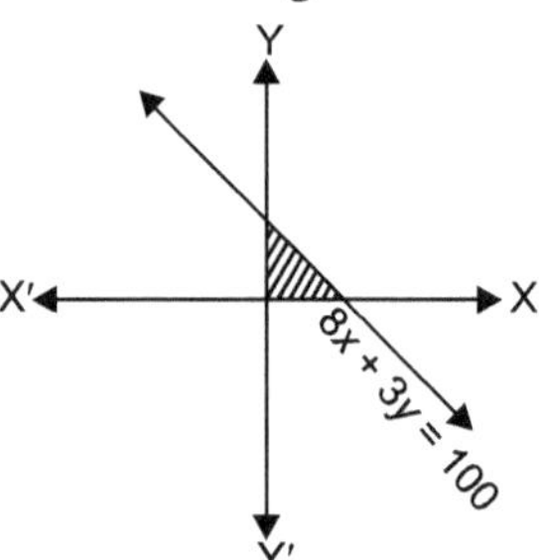

    (a) $8x + 3y \geq 100, x \geq 0, y \geq 0$ (b) $8x + 3y \leq 100, y \geq 0$ (c) $8x + 3y \geq 100$ (d) $8x + 3y \leq 100$

28. The values of a for which $y = x^2 + ax + 25$ touches the axis of x are:

    (a) ± 5 (b) ± 10 (c) ± 2 (d) ± 1

29. LPP of how many variables can be solved by graphical method?
   (a) Three variables
   (b) Two variables
   (c) More than three variables
   (d) None of the above

30. Let $A = \begin{bmatrix} \cos^2\theta & \sin\theta\cos\theta \\ \cos\phi\sin\phi & \sin^2\theta \end{bmatrix}$ and $B = \begin{bmatrix} \cos^2\phi & \sin\phi\cos\phi \\ \cos\phi\sin\phi & \sin^2\phi \end{bmatrix}$, then AB = 0, if:

   (a) $\theta = n\phi$, $n = 0, 1, 2, \ldots$
   (b) $\theta + \phi = n\pi$, $n = 0, 1, 2, \ldots$
   (c) $\theta = \phi + (2n+1)\dfrac{\pi}{2}$, $n = 0, 1, 2, \ldots$
   (d) $\theta = \phi + \dfrac{n\pi}{2}$, $n = 0, 1, 2, \ldots$

31. If $(6, 0)$, $(4, 3)$, $(2, 1)$ is the vertices of a triangle then the area of the triangle is:
   (a) 3 square unit
   (b) 4 square unit
   (c) 5 square unit
   (d) 6 square unit

32. Corner points of the feasible region for an LPP are $(0, 2)$, $(3, 0)$, $(6, 0)$, $(6, 8)$ and $(0, 5)$. Let F = $4x + 6y$ be the objective function. The minimum value of F occurs at:
   (a) $(0, 2)$ only
   (b) $(3, 0)$ only
   (c) The mid-point of the line segment joining the points $(0, 2)$ and $(3, 0)$ only
   (d) Any point on the line segment joining the points $(0, 2)$ and $(3, 0)$

33. If $\sin y = x \sin(a + y)$, then $\dfrac{dy}{dx}$ is equal to:

   (a) $\dfrac{\sin a}{\sin^2(a+y)}$
   (b) $\dfrac{\sin^2(a+y)}{\sin a}$
   (c) $\sin a \sin^2(a+y)$
   (d) $\dfrac{\sin^2(a-y)}{\sin a}$

34. If $A = \begin{bmatrix} 1 & 2 & x \\ 0 & 1 & 0 \\ 0 & 0 & 1 \end{bmatrix}$ and $B = \begin{bmatrix} 1 & -2 & y \\ 0 & 1 & 0 \\ 0 & 0 & 1 \end{bmatrix}$ and $AB = I_3$, then $x + y$ equals:

   (a) 0
   (b) -1
   (c) 2
   (d) None of these

35. The area of the triangle with vertices $(-2, -3)$ $(3, 2)$ and $(-1, -8)$ is:
   (a) $\dfrac{15}{2}$ sq. units
   (b) $\dfrac{47}{2}$ sq. units
   (c) 15 sq. units
   (d) None of these

36. Fesible region for an LPP is shown shaded in the following figure. Minimum of $Z = 4x + 3y$ occurs at the point:

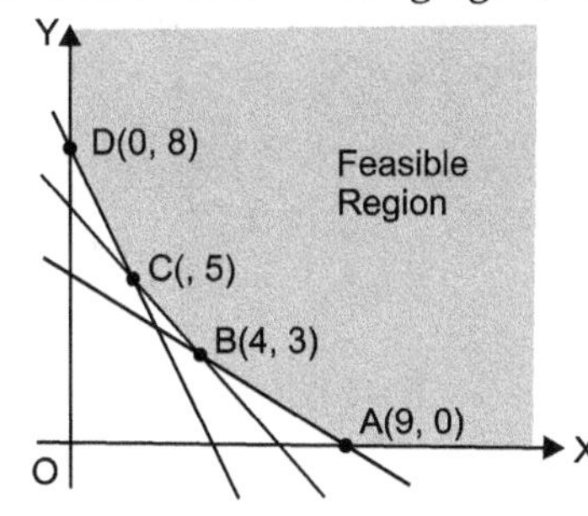

   (a) $(0, 8)$
   (b) $(2, 5)$
   (c) $(4, 3)$
   (d) $(9, 0)$

37. Function $2x + 3y = \sin x$, then the value of $\dfrac{dy}{dx}$ is:

   (a) $-\dfrac{(\cos x + 2)}{3}$
   (b) $\dfrac{\cos x - 2}{3}$
   (c) $\cos x - 2$
   (d) $\dfrac{\cos x - 3}{2}$

38. If A_{ij} denotes the cofactor of the element a_{ij} of the determinant $\begin{vmatrix} 2 & -3 & 5 \\ 6 & 0 & 4 \\ 1 & 5 & -7 \end{vmatrix}$ then value of

   $a_{11}A_{31} + a_{12}A_{32} + a_{13}A_{33}$ is:
   (a) 0
   (b) 5
   (c) 10
   (d) -5

39. If the function $f(x) = \dfrac{\sin(10x)}{x}$, $x \neq 0$ is continuous at $x = 0$, find $f(0)$.

   (a) 0
   (b) 1
   (c) 10
   (d) None of these

40. Region represented by $x \geq 0$, $y \geq 0$ is:

    (a) First quadrant (b) Second quadrant (c) Third quadrant (d) Fourth quadrant

Section - C

In this section, attempt any 8 questions. Each question is of 1-mark weightage.

Questions 46–50 are based on a Case-Study.

41. If x is a complex root of the equation $\begin{vmatrix} 1 & x & x \\ x & 1 & x \\ x & x & 1 \end{vmatrix} + \begin{vmatrix} 1-x & 1 & 1 \\ 1 & 1-x & 1 \\ 1 & 1 & 1-x \end{vmatrix} = 0$, then $x^{2007} + x^{-2007} =$

    (a) 1 (b) -1 (c) -2 (d) 2

42. The number of discontinuous functions $y(x)$ on $[-2, 2]$ satisfying $x^2 + y^2 = 4$ is:

    (a) 0 (b) 1 (c) 2 (d) > 2

43. The matrix $\begin{bmatrix} 0 & -5 & 8 \\ 5 & 0 & 12 \\ -8 & -12 & 0 \end{bmatrix}$ is a:

    (a) Diagonal matrix (b) Symmetric matrix
    (c) Skew symmetric matrix (d) Scalar matrix

44. Differential coefficient of $\sec(\tan^{-1} x)$ w.r.t. x is:

    (a) $\dfrac{x}{\sqrt{1+x^2}}$ (b) $\dfrac{x}{1+x^2}$ (c) $x\sqrt{1+x^2}$ (d) $\dfrac{1}{\sqrt{1+x^2}}$

45. On which of the following intervals is the function f given by $f(x) = x^{100} + \sin x - 1$ strictly decreasing?

    (a) $(0, 1)$ (b) $\left(\dfrac{\pi}{2}, \pi\right)$ (c) $\left(0, \dfrac{\pi}{2}\right)$ (d) None of these

A new township is to be constructed along the curve $y = x^3 - 11x + 5$. Two attraction point *i.e.*, Amusement park and shopping mall is to be made on the this curve. At a point $(1, -5)$ on the curve amusement park is to be constructed and on another point shopping mall is to be constructed at which tangent has the equation $y = x - 11$.

Give the answers of the following questions :

46. Find the slope of the normal to the curve at $(1, -5)$ on which amusement park is to be constructed ?

    (a) $\dfrac{1}{8}$ (b) 8 (c) -8 (d) $\dfrac{-1}{8}$

47. Find the equation of normal to the curve along which amusement park is to be constructed ?
    (a) $8y - x - 41 = 0$ (b) $8y + x = 41$
    (c) $8y + x + 41 = 0$ (d) $8y - x + 41 = 0$

48. Find the point of x where curve along which township is parallel to X-axis ?

    (a) $\pm\sqrt{\dfrac{11}{3}}$ (b) $\pm\dfrac{11}{3}$ (c) ± 4 (d) ± 2

49. What is the slope of tangent at the curve ?

    (a) 3 (b) 1 (c) -1 (d) $\dfrac{1}{2}$

50. Find the points on the curve at which tangent $y = x - 11$ is given ?
    (a) $(-2, 19)$ (b) $(2, -9)$
    (c) $(-2, 9)$ (d) $(2, -19)$

❑❑

Sample Paper 3

Mathematics

Section – A

In this section, attempt any 16 questions out of Questions 1 – 20.

Each Question is of 1 mark weightage.

1. What is the principle value of branch of $\sec^{-1}$.

   (a) $[0, \pi]$
   (b) $\left\{\pi, \dfrac{\pi}{2}\right\}$
   (c) $\left\{0, \dfrac{\pi}{2}\right\}$
   (d) $[0, \pi] - \left\{\dfrac{\pi}{2}\right\}$

2. The relation R in the set $\{1, 2, 3\}$ given by $R = \{(1, 2), (2, 1)\}$ is :

   (a) Transitive
   (b) Symmetric
   (c) Reflexive
   (d) All of these

3. If $x = \begin{bmatrix} 3 & 1 & 1 \\ 5 & 2 & 3 \end{bmatrix}$ and $y = \begin{bmatrix} 2 & 1 & 1 \\ 7 & 2 & 4 \end{bmatrix}$, what is matrix z, such that $x + y + z = 0$.

   (a) $\begin{bmatrix} -5 & -2 & -2 \\ -12 & -4 & -7 \end{bmatrix}$
   (b) $\begin{bmatrix} -2 & -1 & -1 \\ -7 & -2 & -4 \end{bmatrix}$
   (c) $\begin{bmatrix} -3 & -1 & -1 \\ -5 & -2 & -3 \end{bmatrix}$
   (d) None of these

4. If matrix $A = [1 \ -3 \ \ 0]$, then what is AA', where A' is transpose of A.

   (a) -10
   (b) 10
   (c) 0
   (d) 1

5. For what value of x, is the matrix $A = \begin{bmatrix} 0 & 1 & -2 \\ -1 & 0 & 3 \\ x & -3 & 0 \end{bmatrix}$ a skew-symmetric matrix ?

   (a) 2
   (b) 1
   (c) -1
   (d) 0

6. What is the differential coefficient of $\sec(\tan^{-1} x)$ w.r.t. x.

   (a) $\dfrac{x}{1+x^2}$
   (b) $\dfrac{1}{x}$
   (c) $\dfrac{x}{\sqrt{1+x^2}}$
   (d) $\dfrac{2}{x}$

7. The two curves $x^3 - 3xy^2 + 2 = 0$ and $3x^2y - y^3 = 2$, are :

   (a) Parallel
   (b) Perpendicular
   (c) No common point of intersection
   (d) None of these

8. If a matrix has 12 elements, what are the possible number of orders it can have ?

   (a) 12
   (b) 24
   (c) 6
   (d) 13

9. What is the principal value of $\sin^{-1}\left(\dfrac{-\sqrt{3}}{2}\right)$?

   (a) $\dfrac{\pi}{3}$
   (b) $\dfrac{-\pi}{3}$
   (c) $\dfrac{-\pi}{2}$
   (d) $\dfrac{\pi}{2}$

10. Find $\dfrac{dy}{dx}$ if $y = 8x^6 - 4x^3$.

    (a) $24x^5 - 8x^2$
    (b) $48x^5 - 12x^2$
    (c) $4x^5 - x^2$
    (d) $3x^5 - 2x^2$

11. How many possible orders a matrix having 8 elements can have?

    (a) 5
    (b) 2
    (c) 4
    (d) 3

12. If $f(x) = \sin^{-1}(4x + 3)$, then the domain of f is:

    (a) $[\infty, 0]$
    (b) $\left[-1, \dfrac{-1}{2}\right]$
    (c) $[-1, \infty]$
    (d) $[-\infty, \infty]$

13. If $f(x) = \dfrac{\sqrt{4+x}-2}{x}$, $x \neq 0$ be continuous at $x = 0$, then $f(0) =$

    (a) $\dfrac{1}{2}$
    (b) $\dfrac{1}{4}$
    (c) 2
    (d) $\dfrac{3}{2}$

14. The equation of the normal to the curve $y = \sin x$ at $(0, 0)$ is:
    (a) $x = y$
    (b) $x = 2y$
    (c) $x + y = 0$
    (d) $x + 2y = 0$

15. If $y = (3x^2 - 9x + 5)^2$ then $\dfrac{dy}{dx} =$

    (a) $2(3x^2 - 9x + 5)(6x - 5)$
    (b) $2(3x^2 - 9x + 5)$
    (c) $3(3x^2 - 9x + 5)$
    (d) $6(3x^2 - 9x + 5)(2x - 3)$

16. The number of all one-one functions from the set $\{1, 2, 3, \ldots, n\}$ to itself is:
    (a) n
    (b) n^2
    (c) n^n
    (d) $n\,!$

17. Let $f : R \to R$ be a function defined by $f(x) = \dfrac{x^2 - 8}{x^2 + 2}$, then f is:

    (a) One-one but not onto
    (b) One-one and onto
    (c) Onto but not one-one
    (d) Neither one-one nor onto

18. Let $\theta = \sin^{-1}(\sin(-600°))$, then value of θ is:

    (a) $\dfrac{\pi}{3}$
    (b) $\dfrac{\pi}{2}$
    (c) $\dfrac{2\pi}{3}$
    (d) $\dfrac{-2\pi}{3}$

19. If $\tan(\sec^{-1} x) = \sin\left(\cos^{-1}\dfrac{1}{\sqrt{5}}\right)$, then x is equal to:

    (a) $\pm\dfrac{3}{\sqrt{5}}$
    (b) $\pm\dfrac{\sqrt{5}}{3}$
    (c) $\pm\dfrac{\sqrt{3}}{5}$
    (d) None of these

20. If $U = [2 \;\; -3 \;\; 4]$, $V = \begin{bmatrix} 3 \\ 2 \\ 1 \end{bmatrix}$, $X = [0 \;\; 2 \;\; 3]$ and $Y = \begin{bmatrix} 2 \\ 2 \\ 4 \end{bmatrix}$, then the value of $UV + XY$ is:

    (a) 20
    (b) $[-20]$
    (c) -20
    (d) $[20]$

Section - B

In this section, attempt any 16 questions out of the Questions 21 – 40.

Each Question is of 1 mark weightage.

21. The function $f : R \to R$ given by $f(x) = x^3 - 1$ is:
    (a) One-one but not onto
    (b) Onto but not one-one
    (c) A bijection
    (d) Neither one-one nor onto

22. After the lockdown period of Covid-19, it is difficult to restart the business of Touring Agency. A tour operator charges ₹ 200 per passenger for 50 passengers. He is giving a discount of ₹ 5 for each 10 passenger in excess of 50. He wants to maximise his earning during this pandemic period.

    What is the total earning function ?

    (a) $225 - \dfrac{x}{2}$
    (b) $225x - \dfrac{x^2}{2}$
    (c) $220 - \dfrac{x}{2}$
    (d) $220 - \dfrac{x^2}{3}$

23. A cooperative society of farmers has 50 hectare of land to grow two crops X and Y. The estimation of income from crops per hectare is 10,500 and 9,000 respectively. To control weeds, a runny herbicide has used for both crops at rates of 20 litres and 10 litres per hectare. Additionally, not more than 800 litres of

herbicide should be used for protecting fish and natural world using a fishpond which collect drainage from this ground.

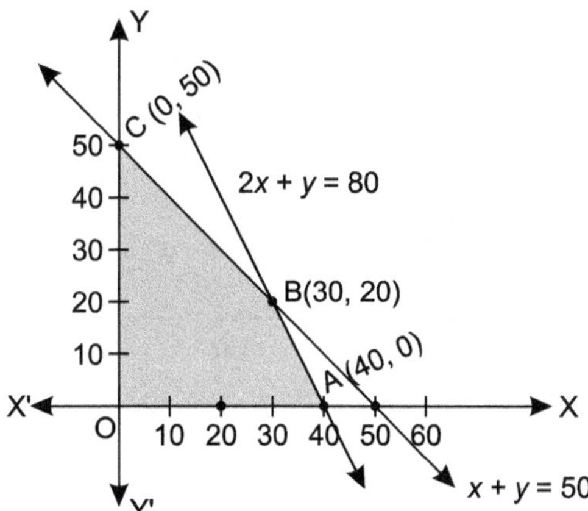

Fig. : Graph of OABC is the feasible region (shaded)

Corner Point	$Z = 10500x + 9000y$
$O(0,\ 0)$	0
$A(40,\ 0)$	420000
$B(30,\ 20)$	495000
$C(0,\ 50)$	450000

The maximum income would be got by people is :

(a) ₹ 4,95,000 (b) ₹ 4,90,000 (c) ₹ 4,85,000 (d) ₹ 4,80,000

24. The function $(x) = |x| + |x - 1|$ is:
(a) Continuous at $x = 0$ as well as at $x = 1$ (b) Continuous at $x = 1$ but not at $x = 0$
(c) Discontinuous at $x = 0$ as well as at $x = 1$ (d) Continuous at $x = 0$ but not at $x = 1$

25. For $A = \begin{bmatrix} 4 & 2i \\ i & 1 \end{bmatrix}$, $(A - 2I)(A - 3I)$ is a:

(a) Null matrix (b) Hermitian matrix (c) Unit matrix (d) None of these

26. Determine the value of 'k' for which the following is continuous at $x = 3$:

$$f(x) = \begin{cases} \dfrac{(x+3)^2 - 36}{x - 3}, & x \neq 3 \\ k, & x = 3 \end{cases}$$

(a) 9 (b) 12 (c) 3 (d) 15

27. If $[1 \quad x \quad 1] \begin{bmatrix} 1 & 2 & 3 \\ 0 & 5 & 1 \\ 0 & 3 & 2 \end{bmatrix} \begin{bmatrix} x \\ 1 \\ -2 \end{bmatrix} = O$ (null matrix), then the value of x is:

(a) 0 (b) $\dfrac{2}{3}$ (c) $\dfrac{5}{4}$ (d) $-\dfrac{4}{5}$

28. The differential coefficient of the function $\cot^3 2x$ is:
(a) $-6\cot^2 2x \cdot \operatorname{cosec}^2 2x$ (b) $-3\cot^2 2x \cdot \operatorname{cosec}^2 2x$
(c) $-6\cot^2 2x \cdot \operatorname{cosec} 2x$ (d) $-3\cot^2 2x \cdot \operatorname{cosec} 2x$

29. If $A = \begin{bmatrix} a & 0 & 0 \\ 0 & a & 0 \\ 0 & 0 & a \end{bmatrix}$, then the value of $|A|\ |\operatorname{adj} A|$ is:

(a) a^3 (b) a^6 (c) a^9 (d) a^{27}

30. The feasible region for an LPP is shown shaded in the figure. Let F = $3x - 4y$ be objecive function. Maximum value of F is:

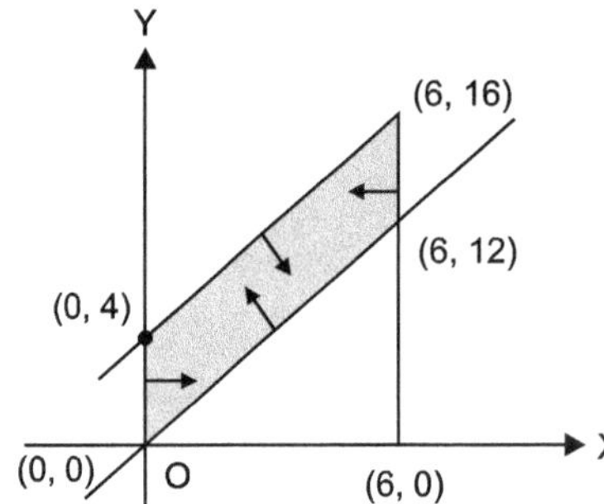

(a) 0   (b) 8   (c) 12   (d) – 18

31. If $y = (1 + x)(1 + x^2)(1 + x^4)$, then $\dfrac{dy}{dx}$ at $x = 1$ is:

(a) 20   (b) 28   (c) 1   (d) 0

32. The derivative of $\cos^{-1}(2x^2 - 1)$ w.r.t. $\cos^{-1} x$ is:

(a) 2   (b) $\dfrac{-1}{2\sqrt{1-x^2}}$ (c) $\dfrac{2}{x}$ (d) $1 - x^2$

33. The corner points of the feasible region determined by the system of linear constraints are (0, 10), (5, 5), (15, 15), (0, 20). Let $Z = px + qy$, where $p, q > 0$. Condition on p and q so that the maximum of Z occurs at both the points (15, 15) and (0, 20) is:

(a) $p = q$ (b) $p = 2q$ (c) $q = 2p$ (d) $q = 3p$

34. Variables of the objective function of the linear programming problem are:

(a) Zero   (b) Zero or positive   (c) Negative   (d) Zero or negative

35. If $x = \dfrac{a}{1+m^3}$, $y = \dfrac{am}{1+m^3}$, then $\dfrac{dy}{dx}$ is:

(a) $\dfrac{1+2m^3}{3m^2}$ (b) $\dfrac{1-2m^3}{3m^2}$ (c) $\dfrac{-1+2m^3}{3m^2}$ (d) 1

36. The value of x for which the function $y = x^4 - \dfrac{4x^3}{3}$ is increasing is:

(a) $(-\infty, 1)$ (b) $(1, \infty)$ (c) $(1, \infty)$ (d) $(-\infty, 0)$

37. The point on the curve $y^2 = x$, where the tangent makes an angle of $\dfrac{\pi}{4}$ with X-axis is:

(a) $\left(\dfrac{1}{2}, \dfrac{1}{4}\right)$ (b) $\left(\dfrac{1}{4}, \dfrac{1}{2}\right)$ (c) (4, 2)   (d) (1, 1)

38. The angle of intersection of the curves $y = 2\sin^2 x$ and $y = \cos 2x$ at $x = \dfrac{\pi}{6}$ is:

(a) $\dfrac{\pi}{4}$ (b) $\dfrac{\pi}{3}$ (c) $\dfrac{\pi}{2}$ (d) None of these

39. The maximum value of $(\sin x + \cos x)$ is:

(a) $\dfrac{1}{\sqrt{2}}$ (b) $\sqrt{2}$ (c) $\dfrac{\sqrt{2}}{2}$ (d) 0

40. Which of the following statement is correct?
    (a) Every LPP has at least one optimal solution
    (b) Every LPP has a unique optimal solution
    (c) If an LPP has two optimal solutions, then it has infinitely many solutions
    (d) None of these

Section - C

In this section, attempt any 8 questions. Each question is of 1-mark weightage.

Questions 46-50 are based on a Case-Study.

41. If the value of $y = a \log x + bx^2 + x$ is maximum or minimum at $x = -1$ and $x = 2$, find the values of a and b.

(a) $2, -\dfrac{1}{2}$ (b) $2, -4$ (c) $3, -\dfrac{1}{2}$ (d) $-3, 2$

42. The function $f : A \to B$ defined by $f(x) = 4x + 7$, $x \in R$ is:

(a) One-one (b) Many-one (c) Odd (d) Even

43. A missile is fired from the ground level rises x metre vertically upwards in t s, where $x = 100t - \dfrac{25}{2} t^2$. The maximum height reached is:

(a) 200 m (b) 125 m (c) 160 m (d) 190 m

44. If the two positive numbers x and y such that $x + y = 60$ and x^3y is maximum, then:

(a) $x = 15, y = 45$ (b) $x = 45, y = 15$ (c) $x = 30, y = 30$ (d) $x = 20, y = 40$

45. The value of a, so that the sum of the squares of the roots of the equation $x^2 - (a - 2)x - a + 1 = 0$ assume the least value, is:

(a) 2 (b) 0 (c) 3 (d) 1

A concert is organised to earn the revenue of ₹ 1,80,000 which can be distributed among the needy people during the period of Covid-19. The concert hall has 4,000 seats which are divided into two sections A and B. The cost of a ticket in Section A is ₹ 50 and that of Section B is ₹ 40. All the seats are occupied.

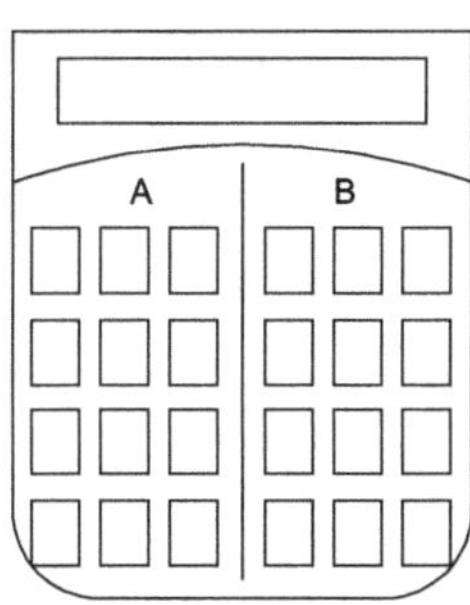

Attempt the following questions :

46. If x and y are number of seats of Section A and B respectively, then write the equation related to number of seats :

(a) $x - y = 4000$ (b) $x + y = 400$ (c) $x + y = 4000$ (d) $2x + y = 4000$

47. What will be relation between x and y for the total revenue ?

(a) $5x + 4y = 18000$ (b) $50x + 40y = 18000$ (c) $5x + 4y = 1800$ (d) $x + y = 180$

48. If equations are to be solved through the matrix method in the form of $AX = B$, then what will be matrix A and matrix B :

(a) $A = \begin{bmatrix} 1 & 1 \\ 5 & 4 \end{bmatrix}, B = \begin{bmatrix} 4000 \\ 18000 \end{bmatrix}$ (b) $A = \begin{bmatrix} 5 & 4 \\ 1 & 1 \end{bmatrix}, B = \begin{bmatrix} 4000 \\ 18000 \end{bmatrix}$

(c) $A = \begin{bmatrix} 1 & 5 \\ 1 & 4 \end{bmatrix}, B = \begin{bmatrix} 18000 \\ 4000 \end{bmatrix}$ (d) $A = \begin{bmatrix} 1 & 4 \\ 1 & 5 \end{bmatrix}, B = \begin{bmatrix} 4000 \\ 18000 \end{bmatrix}$

49. The value of X will be equal to $A^{-1}B$, then A^{-1} :

(a) $\begin{bmatrix} -4 & 1 \\ -5 & 1 \end{bmatrix}$ (b) $\begin{bmatrix} -4 & 1 \\ 5 & -1 \end{bmatrix}$ (c) $\begin{bmatrix} 4 & -5 \\ -1 & 1 \end{bmatrix}$ (d) $\begin{bmatrix} -4 & 5 \\ -1 & -1 \end{bmatrix}$

50. How many seats are there in Section A and Section B of Concert Hall ?

(a) 2000, 4000 (b) 4000, 2000 (c) 2000, 2000 (d) 6000, 4000

Sample Paper 4

Mathematics

Section - A

In this section, attempt any 16 questions out of Questions 1 – 20.

Each Question is of 1 mark weightage.

1. The value of the expression $\sin [\cot^{-1} \{\cos (\tan^{-1} 1)\}]$ is :

    (a) $\sqrt{\dfrac{2}{3}}$ (b) $\sqrt{\dfrac{3}{2}}$ (c) 1   (d) 0

2. If $\begin{bmatrix} a+b & 2 \\ 5 & b \end{bmatrix} = \begin{bmatrix} 6 & 2 \\ 5 & 2 \end{bmatrix}$, then the value of a is :

    (a) 4   (b) 2   (c) 0   (d) 1

3. The slope of the tangent to the curve $y = x^4 - 4x$ at $x = 4$ is :

    (a) 100   (b) 200   (c) 50   (d) 252

4. At what value of x, the function $g(x) = \dfrac{x}{2} + \dfrac{2}{x}$ will have a local minimum.

    (a) -2 (b) 2   (c) 0   (d) 1

5. If $y = ae^{mx} + be^{-mx}$; then $\dfrac{d^2y}{dx^2} =$

    (a) my (b) $m^2 y$ (c) y (d) $\dfrac{y}{m^2}$

6. What do we call the linear function Z, which is to be maximized or minimized ?

    (a) Constraints   (b) Dependent variable

    (c) Objective function   (d) None of these

7. Name the region in linear programming problem that gives the most feasible value of the objective function.

    (a) Concave set   (b) Feasible   (c) Convex set   (d) Bounded region

8. If matrix $A = \begin{bmatrix} 3 & 2 & -1 \\ 4 & 1 & 6 \end{bmatrix}$, then additive inverse of A is:

    (a) $\begin{bmatrix} -3 & -2 & 1 \\ -4 & -1 & -6 \end{bmatrix}$ (b) $\begin{bmatrix} 6 & 4 & -2 \\ 8 & 2 & 12 \end{bmatrix}$ (c) $\begin{bmatrix} 0 & 0 & 0 \\ 0 & 0 & 0 \end{bmatrix}$ (d) $\begin{bmatrix} 3 & 2 & -1 \\ 4 & -1 & -6 \end{bmatrix}$

9. If $A = \begin{bmatrix} 3 & 2 \\ 2 & -1 \end{bmatrix}$ and $B = \begin{bmatrix} 1 & -2 \\ 3 & 0 \end{bmatrix}$, then the value of AB is:

    (a) $\begin{bmatrix} 9 & 6 \\ 1 & 4 \end{bmatrix}$ (b) $\begin{bmatrix} -9 & -6 \\ -1 & -4 \end{bmatrix}$ (c) $\begin{bmatrix} 9 & -6 \\ -1 & -4 \end{bmatrix}$ (d) None of these

10. What would be the graph of the inequation $2x + y > 5$ represent ?

    (a) Open half plane containing the origin   (b) Open half plane not containing the origin

    (c) Second half plane not containing the origin   (d) None of these

11. The range of the function $\cos 2x$ is :

   (a) $[1, 0]$ (b) $[0, 1]$ (c) $[-1, 1]$ (d) $[\infty, 0]$

12. Find $\dfrac{dy}{dx}$, if $y = \sin^3 x \cos x$.

   (a) $\sin^2 x\,(3\cos^2 x - \sin^2 x)$ (b) $3\cos^3 x\,(1 - \sin^2 x)$ (c) $3\cos^4 x$ (d) $3\sin^4 x$

13. The number of values of x in the interval $[0, 3\pi]$ satisfying the equation $2\sin^2 x + 5\sin x - 3 = 0$ is:

   (a) $\dfrac{\pi}{6}, \dfrac{5\pi}{6}, \dfrac{13\pi}{6}, \dfrac{8\pi}{3}$ (b) $\dfrac{\pi}{3}, \dfrac{5\pi}{6}, \dfrac{13\pi}{6}, \dfrac{8\pi}{3}$ (c) $\dfrac{\pi}{6}, \dfrac{5\pi}{6}, \dfrac{7\pi}{6}, \dfrac{8\pi}{3}$ (d) $\dfrac{\pi}{3}, \dfrac{13\pi}{6}, \dfrac{8\pi}{3}, \dfrac{7\pi}{6}$

14. The value of b for which $f(x) = \begin{cases} 5x - 4, & 0 < x < 1 \\ 4x^2 + 3bx, & 1 < x < 2 \end{cases}$ is continuous at $x = 1$ is:

   (a) 1 (b) -1 (c) 2 (d) 3

15. If $y = e^x \tan^{-1} x$, then $\dfrac{dy}{dx}$ is:

   (a) $e^x\left[\tan^{-1} x + \dfrac{1}{1 + x^2}\right]$ (b) $e^x\left[\tan^{-1} x + \dfrac{1}{1 - x^2}\right]$

   (c) $e^x\left[\tan^{-1} x + \dfrac{1}{\sqrt{1 + x^2}}\right]$ (d) $e^x\left[\tan^{-1} x - \dfrac{1}{1 + x^2}\right]$

16. A feasible region of a system of linear inequalities is said to be .... it can be enclosed within a circle.

   (a) Unbounded (b) Bounded (c) Infeasible (d) None ofthese

17. Let $f(x) = \dfrac{\ln\,(1 + ax) - \ln\,(1 - bx)}{x}$, $x \neq 0$. If $f(x)$ is continuous at $x = 0$, then $f(0) =$

   (a) $a - b$ (b) $a + b$ (c) $b - a$ (d) $\ln a + \ln b$

18. The value of $\tan^{-1}\left[2\cos\left(2\sin^{-1}\dfrac{1}{2}\right)\right]$ is:

   (a) $-\dfrac{\pi}{4}$ (b) $\dfrac{\pi}{4}$ (c) $\dfrac{\pi}{2}$ (d) None of these

19. The value of $\cos^{-1}\left(\cos\dfrac{5\pi}{3}\right) + \sin^{-1}\left(\sin\dfrac{5\pi}{3}\right)$ is:

   (a) $\dfrac{\pi}{2}$ (b) $\dfrac{5\pi}{3}$ (c) $\dfrac{10\pi}{3}$ (d) 0

20. If $AB = A$ and $BA = B$, then $A^2 + B^2$ is equal to:

   (a) $A + B$ (b) $A - B$ (c) $2A + B$ (d) None of these

Section - B

In this section, attempt any 16 questions out of the Questions 21 - 40.

Each Question is of 1 mark weightage.

21. The relation R defined in the set $A = \{1, 2, 3, 4, 5, 6, 7\}$ by $R = \{(a, b) : \text{both } a \text{ and } b \text{ are either odd or even}\}$, then, R is:

   (a) Symmetric (b) Transitive

   (c) An equivalence relation (d) Reflexive

22. The area of the feasible region for the following constraints $3y + x \geq 3$, $x \geq 0$ and $y \geq 0$ will be:

   (a) Bounded (b) Unbounded (c) Convex (d) Concave

23. Raj is playing with a spring by throwing it in the air which is moving along the function :
$$f(x) = 3x^4 - 4x^3 - 12x^2 + 5.$$

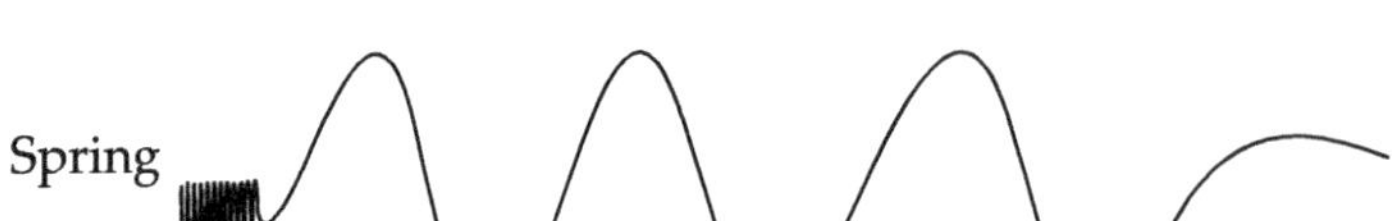

Find the critical points of x which it touches the x-axis :

(a) 0, 1, 2 (b) 0, – 1, 2 (c) 0, 1, – 2 (d) 1, 2, – 2

24. A mobile shop purchases three types of mobiles namely LG, I-phone and samsung and sells them in two malls of Gurugram. The annual sales in units are given below :

	LG	I-phone	Samsung
Mall I	20	15	35
Mall II	10	20	30

If the sale prices of per unit of LG phone is ₹20,000, I-phone ₹50,000 and Samsung is ₹15,000 respectively and costs per unit for LG ₹15,000, I-phone ₹40,000 and Samsung ₹12,000 respectively.

What is the total amount of profit in Mall I and Mall II if all goods are sold ?

(a) $\begin{bmatrix} 35,500 \\ 34,000 \end{bmatrix}$ (b) $\begin{bmatrix} 3,40,000 \\ 3,55,000 \end{bmatrix}$ (c) $[34,000 \ \ 35,500]$ (d) $\begin{bmatrix} 3,55,000 \\ 3,40,000 \end{bmatrix}$

25. If $A = [a_{ij}]_{4 \times 3}$, where $a_{ij} = \dfrac{i-j}{i+j}$, then find A.

(a) $\begin{bmatrix} 0 & -1/3 & -1/2 \\ 1/2 & 0 & 1/5 \\ 1/3 & 1/5 & 0 \\ 3/5 & 1/3 & 1/7 \end{bmatrix}$ (b) $\begin{bmatrix} 0 & -1/3 & -1/2 \\ 1/3 & 0 & -1/5 \\ 1/2 & 1/5 & 0 \\ 3/5 & 1/3 & 1/7 \end{bmatrix}$

(c) $\begin{bmatrix} 0 & -3 & -1/2 \\ 2 & 0 & 5 \\ 3 & 5 & 0 \\ 3/5 & 3 & 7 \end{bmatrix}$ (d) $\begin{bmatrix} 0 & 1/3 & 1/2 \\ -1/3 & 0 & 1/5 \\ -1/2 & -1/5 & 0 \\ -3/5 & -1/3 & -1/7 \end{bmatrix}$

26. $\begin{vmatrix} \cos 15° & \sin 15° \\ \sin 75° & \cos 75° \end{vmatrix}$

(a) 0 (b) 5 (c) 3 (d) 7

27. The function $f(x) = x - [x]$, where [ ] denotes the greatest integer function, is:

(a) continuous everywhere (b) continuuos at integer points only
(c) continuous at non-integer points only (d) nowhere continuous

28. Determine the value of the constant 'k' so that the function $f(x) = \begin{cases} \dfrac{kx}{|x|}, & \text{if } x < 0 \\ 3, & \text{if } x \geq 0 \end{cases}$ is continuous at $x = 0$.

(a) – 3 (b) 0 (c) 3 (d) – 1

29. If $A = \begin{bmatrix} -3 & 5 & -8 \\ x & 5 & 5 \\ 0 & y & 4 \end{bmatrix}$ is upper triangular matrix, then $x + y$ is:

(a) 3 (b) – 3 (c) 0 (d) 1

30. If $f(x) = \left(\dfrac{x^a}{x^b}\right)^{a+b} \left(\dfrac{x^b}{x^c}\right)^{b+c} \left(\dfrac{x^c}{x^a}\right)^{c+a}$ then $f'(x)$ is equal to:

(a) 1
(b) 0
(c) x^{a+b+c}
(d) None of these

31. The differential coefficient of the function $\dfrac{\tan x}{3+2\tan x}$ with respect to x is:

(a) $\dfrac{3}{(3+2\tan x)^2}$
(b) $\dfrac{3+\tan x}{(3+2\tan x)^2}$
(c) $\dfrac{3\sec^2 x}{3+2\tan x}$
(d) $\dfrac{3\sec^2 x}{(3+2\tan x)^2}$

32. If A and B are any 2 × 2 matrices, then det (A + B) = 0 implies:

(a) det A = 0 and det B = 0
(b) det A + det B ≠ 0
(c) det A = 0 or det B = 0
(d) None of these

33. Let A = {1, 2, 3} and R = {(1, 2), (2, 3)} be a relation in A. Then, the minimum number of ordered pairs may be added, so that R becomes an equivalence relation, is:

(a) 7
(b) 5
(c) 1
(d) 4

34. Find the area of the triangle with vertices P(4, 5), Q(4, – 2) and R(– 6, 2).

(a) 21 sq. units
(b) 35 sq. units
(c) 30 sq. units
(d) 40 sq. units

35. $\cos^{-1}\left(\dfrac{1}{2}\right) + 2\sin^{-1}\left(\dfrac{1}{2}\right)$ is equal to:

(a) $\dfrac{\pi}{4}$
(b) $\dfrac{\pi}{6}$
(c) $\dfrac{\pi}{3}$
(d) $\dfrac{2\pi}{3}$

36. Let $f : [2, \infty) \to R$ be the function defined by $f(x) = x^2 - 4x + 5$, then the range of f is:

(a) R
(b) $[1, \infty)$
(c) $[4, \infty)$
(d) $[5, \infty)$

37. If $xe^{xy} - y = \sin^2 x$, then $\dfrac{dy}{dx}$ at $x = 0$, is:

(a) 0
(b) 1
(c) – 1
(d) None of these

38. If $\begin{bmatrix} x \\ y \\ z \end{bmatrix} = \dfrac{1}{40} \begin{bmatrix} 5 & 10 & -5 \\ -5 & -2 & 13 \\ 10 & -4 & 6 \end{bmatrix} \begin{bmatrix} 5 \\ 0 \\ 5 \end{bmatrix}$, then the value of $x + y + z$ is:

(a) 3
(b) 0
(c) 2
(d) 1

39. The function $f(x) = 2 \log (x - 2) - x^2 + 4x + 1$ increases on the interval:

(a) (1, 2)
(b) (2, 3)
(c) (1, 3)
(d) (2, 4)

40. The tangent to the curve $5x^2 + y^2 = 1$ at $\left(\dfrac{1}{3}, -\dfrac{2}{3}\right)$ passes through the point:

(a) (0, 0)
(b) (1, – 1)
(c) (– 1, 1)
(d) None of these

Section - C

In this section, attempt any 8 questions. Each question is of 1-mark weightage.

Questions 46–50 are based on a Case-Study.

41. Two towns A and B are 60 km apart. A school is to be built to serve 150 students in town A and 50 students in twon B. If the total distance to be travelled by 200 students is to be as small as possible, then the school be built at:

(a) Town B
(b) 45 km from town A
(c) town A
(d) 45 km from town B

42. Find the cofactors of elements a_{12}, a_{22}, a_{32} respectively of the matrix $\begin{bmatrix} 1 & \sin\theta & 1 \\ -\sin\theta & 1 & \sin\theta \\ -1 & -\sin\theta & 1 \end{bmatrix}$:

(a) $0, 2, -2\sin\theta$
(b) $2, 0, 2\sin\theta$
(c) $2, 0, -2\sin\theta$
(d) $-2\sin\theta, 2, 0$

43. The principal value branch of $\sec^{-1}$ is:

(a) $\left[-\dfrac{\pi}{2}, \dfrac{\pi}{2}\right] - \{0\}$ (b) $[0, \pi] - \left\{\dfrac{\pi}{2}\right\}$ (c) $(0, \pi)$ (d) $\left(-\dfrac{\pi}{2}, \dfrac{\pi}{2}\right)$

44. Let $A = \{a, b\}$, then number of one-one functions from A to A possible are:

(a) 1   (b) 2   (c) 3   (d) 4

45. Let $A = \begin{bmatrix} 1 & 2 \\ 3 & -5 \end{bmatrix}$, $B = \begin{bmatrix} 1 & 0 \\ 0 & 2 \end{bmatrix}$ and X be a matrix such that $A = BX$, then X is equal to:

(a) $\dfrac{1}{2}\begin{bmatrix} 2 & 4 \\ 3 & -5 \end{bmatrix}$ (b) $\dfrac{1}{2}\begin{bmatrix} -2 & 4 \\ 3 & 5 \end{bmatrix}$ (c) $\begin{bmatrix} 2 & 4 \\ 3 & -5 \end{bmatrix}$ (d) None of these

Sita is celebrating her birthday in fun city where she has invited her friends. There is a swing which is moving along the function $f(x) = x^3 + \dfrac{1}{x^3}$.

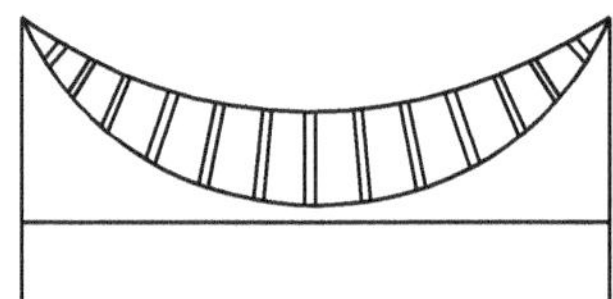 

Answer the following questions :

46. Find the slope of the given function :

(a) $x^2 + \dfrac{3}{x^4}$ (b) $3x^2 - \dfrac{3}{x^4}$ (c) $\dfrac{3}{x^2} + \dfrac{3}{x^4}$ (d) $\dfrac{3}{x^2} - 3x^4$

47. Find the critical values of x.

(a) ± 1 (b) ± 2 (c) $1, 0$ (d) $-1, 0$

48. In which interval swing is strictly increasing.

(a) $(-\infty, -1) \cup (1, \infty)$ (b) $(-\infty, -1) \cap (1, \infty)$

(c) $(-1, 1)$ (d) $(0, 1)$

49. In which interval swing is strictly decreasing ?

(a) $(0, 0)$ (b) $(-\infty, -1) \cup (1, \infty)$ (c) $(-1, 1)$ (d) $(-\infty, \infty)$

50. In which interval function is neither increasing nor decreasing ?

(a) $(-\infty, \infty)$ (b) $(-1, 1)$ (c) $(-\infty, -1)$ (d) $(1, \infty)$

❑❑

Sample Paper 5

Mathematics

Section – A

In this section, attempt any 16 questions out of Questions 1 – 20.

Each Question is of 1 mark weightage.

1. What corresponds to the principal value branch of $\tan^{-1}$?

   (a) $\left(-\dfrac{\pi}{2},\dfrac{\pi}{2}\right)$

   (b) $\left(0,\dfrac{\pi}{2}\right)$

   (c) $\left(\dfrac{-\pi}{2},0\right)$

   (d) $(-\infty,\infty)$

2. What type of a matrix is $A = \begin{bmatrix} 0 & 0 & 5 \\ 0 & 5 & 0 \\ 5 & 0 & 0 \end{bmatrix}$?

   (a) Identity matrix

   (b) Upper triangular matrix

   (c) Square maxtrix

   (d) Lower triangular matix

3. The limit on which the given function $f(x) = x^{100} + \sin x - 1$ is strictly decreasing ?

   (a) $\left(0,\dfrac{\pi}{2}\right)$

   (b) $\left(\dfrac{-\pi}{2},0\right)$

   (c) $(-1,1)$

   (d) None of the intervals

4. What do we call a set of values of the variable satisfying all the constraints ?

   (a) Optimal solution

   (b) Feasible solution

   (c) Objective solution

   (d) None of them

5. What is the objective of LPP ?

   (a) Finding solution

   (b) Optimization technique

   (c) Value method

   (d) None of these

6. What is the slope of normal to the curve $y = 2x^2 + 3 \sin x$ at $x = 0$?

   (a) $\dfrac{-1}{3}$

   (b) $\dfrac{1}{2}$

   (c) 0

   (d) -1

7. The line $y = x + 1$ is a tangent to the curve $y^2 = 4x$ at the point:

   (a) $(1, 2)$

   (b) $(2, 1)$

   (c) $(-1, 2)$

   (d) $(1, 2)$

8. Find the value of $\sin^{-1}\left(\sin\dfrac{3\pi}{5}\right)$.

   (a) $\dfrac{2\pi}{5}$

   (b) $\dfrac{\pi}{4}$

   (c) $\dfrac{3\pi}{5}$

   (d) $\dfrac{\pi}{2}$

9. If $\begin{bmatrix} 3 & -2 \\ -1/6 & 4 \end{bmatrix}\begin{bmatrix} 2x \\ 1 \end{bmatrix} + 2\begin{bmatrix} -4 \\ 5 \end{bmatrix} = 4\begin{bmatrix} 2 \\ y \end{bmatrix}$ then find the values of x and y.

   (a) $\dfrac{13}{4},1$

   (b) $0, 3$

   (c) $3,\dfrac{13}{4}$

   (d) $3, 0$

10. $Z = 8x + 10y$, subject to $2x + y \ge 7$, $2x + 3y \ge 15$, $y \ge 2$, $x \ge 0$, $y \ge 0$. The minimum value of Z occurs at:

    (a) $(4.5, 2)$

    (b) $(1.5, 4)$

    (c) $(0, 7)$

    (d) $(7, 0)$

11. If $A = \begin{bmatrix} 2 & 3 \\ 1 & 0 \end{bmatrix} = P + Q$, where P is symmetric matrix and Q is skew-symmetric matrix then the value of matrix P is:

(a) $\begin{bmatrix} 0 & -2 \\ 2 & 0 \end{bmatrix}$

(b) $\begin{bmatrix} 2 & 2 \\ 2 & 0 \end{bmatrix}$

(c) $\begin{bmatrix} 2 & -2 \\ -2 & 0 \end{bmatrix}$

(d) $\begin{bmatrix} 1 & 2 \\ 0 & 1 \end{bmatrix}$

12. If $\begin{bmatrix} x+3y & y \\ 7-x & 4 \end{bmatrix} = \begin{bmatrix} 4 & -1 \\ 0 & 4 \end{bmatrix}$ then the values of x and y is:

(a) $x = 7, y = -1$

(b) $x = -7, y = 1$

(c) $x = -7, y = -1$

(d) None of these

13. If $A \,(\text{adj. } A) = \begin{bmatrix} 8 & 0 \\ 0 & 8 \end{bmatrix}$, then value of $|A| =$

(a) $|A| = 6$

(b) $|A| = 8$

(c) $|A| = 0$

(d) $|A| = 1$

14. In a LPP, what is the linear function $Z = ax + by$ called ?

(a) Profit function

(b) Loss function

(c) Objective function

(d) None of these

15. The value of $\tan^2 (\sec^{-1} 2) + \cot^2 (\operatorname{cosec}^{-1} 3)$ is:

(a) 11

(b) 10

(c) 0

(d) 5

16. If $y = e^{-x}(6 \cos ax + 5 \sin bx)$ then $\dfrac{dy}{dx} =$

(a) $\dfrac{dy}{dx} = e^{-x}[-6a \sin ax + 5b \cos bx - 6 \cos ax - 5 \sin bx]$

(b) $\dfrac{dy}{dx} = e^{-x}[6a \sin ax - 5b \cos bx - 6a \cos ax - 5 \sin bx]$

(c) $\dfrac{dy}{dx} = e^{-x}[-6a \sin ax + 5b \cos bx + 6 \cos ax + 5 \sin bx]$

(d) None of these

17. $\dfrac{d}{dx}[\sin^{-1}(x\sqrt{1-x} - \sqrt{x}\,\sqrt{1-x^2})]$ is equal to:

(a) $\dfrac{1}{2\sqrt{x(1-x)}} - \dfrac{1}{\sqrt{1-x^2}}$

(b) $\dfrac{1}{\sqrt{1-\{x\sqrt{1-x}-\sqrt{x(1-x^2)}\}^2}}$

(c) $\dfrac{1}{\sqrt{1-x^2}-2\sqrt{x(1-x)}}$

(d) $\dfrac{1}{\sqrt{x(1-x)(1-x)^2}}$

18. If $f(x) = \cos x \cdot \cos 2x \cdot \cos 4x \cdot \cos 8x \cdot \cos 16x$, then the value of $f'\left(\dfrac{\pi}{4}\right)$ is:

(a) 1

(b) $\sqrt{2}$

(c) $\dfrac{1}{\sqrt{2}}$

(d) 0

19. $\operatorname{cosec}^{-1}\left(\dfrac{-2}{\sqrt{3}}\right) =$

(a) $-\dfrac{\pi}{3}$

(b) $\dfrac{\pi}{3}$

(c) $\dfrac{\pi}{2}$

(d) $-\dfrac{\pi}{2}$

20. Let R be a relation on N defined by $x + 2y = 8$. The domain of R is:

(a) $\{2, 4, 8\}$

(b) $\{2, 4, 6, 8\}$

(c) $\{2, 4, 6\}$

(d) None of these

Section – B

In this section, attempt any 16 questions out of the Questions 21 – 40.

Each Question is of 1 mark weightage.

21. The number of all possible matrices of order 3×3 with each entry 0 or 1 is:
    (a) 27   (b) 18   (c) 81   (d) 512

22. Which of the following functions from Z into Z are bijective?
    (a) $f(x) = x^3$ (b) $f(x) = x + 2$ (c) $f(x) = 2x + 1$ (d) $f(x) = x^2 + 1$

23. The maximum value of $P = x + 3y$ such that $2x + y \le 20$, $x + 2y \le 20$, $x \ge 0$, $y \ge 0$, is:
    (a) 10   (b) 60   (c) 30   (d) None of the above

24. Gita, Rita and Sita are three friends and want to plant different types of flowers namely Rose, Lilly and Sunflower respectively in the garden in three different section which is fenced by 600 m of wire to make it enclosed for each type of flowers as shown in figure :

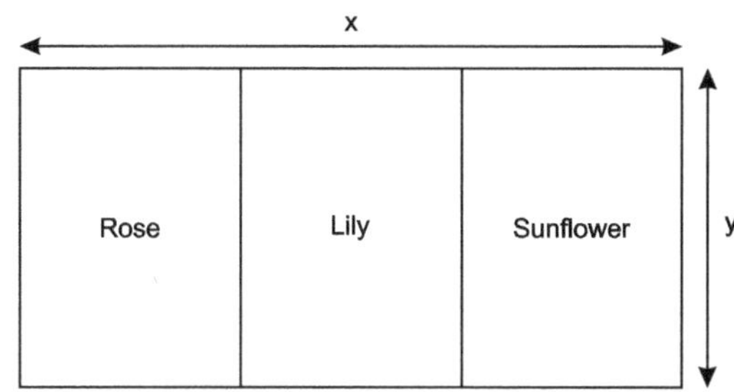

Maximum area will be when $x =$
    (a) 150   (b) 100   (c) 75   (d) 125

25. Three friends, Rajesh, Suresh and Mahesh went to Agra to visit Taj Mahal. They are carrying some visiting card, but don't want to reveal the actual number. They start playing in the Mehtaab Baag. Total no. of visiting cards they have is 18. Twice the number of visiting cards Mahesh has when added to Rajesh's number of cards given on adding Suresh and Mahesh's visiting cards to thrice the Rajesh's number of cards, they give 36. (Assume that Rajesh, Suresh and Mahesh has x, y and z cards respectively.)

    The system of linear equations formed from the given situation, is:
    (a) $x + y + z = 18$, $x + 2y = 21$, $x + 3y + z = 36$ (b) $x + y + z = 18$, $x + 2z = 21$, $3x + y + z = 36$
    (c) $x + y + z = 18$, $y + 2z = 21$, $x + y + z = 36$ (d) $x + y + z = 18$, $2x + z = 21$, $x + 3y + 3z = 36$

26. Two matrices of same order are said to be equal if the .... of the matrices are equal.
    (a) Corresponding elements   (b) Diagonal elements
    (c) Only non-diagonal elements   (d) None of the above

27. Let R be a relation on D defined by
    $$R = \{(1 + x, 1 + x^2) : x \le 5, x \in N\}$$
    Which of the following is false?
    (a) $R = \{(2, 2), (3, 5), (4, 10), (5, 17), (6, 26)\}$ (b) Domain of $R = \{2, 3, 4, 5, 6\}$
    (c) Range of $R = \{2, 3, 4, 5, 6\}$ (d) None of the above

28. If $f(x) = \begin{cases} \dfrac{x^3 + x^2 - 16x + 20}{(x-2)^2}, & x \ne 2 \\ k, & x = 2 \end{cases}$, is continous at $x = 2$, then the value of k is:
    (a) 2   (b) 5   (c) 7   (d) 3

29. The domain of $y = \cos^{-1}(x^2 - 4)$ is:
    (a) $[3, 5]$ (b) $[0, \pi]$
    (c) $[-\sqrt{5}, -\sqrt{3}] \cap [-\sqrt{5}, \sqrt{3}]$ (d) $[-\sqrt{5}, -\sqrt{3}] \cup [\sqrt{3}, \sqrt{5}]$

30. $f + g$ may be a continuous function, if:
    (a) f is continuous and g is discontinuous
    (b) f is discontinuous and g is continuous
    (c) f and g both are discontinous
    (d) None of the above

31. Which of the following is correct:
    (a) Determinant is a square matrix
    (b) Determinant is a number associated to a matrix
    (c) Determinant is a number associated to a square matrix
    (d) None of the above

32. If every element of third order determinant of value Δ is multiplied by 5, then value of determinant is:
    (a) Δ
    (b) 5Δ
    (c) 25Δ
    (d) 125Δ

33. Differential coefficient of $\sqrt{\sec \sqrt{x}}$ is:

    (a) $\dfrac{1}{4\sqrt{x}} \sec \sqrt{x} \sin \sqrt{x}$
    (b) $\dfrac{1}{4\sqrt{x}} (\sec \sqrt{x})^{3/2}. \sin \sqrt{x}$

    (c) $\dfrac{1}{2} \sqrt{x} \sec \sqrt{x} \sin \sqrt{x}$
    (d) $\dfrac{1}{2} \sqrt{x}(\sec \sqrt{x})^{3/2}. \sin \sqrt{x}$

34. If $a_{ij} = |2i + 3j^2|$, then matrix $A_{2 \times 2} = [a_{ij}]$ will be:

    (a) $\begin{bmatrix} 5 & -14 \\ 7 & 16 \end{bmatrix}$
    (b) $\begin{bmatrix} 5 & 14 \\ -7 & 16 \end{bmatrix}$
    (c) $\begin{bmatrix} 5 & 14 \\ 7 & 16 \end{bmatrix}$
    (d) $\begin{bmatrix} 5 & 14 \\ 7 & -16 \end{bmatrix}$

35. If R and R′ are symmetric relations (not disjoint) on a set A, then the relation $R \cap R'$ is:
    (a) reflexive
    (b) symmetric
    (c) transitive
    (d) None of these

36. Differentiate $x^{3e^{3x}}$ with respect to x.

    (a) $3e^{3x}\left(3\log x + \dfrac{1}{x}\right)$
    (b) $x^{3e^{3x}}.3e^{3x}\left(3\log x - \dfrac{1}{x}\right)$

    (c) $x^{3e^{3x}}\left(3\log x + \dfrac{1}{x}\right)$
    (d) $x^{3e^{3x}}.3e^{3x}\left(3\log x + \dfrac{1}{x}\right)$

37. Using determinants, find the equation of the line joining the points (1, 2) and (3, 6):
    (a) $y = 2x$
    (b) $x = 3y$
    (c) $y = x$
    (d) $4x - y = 5$

38. The equation of the normal to the curve $y = \sin x$ at (0, 0) is:
    (a) $x = 0$
    (b) $y = 0$
    (c) $x + y = 0$
    (d) $x - y = 0$

39. If the set A contains 5 elements and the set B contains 6 elements, then the number of one-one and onto mappings from A to B is:
    (a) 720
    (b) 120
    (c) 0
    (d) None of these

40. If $\begin{bmatrix} 1/25 & 0 \\ x & 1/25 \end{bmatrix} = \begin{bmatrix} 5 & 0 \\ -a & 5 \end{bmatrix}^{-2}$, then the value of x is:

    (a) $\dfrac{a}{125}$
    (b) $\dfrac{2a}{25}$
    (c) $\dfrac{2a}{125}$
    (d) None of these

Section – C

In this section, attempt any 8 questions. Each question is of 1-mark weightage.

Questions 46–50 are based on a Case-Study.

41. The condition for the curves $\dfrac{x^2}{a^2} - \dfrac{y^2}{b^2} = 1;\ xy = c^2$ to intersect orthogonally is:

    (a) $\dfrac{b^2}{a^2} = -1$
    (b) $a^2 - b^2 = 0$
    (c) $a^2 + b^2 = 0$
    (d) None of these

42. If the sum of the lengths of the hypotenuse and another side of a right-angled triangle is given, the area of the triangle is maximum when the angle between these sides is:

(a) $\dfrac{\pi}{6}$ (b) $\dfrac{\pi}{4}$ (c) $\dfrac{\pi}{3}$ (d) $\dfrac{\pi}{2}$

43. The value of the expression $\sin\left[\cot^{-1}\left(\cos\left(\tan^{-1} 1\right)\right)\right]$ is:

(a) 0   (b) 1   (c) $\dfrac{1}{\sqrt{3}}$ (d) $\sqrt{\dfrac{2}{3}}$

44. If the function $f(x) = x^2 e^{-2x}$, $x > 0$, then the maximum value of $f(x)$ is:

(a) $\dfrac{1}{e}$ (b) $\dfrac{1}{2e}$ (c) $\dfrac{1}{e^2}$ (d) $\dfrac{4}{e^4}$

45. $\dfrac{d}{dx}\left[\tan^{-1}\left(\dfrac{a-x}{1+ax}\right)\right]$ is equal to:

(a) $-\dfrac{1}{1+x^2}$ (b) $\dfrac{1}{1+a^2} - \dfrac{1}{1+x^2}$ (c) $\dfrac{1}{1+\left(\dfrac{a-x}{1+ax}\right)^2}$ (d) $\dfrac{-1}{\sqrt{1-\left(\dfrac{a-x}{1+ax}\right)^2}}$

A Tangocola Company wants to produce a new cylindrical tin as healthy protein drink which contain 300 cubic cm of protein drink. The cost of material used to make the sides of the container is ₹5 per square cm. While the cost of material used to make top and bottom of container is ₹10 per sq. meter. He wants to minimise the cost of container.

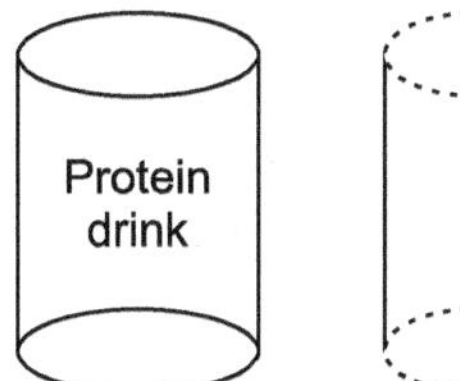

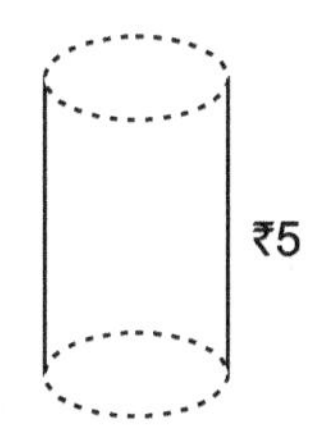

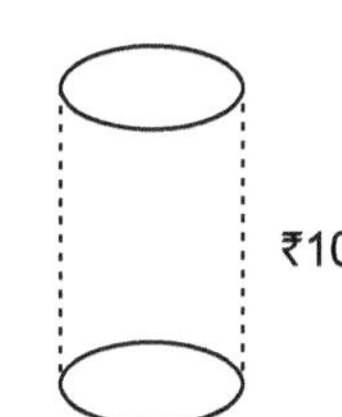

Give the answers of the following questions :

46. Being h be height and r be the radius, express the relationship between h and r :

(a) $h = \dfrac{300}{\pi r^2}$ (b) $h = \dfrac{100}{\pi r}$ (c) $h = \dfrac{300}{\pi r}$ (d) $h = \dfrac{300}{\pi r^3}$

47. What is the cost function which is to be minimised ?

(a) $\dfrac{3000}{r} + 20\pi r^2$ (b) $\dfrac{300}{r^2} + 20\pi r^2$ (c) $\dfrac{3000}{r} - 20\pi r^2$ (d) $\dfrac{300}{r} - 20\pi r^2$

48. At what value of r, cost can be minimised ?

(a) $r = \left(\dfrac{75}{\pi}\right)^{1/3}$ (b) $r = \left(\dfrac{\pi}{75}\right)^{1/3}$ (c) $r = \left(\dfrac{75}{\pi^2}\right)^{2/3}$ (d) $r = (75\pi)^{1/3}$

49. Find the value of h :

(a) $\dfrac{300}{(75)^{2/3}}\cdot(\pi)^{-1/3}$ (b) $\dfrac{300}{(75)^{1/3}}\cdot(\pi)^{-1/3}$ (c) $\dfrac{300}{(75)^{-1/3}}\cdot(\pi)^{2/3}$ (d) $\dfrac{300}{(75)^{2/3}}\cdot(\pi)^{2/3}$

50. Find total cost :

(a) $4500\left(\dfrac{75}{\pi}\right)^{1/3}$ (b) $4500\left(\dfrac{75}{\pi}\right)^{-1/3}$ (c) $4500\left(\dfrac{75}{\pi}\right)^{2/3}$ (d) $4500\left(\dfrac{75}{\pi}\right)^{-2/3}$

❏❏

Sample Paper 6

Mathematics

Questions

Section – A

In this section, attempt any 16 questions out of Questions 1 – 20.

Each Question is of 1 mark weightage.

1. If $\begin{vmatrix} 2 & 5 \\ 8 & x^2 \end{vmatrix} = \begin{vmatrix} 6 & 5 \\ 8 & 3 \end{vmatrix}$, then find the value of x.

   (a) ± 2 (b) ± 3 (c) 0 (d) -1

2. What is the principal value of $\operatorname{cosec}^{-1}(2)$?

   (a) $\dfrac{\pi}{6}$ (b) $\dfrac{\pi}{3}$ (c) $\dfrac{\pi}{4}$ (d) $\dfrac{\pi}{2}$

3. The derivative of $f(x) = |x|^3$ at $x = 0$ is :

   (a) $\dfrac{1}{2}$ (b) $\dfrac{-1}{2}$ (c) -1 (d) 0

4. The maximum value of slope of the curve $y = -x^3 + 3x^2 + 12x - 5$ is :

   (a) 15 (b) 12 (c) a (d) 0

5. What kind of matrix is $(AB' - BA')$. If A and B are symmetric matrices of the same order ?

   (a) Symmetric matrix (b) Skew-symmetric matrix

   (c) Diagonal matrix (d) Identity matrix

6. What is the value of $\sin^{-1}\left[\cos\left(\dfrac{43\pi}{5}\right)\right]$?

   (a) $\dfrac{-\pi}{10}$ (b) $\dfrac{\pi}{10}$ (c) $\dfrac{\pi}{2}$ (d) $\dfrac{-\pi}{3}$

7. If $A = \begin{bmatrix} 5 & -3 & 2 \\ -3 & 8 & 1 \end{bmatrix}$ and $B = \begin{bmatrix} 2 & 3 \\ 5 & 6 \\ 2 & -3 \end{bmatrix}$, then find BA.

   (a) $\begin{bmatrix} 1 & 18 & 7 \\ 7 & 33 & 16 \\ 19 & -30 & 1 \end{bmatrix}$ (b) $\begin{bmatrix} -1 & -19 \\ 36 & 30 \end{bmatrix}$ (c) $\begin{bmatrix} 1 & 7 & 19 \\ 18 & 33 & 1 \\ 7 & 30 & -10 \end{bmatrix}$ (d) $\begin{bmatrix} 36 & -36 \\ 19 & -1 \end{bmatrix}$

8. The absolute minimum value of the function $f(x) = x^3 - 12x$ on the interval $[0, 3]$ is :

   (a) 0 (b) -9 (c) -16 (d) -19

9. The line $y = x + 1$ is a tangent to the curve $y^2 = 4x$ at the point :

   (a) 1, 2 (b) $-1, -2$ (c) 3, 2 (d) $-3, 2$

10. Using determinants, find the area of triangle with vertices $(0, 0), (2, 3), (0, 5)$.

    (a) 10 sq. units (b) 6 sq. units (c) 5 sq. units (d) 12 sq. units

11. What is the domain of $\sin^{-1} 2x$?

    (a) $-1 \le x \le 1$ (b) $0 \le x \le 1$ (c) $\dfrac{-1}{2} \le x \le \dfrac{1}{2}$ (d) $-\infty \le x \le \infty$

12. Write the order of the product matrix $\begin{bmatrix} 1 \\ 2 \\ 3 \end{bmatrix}$ [2 3 4].

    (a) 1 × 3   (b) 3 × 1   (c) 3 × 3   (d) 2 × 2

13. Find the value of $\sec^{-1} 2 + \sin^{-1}\left(\dfrac{1}{\sqrt{2}}\right)$.

    (a) $\dfrac{5\pi}{12}$ (b) $\dfrac{7\pi}{12}$ (c) $\dfrac{\pi}{4}$ (d) $\dfrac{3\pi}{4}$

14. The maximum value of $\sin x . \cos x$ is :

    (a) $\dfrac{1}{4}$ (b) $\dfrac{1}{2}$ (c) $\sqrt{2}$ (d) $2\sqrt{2}$

15. The second derivative of $y = \sin^2 x$ is :

    (a) $\cos 2x$ (b) $2 \sin 2x$ (c) $2 \sin x \cos^2 x$ (d) $2 \cos 2x$

16. Find the value of $\begin{vmatrix} 8 & 4 \\ 5 & 6 \end{vmatrix}$.

    (a) 38   (b) 28   (c) 10   (d) 12

17. The relation R = {$(x, x^3) : x$ is a prime number less than 10} in roster form is:

    (a) {(2, 8), (3, 27), (5, 125), (7, 343, (9, 729)}   (b) {(3, 27), (5, 125), (7, 343)}

    (c) {(2, 8), (3, 27), (5, 125), (7, 343)}   (d) {(1, 1), (2, 8), (3, 27), (5, 125), (7, 343)}

18. Let A = {1, 2, 3}, B = {1, 3, 5}. If relation R from A to B is given by R = {(1, 3), (2, 5), (3, 3)}. Then R^{-1} is:

    (a) {(3, 3), (3, 1), (5, 2)}   (b) {(1, 3), (2, 5), (3, 3)}   (c) {(1, 3), (5, 2)}   (d) None of the above

19. $\tan^{-1}\left\{\sin\left(-\dfrac{\pi}{2}\right)\right\}$ is equal to:

    (a) – 1   (b) 1   (c) $\dfrac{\pi}{2}$ (d) $-\dfrac{\pi}{4}$

20. $\sin\left\{2\cos^{-1}\left(\dfrac{-3}{5}\right)\right\}$ is equal to:

    (a) $\dfrac{6}{26}$ (b) $\dfrac{24}{25}$ (c) $\dfrac{4}{5}$ (d) $-\dfrac{24}{25}$

Section – B

In this section, attempt any 16 questions out of the Questions 21 – 40.

Each Question is of 1 mark weightage.

21. If the matrix $\begin{bmatrix} a & b \\ c & d \end{bmatrix}$ is commutative with the matrix $\begin{bmatrix} 1 & 1 \\ 0 & 1 \end{bmatrix}$, then:

    (a) $a = 0, b = c$ (b) $b = 0, c = d$ (c) $c = 0, d = a$ (d) $d = 0, a = b$

22. For what value of k will the function $f(x) = \begin{cases} \dfrac{x^2 - 25}{x - 5}, & x \neq 5 \\ k, & x = 5 \end{cases}$ is continuous at $x = 5$:

    (a) 10   (b) 0   (c) Not defined   (d) 5

23. A relation is a set of all:

    (a) Ordered pairs   (b) Functions   (c) y-values   (d) None of these

24. Matrix A has x rows and $(x + 5)$ columns. Matrix B has y rows and $(11 - y)$ columns. If both AB and BA exist, then the respective values of x and y are:

    (a) 3, 9   (b) 8, 3   (c) 3, 8   (d) 4, 8

25. The region represented by the inequation system $x, y \geq 0$, $y \leq 6$, $x + y \leq 3$ is:
    (a) Unbounded in first quadrant
    (b) Unbounded in first and second quadrants
    (c) Bounded in first quadrant
    (d) None of the above

26. If $f(x) = \begin{cases} \dfrac{x^3 + x^2 - 16x + 20}{(x-2)^2}, & x \neq 2 \\ k, & x = 2 \end{cases}$, is continuous at $x = 2$, then the value of k is:

    (a) 2
    (b) 5
    (c) 7
    (d) 3

27. The set of points, where the function $f(x) = |x - 2| \cos x$ is differentiable is:
    (a) $(-\infty, \infty)$
    (b) $(-\infty, \infty) - \{2\}$
    (c) $(0, \infty)$
    (d) None of these

28. If $A = \begin{bmatrix} 2 & -1 \\ -1 & 2 \end{bmatrix}$ and I is the unit matrix of order 2, then A^2 equals:

    (a) $4A - 3I$
    (b) $3A - 4I$
    (c) $A - I$
    (d) $A + I$

29. If $y = ax^2 + b$, then $\dfrac{dy}{dx}$ at $x = 2$ is equal to:

    (a) $4a$
    (b) $3a$
    (c) $2a$
    (d) None of these

30. The optimal value of the objective function is attained at the point is:
    (a) Given by intersection of inequations with axes only
    (b) Given by intersection of inequtions with X-axis only
    (c) Given by corner points of the feasible region
    (d) None of the above

31. Differential coefficient of $\sqrt{\sec \sqrt{x}}$ is:

    (a) $\dfrac{1}{4\sqrt{x}} \sec \sqrt{x} \sin \sqrt{x}$

    (b) $\dfrac{1}{4\sqrt{x}} (\sec \sqrt{x})^{3/2} . \sin \sqrt{x}$

    (c) $\dfrac{1}{2} \sqrt{x} \sec \sqrt{x} \sin \sqrt{x}$

    (d) $\dfrac{1}{2} \sqrt{x} (\sec \sqrt{x})^{3/2} . \sin \sqrt{x}$

32. If $A^3 = 0$, then $A^2 + A + I =$
    (a) $I - A$
    (b) $(I - A)^{-1}$
    (c) $(I + A)^{-1}$
    (d) $I + A$

33. The differential coefficient of $\tan^{-1}\left(\dfrac{\sqrt{1+x} - \sqrt{1-x}}{\sqrt{1+x} + \sqrt{1-x}}\right)$:

    (a) $\sqrt{1-x^2}$
    (b) $\dfrac{1}{\sqrt{1-x^2}}$
    (c) $\dfrac{1}{2\sqrt{1-x^2}}$
    (d) x

34. The second order derivative if $y = e^{2x^2}$ is:

    (a) $4e^{2x^2}(4x^2 + 3)$
    (b) $4e^{2x^2}(4x^2 - 1)$
    (c) $4e^{2x^2}(4x^2 + 1)$
    (d) $e^{2x^2}(4x^2 + 1)$

35. If the value of the objective function Z of a LPP can be increased or decreased indefinitely. Such solutions are called:
    (a) Bounded solutions
    (b) No solution
    (c) Unique solutions
    (d) Unbounded solutions

36. The value of the determinant $\begin{vmatrix} x & x+1 \\ x-1 & 1 \end{vmatrix}$ is:

    (a) 1
    (b) -1
    (c) 2
    (d) 0

37. The equation of the normal to the curve $y = \sin x$ at $(0, 0)$ is:
    (a) $x = 0$
    (b) $y = 0$
    (c) $x + y = 0$
    (d) $x - y = 0$

38. If the points $(2, -3)$, $(k, -1)$ and $(0, 4)$ are collinear, then find the value of $4k$.

    (a) 4
    (b) $\dfrac{7}{140}$
    (c) 47
    (d) $\dfrac{40}{7}$

39. The equation of the tangent to the curve $y = \sqrt{9 - 2x^2}$ at the point where the ordinate and the abscissa are equal, is:

   (a) $2x + y - 3\sqrt{3} = 0$ (b) $2x + y + 3\sqrt{3} = 0$ (c) $2x - y - 3\sqrt{3} = 0$ (d) None of these

40. If A′ is the transpose of a square matrix A, then:

   (a) $|A| \neq |A'|$

   (b) $|A| = |A'|$

   (c) $|A| + |A'| = 0$

   (d) $|A| = |A'|$ only, when A is symmetric

Section - C

In this section, attempt any 8 questions. Each question is of 1-mark weightage.

Questions 46–50 are based on a Case-Study.

41. If $A = \begin{bmatrix} \alpha & \beta \\ \gamma & -\alpha \end{bmatrix}$ is such that $A^2 = I$, then:

   (a) $1 + \alpha^2 + \beta\gamma = 0$ (b) $1 - \alpha^2 + \beta\gamma = 0$ (c) $1 - \alpha^2 - \beta\gamma = 0$ (d) $1 + \alpha^2 - \beta\gamma = 0$

42. The point at which the maximum value of $3x + 2y$ subject to the constraints $x + y \leq 2$, $x \geq 0$, $y \geq 0$, obtained is:

   (a) $(0, 0)$ (b) $(1.5, 1.5)$ (c) $(2, 0)$ (d) $(0, 2)$

43. If the slope of the curve $y = \dfrac{ax}{b - x}$ at the point $(1, 1)$ is 2, then the values of a and b are respectively:

   (a) $1, -2$ (b) $-1, 2$ (c) $1, 2$ (d) None of these

44. The minimum value of $\dfrac{x}{\log x}$ is:

   (a) e (b) $\dfrac{1}{e}$ (c) 1   (d) None of these

45. A furniture dealer deals in only two items namely tables and chairs. He has ₹ 5000 to invest and space to store atmost 60 pieces. A table cost him ₹ 250 and a chair ₹ 60. He can sell a table at a profit of ₹ 15. Assume that, he can sell all the items that he produced. The number of constraints in the problem are:

   (a) 2   (b) 3   (c) 4   (d) 5

There is a rectangular land on the bank of the river on which the farmer and his family grows the crops but wild animals graze all the crops. So farmer and his family decided to enclose his rectangular field with 4000 meter fencing leaving from the side of river.

Give answer for the following questions :

46. If length is expressed in terms of y and breadth in terms of x, express the relationship of y in terms of x :

   (a) $2y = 4000 - x$ (b) $x = 4000 - 2y$ (c) $y = 4000 - 2x$ (d) $y = 2000 - 2x$

47. The area of rectangular plot A expressed as a function of x is :

   (a) $A = x(4000 - 2x)$ (b) $A = 4000x^2 - 2x$ (c) $A = 2000 - x^2$ (d) $A = 4000 - x^2$

48. The maximum area will be at $x = $?

   (a) 2000   (b) 1200   (c) 1000   (d) 1500

49. What is the maximum area of the plot ?

   (a) 2000 m^2 (b) 2 km^2 (c) 200 km^2 (d) $20,000 \text{ m}^2$

50. What are the dimensions of the plot ?

   (a) $200 \text{ m} \times 100 \text{ m}$ (b) $2 \text{ km} \times 1 \text{ km}$ (c) $20 \text{ m} \times 1000 \text{ m}$ (d) $2000 \text{ m} \times 10 \text{ m}$

❑❑

Sample Paper 7

Mathematics

🧠 Questions

Section – A

In this section, attempt any 16 questions out of Questions 1 – 20.

Each Question is of 1 mark weightage.

1. What is the principal value of $\tan^{-1}\left(\tan\dfrac{9\pi}{8}\right)$?

   (a) $\dfrac{\pi}{8}$ (b) $\dfrac{\pi}{4}$ (c) $\dfrac{\pi}{2}$ (d) $\dfrac{\pi}{6}$

2. Find a matrix of order 2×2, whose elements are determined by $a_{ij} = (2i - j)^2$.

   (a) $\begin{bmatrix} 9 & 4 \\ 1 & 0 \end{bmatrix}$ (b) $\begin{bmatrix} 0 & 2 \\ 1 & 3 \end{bmatrix}$ (c) $\begin{bmatrix} 1 & 0 \\ 9 & 4 \end{bmatrix}$ (d) $\begin{bmatrix} 4 & 1 \\ 0 & 8 \end{bmatrix}$

3. If $x = t^2$ and $y = t^3$, then $\dfrac{d^2y}{dx^2}$ is equal to :

   (a) $\dfrac{3}{2}$ (b) $\dfrac{3}{4t}$ (c) $\dfrac{3}{2t}$ (d) $\dfrac{3}{4}$

4. If $\begin{bmatrix} 2x+y & 3y \\ 0 & 4 \end{bmatrix} = \begin{bmatrix} 6 & 0 \\ 0 & 4 \end{bmatrix}$, then find the value of x.

   (a) 2   (b) 3   (c) – 1   (d) 0

5. The derivative of $\sin^{-1} x$ w.r.t. $\cos^{-1} \sqrt{1-x^2}$ is :

   (a) 1   (b) 0   (c) $\cos^{-1} x$ (d) $\dfrac{x}{\sqrt{1-x^2}}$

6. What is the domain of the function $\cos^{-1}(2x - 1)$?

   (a) $(-1, 0)$ (b) $(0, 1)$ (c) $[0, 1]$ (d) $(0, -1)$

7. If A is an invertible square matrix and K is non-negative real number, then what will be the value of $(K.A)^{-1}$?

   (a) KA^{-1} (b) $\dfrac{1}{K}A^{-1}$ (c) $\dfrac{K}{A^{-1}}$ (d) $K^2 A^{-1}$

8. Find the value of $\begin{vmatrix} -8 & 6 \\ 5 & 4 \end{vmatrix}$.

   (a) -62 (b) -30 (c) -32 (d) -62

9. The derivative of $\tan^{-1}(2x)$ w.r.t x is :

   (a) $\dfrac{1}{1+4x^2}$ (b) $\dfrac{2}{1+4x^2}$ (c) $\dfrac{2}{\sqrt{1-4x^2}}$ (d) $\dfrac{-2}{\sqrt{1-4x^2}}$

10. Let $f(x) = \dfrac{1 - \tan x}{4x - \pi}, x \neq \dfrac{\pi}{4}, x \in \left(0, \dfrac{\pi}{2}\right)$

If $f(x)$ is continuous in $\left(0, \dfrac{\pi}{2}\right)$, then $f\left(\dfrac{\pi}{4}\right) =$

(a) 1
(b) $\dfrac{1}{2}$
(c) $-\dfrac{1}{2}$
(d) -1

11. If A is a matrix of order 3×3, then number of minors in determinant of A are:

(a) 3
(b) 6
(c) 9
(d) 18

12. Differentiate the function $y = \sec(x^2 + 2)$ w.r.t. x **is:**

(a) $2x \sec(x^2 + 2) \tan(x^2 + 2)$
(b) $\sec(x^2 + 2) \tan(x^2 + 2)$
(c) $2x \sec^2(x^2 + 2)$
(d) $2x \tan^2(x^2 + 2)$

13. The value of $\sin\left[\dfrac{\pi}{3} - \sin^{-1}\left(\dfrac{-1}{2}\right)\right]$ is:

(a) -1
(b) 0
(c) 1
(d) ∞

14. It is given that at $x = 1$, the function $x^4 - 62x^2 + ax + 9$ attains its maximum value, on the interval $[0, 2]$. Find the value of a is:

(a) 100
(b) 120
(c) 80
(d) 140

15. The value of $\cot(\sin^{-1} x)$ is:

(a) $\dfrac{\sqrt{1-x^2}}{x}$
(b) $\dfrac{x}{\sqrt{1-x^2}}$
(c) $\dfrac{2x}{\sqrt{1-x^2}}$
(d) $\dfrac{\sqrt{1-x^2}}{2x}$

16. If $f(x) = |\cos x|$, then $f'\left(\dfrac{3\pi}{4}\right)$ is equal to:

(a) $\dfrac{\sqrt{3}}{2}$
(b) 1
(c) $\dfrac{1}{\sqrt{2}}$
(d) 0

17. The value of $\tan^{-1}\left(\tan\dfrac{5\pi}{6}\right) + \cos^{-1}\left(\cos\dfrac{13\pi}{6}\right)$ is:

(a) 0
(b) -1
(c) 2
(d) 1

18. The set of points where the function f given by $f(x) = |2x - 1| \sin x$ is differentiable is:

(a) R
(b) $R - \left\{\dfrac{1}{2}\right\}$
(c) $(0, \infty)$
(d) None of these

19. Let $f : R \to R$ be defined by $f(x) = \dfrac{1}{x} \; \forall \, x \in R$. then f is:

(a) one-one
(b) onto
(c) bijective
(d) f is not defined

20. If $\cos^{-1}\alpha + \cos^{-1}\beta + \cos^{-1}\gamma = 3\pi$, then $\alpha(\beta + \gamma) + \beta(\gamma + \alpha) + \gamma(\alpha + \beta)$ equals:

(a) 0
(b) 1
(c) 6
(d) 12

Section - B

In this section, attempt any 16 questions out of the Questions 21 – 40.

Each Question is of 1 mark weightage.

21. The matrix $\begin{bmatrix} 1 & 0 & 0 \\ 0 & 2 & 0 \\ 0 & 0 & 0 \end{bmatrix}$ is a:

(a) Identity matrix
(b) Symmetric matrix
(c) Skew symmetric matrix
(d) None of these

22. The number of bijective functions from set A to itself when A contains 106 elements is:

    (a)   106   (b) $(106)^2$ (c) $(106)!$ (d) 2^{106}

23. The function $f(x) = \begin{cases} \dfrac{\sin x}{x} + \cos x, & \text{if } x \neq 0 \\ k, & \text{if } x = 0 \end{cases}$, is continuous at $x = 0$, then the value of k is:

    (a)   3   (b) 2   (c) 1   (d) 1.5

24. Corner points of the feasible region for an LPP are (0, 2), (3, 0), (6, 0), (6, 8) and (0, 5).

    Let F = $4x + 6y$ be the objective function.

    The minimum value of F occurs at:

    (a)   (0, 2) only

    (b)   (3, 0) only

    (c)   The mid-point of the line segment joining the points (0, 2) and (3, 0) only

    (d)   Any point on the line segment joining the points (0, 2) and (3, 0)

25. Find the value of constant k when the function f is continuous at $x = 0$, where $f(x) = \begin{cases} \dfrac{1 - \cos 4x}{8x^2}, & x \neq 0 \\ k, & x = 0 \end{cases}$

    (a)   0   (b) -1 (c) 1   (d) $\dfrac{1}{2}$

26. If $\begin{bmatrix} 2x+y & 4x \\ 5x-7 & 4x \end{bmatrix} = \begin{bmatrix} 7 & 7y-13 \\ y & x+6 \end{bmatrix}$, then the values of x, y respectively are:

    (a)   3, 1   (b) 2, 3   (c) 2, 4   (d) 3, 3

27. If $A^2 = A$, then $(I + A)^4$ is equal to:

    (a) $I + A$ (b) $I + 4A$ (c) $I + 15A$ (d) None of these

28. Two matrices of same order are said to be equal if the .... of the two matrices are equal.

    (a)   Corresponding elements   (b) Diagonal elements

    (c)   Only non-diagonal elements   (d) None of the above

29. The optimal value of the objective function is attained at the points:

    (a)   On X-axis   (b) On Y-axis

    (c)   Which are corner points of the feasible region   (d) None of the above

30. The order of the single matrix obtained from $\begin{bmatrix} 1 & -1 \\ 0 & 2 \\ 2 & 3 \end{bmatrix} \left\{ \begin{bmatrix} -1 & 0 & 2 \\ 2 & 0 & 1 \end{bmatrix} - \begin{bmatrix} 0 & 1 & 23 \\ 1 & 0 & 21 \end{bmatrix} \right\}$ is:

    (a) 2×3 (b) 2×2 (c) 3×2 (d) 3×3

31. If $y = \tan(x + y)$, then $\dfrac{dy}{dx}$ is equal to :

    (a) $-\cot^2(x + y)$ (b) $-\csc^2(x + y)$

    (c) $-\cot(x + y)\csc(x + y)$ (d) $-\tan^2(x + y)$

32. If the sum of the lengths of the hypotenuse and another side of a right-angled triangle is given, the area of the triangle is maximum when the angle between these sides is:

    (a) $\dfrac{\pi}{6}$ (b) $\dfrac{\pi}{4}$ (c) $\dfrac{\pi}{3}$ (d) $\dfrac{\pi}{2}$

33. The graphical method of LP problem uses:

    (a)   Objective function equations   (b) Constraint equations

    (c)   Linear equations   (d) All of the above

34. The differential coefficient of the function $\cot(\cos^{-1} x)$ with respect to x is:

(a) $-\csc^2(\cos^{-1} x)/\sqrt{1-x^2}$

(b) $\csc(\cos^{-1} x)/\sqrt{1-x^2}$

(c) $\csc^2(\cos^{-1} x)/\sqrt{1-x^2}$

(d) $-\csc(\cos^{-1} x)/\sqrt{1-x^2}$

35. If $A^T = \begin{bmatrix} 3 & 4 \\ -1 & 2 \\ 0 & 1 \end{bmatrix}$ and $B = \begin{bmatrix} -1 & 2 & 1 \\ 1 & 2 & 3 \end{bmatrix}$, then find $A^T - B^T$.

(a) $\begin{bmatrix} 4 & 3 \\ -3 & 0 \\ -1 & -2 \end{bmatrix}$

(b) $\begin{bmatrix} 4 & 3 \\ 3 & 0 \\ 1 & 2 \end{bmatrix}$

(c) $\begin{bmatrix} 4 & 0 \\ -1 & -3 \\ 3 & -2 \end{bmatrix}$

(d) $\begin{bmatrix} 1 & -3 \\ 2 & 4 \\ 3 & 5 \end{bmatrix}$

36. If the points (a_1, b_1), (a_2, b_2) and $(a_1 + a_2, b_1 + b_2)$ are collinear, then:

(a) $a_1 b_2 = a_2 b_1$

(b) $a_1 + a_2 = b_1 + b_2$

(c) $a_2 b_2 = a_1 b_1$

(d) $a_1 + b_1 = a_2 + b_2$

37. Let $A = R - \{3\}$, $B = R - \{1\}$. Let $f : A \to B$ be defined by $f(x) = \dfrac{x-2}{x-3}$. Then,

(a) f is bijective

(b) f is one-one but not onto

(c) f is onto but not one-one

(d) None of these

38. Find the adjoining of the matrix A, where $A = \begin{bmatrix} 1 & 2 & 3 \\ 0 & 5 & 0 \\ 2 & 4 & 3 \end{bmatrix}$

(a) $\begin{bmatrix} 15 & 6 & 1 \\ 0 & 3 & 0 \\ 10 & 0 & 5 \end{bmatrix}$

(b) $\begin{bmatrix} 15 & 6 & -15 \\ 0 & -3 & 0 \\ -10 & 0 & 5 \end{bmatrix}$

(c) $\begin{bmatrix} 15 & -1 & 5 \\ 0 & 3 & 1 \\ 10 & 1 & 5 \end{bmatrix}$

(d) None of these

39. The slope of tangent to the curve $y = 2\cos^2(3x)$ at $x = \dfrac{\pi}{6}$ is:

(a) 0

(b) 6

(c) -6

(d) π

40. Shaded region is represented by:

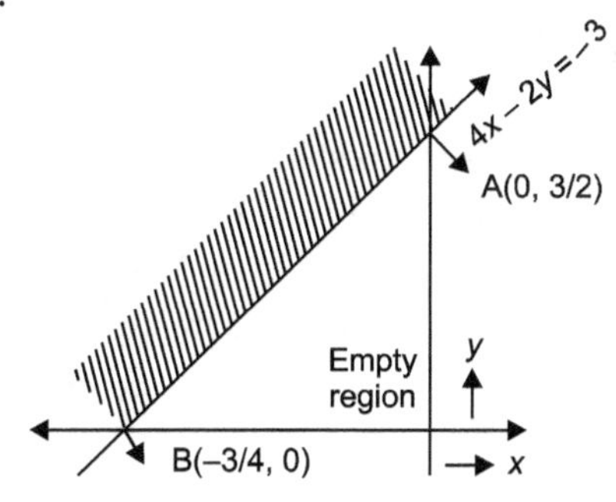

(a) $4x - 2y \le 3$

(b) $4x - 2y \le -3$

(c) $4x - 2y \ge 3$

(d) $4x - 2y \ge -3$

Section - C

In this section, attempt any 8 questions. Each question is of 1-mark weightage.

Questions 46–50 are based on a Case-Study.

41. The angle of intersection of the curves $y^2 = x$ and $x^2 = y$ is:

(a) $\tan^{-1}\left(\dfrac{1}{2}\right)$

(b) $\tan^{-1}\left(\dfrac{5}{2}\right)$

(c) $\tan^{-1}\left(\dfrac{3}{4}\right)$

(d) $\tan^{-1}\left(\dfrac{5}{4}\right)$

42. Derivative of $e^{x \log x}$ is:

(a) $x \log x$

(b) x^x

(c) $x^x(1 + \log x)$

(d) $x(x)^{x-1}$

43. $Z = 20x_1 + 20x_2$, subject to $x_1 \geq 0$, $x_2 \geq 0$, $x_1 + 2x_2 \geq 8$, $3x_1 + 2x_2 \geq 15$, $5x_1 + 2x_2 \geq 20$. The minimum value of Z occurst at:

(a) $(8, 0)$
(b) $\left(\dfrac{5}{2}, \dfrac{15}{4}\right)$
(c) $\left(\dfrac{7}{2}, \dfrac{9}{4}\right)$
(d) $(0, 10)$

44. For what value of x, $A = \begin{bmatrix} 2(x+1) & 2x \\ x & x-2 \end{bmatrix}$ is a singular matrix.

(a) -2
(b) -3
(c) -1
(d) 0

45. If $f(x) = 2x^3 - 21x^2 + 36x - 30$, then which one of the following is correct?

(a) $f(x)$ has maximum at $x = -1$
(b) $f(x)$ has maixmum at $x = 6$
(c) $f(x)$ has maximum at $x = 1$
(d) $f(x)$ has no maximum or minimum

An architect designs a building for a multi-national company. The floor consists of a rectangular region with semicircular ends having a perimeter of 200 m as show below :

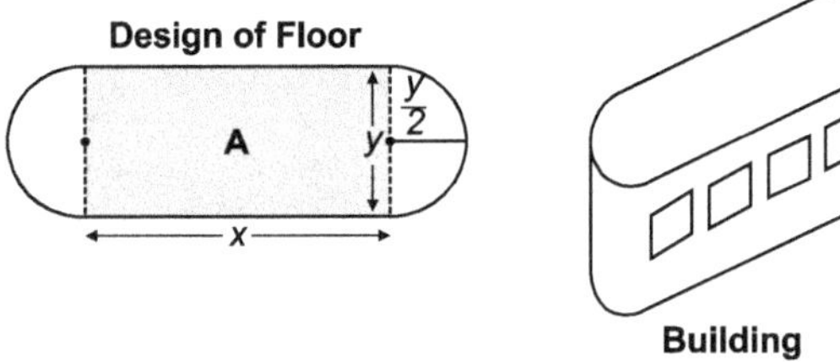

Give the answers of the following questions :

(c) $f(x)$ has maximum at $x = 1$
(d) $f(x)$ has no maximum or minimum

46. If x and y represents the length and breadth of the rectangular region, then the relation between the variables is :

(a) $x + \pi y = 100$
(b) $2x + \pi y = 200$
(c) $\pi x + y = 50$
(d) $x + y = 100$

47. The area of the rectangular region A expressed as a function of x is :

(a) $\dfrac{2}{\pi}(100x - x^2)$
(b) $\dfrac{1}{\pi}(100x - x^2)$
(c) $\dfrac{x}{\pi}(100 - x)$
(d) $\pi y^2 + \dfrac{2}{\pi}(100x - x^2)$

48. The maximum value of area A is :

(a) $\dfrac{\pi}{3200}$ m^2
(b) $\dfrac{3200}{\pi}$ m^2
(c) $\dfrac{5000}{\pi}$ m^2
(d) $\dfrac{1000}{\pi}$ m^2

49. The CEO of the multi-national company is interested in maximizing the area of the whole floor including the semi-circular ends. For this to happen the value of x should be :

(a) 0 m
(b) 30 m
(c) 50 m
(d) 80 m

50. The extra area generated if the area of the whole floor is maximized is :

(a) $\dfrac{3000}{\pi}$ m^2
(b) $\dfrac{5000}{\pi}$ m^2
(c) $\dfrac{7000}{\pi}$ m^2
(d) No change both areas are equal

❑❑

Answers

Section – A

1. (b) $-\dfrac{\pi}{2}$

Explanation: We have, $\tan^{-1}\sqrt{3} - \cot^{-1}(-\sqrt{3}) = \tan^{-1}\left(\tan\dfrac{\pi}{3}\right) - \cot^{-1}\left(\cot\dfrac{5\pi}{6}\right)$

$$= \dfrac{\pi}{3} - \dfrac{5\pi}{6} = \dfrac{2\pi - 5\pi}{6}$$

$$= \dfrac{-3\pi}{6} = -\dfrac{\pi}{2}$$

2. (a) $-1 \le x \le 1$

Explanation:

$y = \sin^{-1}(-x^2) \Rightarrow \sin y = -x^2$

Now,

$-1 \le -x^2 \le 1$ (since $-1 \le \sin y \le 1$)

$\Rightarrow \quad 1 \ge x^2 \ge -1$

$\Rightarrow \quad -1 \le x^2 \le 1$

$\Rightarrow \quad |x| \le 1$

$\Rightarrow \quad -1 \le x \le 1$

3. (b) $\begin{bmatrix} 2 & 2 \\ 2 & 0 \end{bmatrix}$

Explanation: We have,

$A = \begin{bmatrix} 2 & 3 \\ 1 & 0 \end{bmatrix}$

$\therefore \qquad A' = \begin{bmatrix} 2 & 1 \\ 3 & 0 \end{bmatrix}$

Since, P is symmetric matrix

$\therefore \qquad P = \dfrac{1}{2}(A + A')$

$\Rightarrow \qquad P = \dfrac{1}{2}\begin{bmatrix} 2+2 & 3+1 \\ 1+3 & 0+0 \end{bmatrix}$

$\Rightarrow \qquad P = \dfrac{1}{2}\begin{bmatrix} 4 & 4 \\ 4 & 0 \end{bmatrix}$

$\Rightarrow \qquad P = \begin{bmatrix} 2 & 2 \\ 2 & 0 \end{bmatrix}$

4. (b) $\begin{bmatrix} 9/2 & 25/2 \\ 8 & 18 \end{bmatrix}$

Explanation: Here,

$$a_{11} = \frac{(1+2\times1)^2}{2}$$

$$= \frac{9}{2}$$

$$a_{12} = \frac{(1+2\times2)^2}{2}$$

$$= \frac{25}{2}$$

$$a_{21} = \frac{(2+2\times1)^2}{2} = 8$$

and

$$a_{22} = \frac{(2+2\times2)^2}{2} = 18$$

So, the required matrix $A = \begin{bmatrix} 9/2 & 25/2 \\ 8 & 18 \end{bmatrix}$

5. (a) -15

Explanation: Given :

$$|A| = -15$$

Let

$$A = \begin{bmatrix} a_{11} & a_{12} \\ a_{21} & a_{22} \end{bmatrix}$$

So,

$$|A| = a_{11}a_{22} - a_{12}a_{21}$$

$$\Rightarrow \quad -15 = a_{11}a_{22} - a_{12}a_{21} \qquad \qquad \dots(i)$$

Let c_{ij} represent the cofactor of a_{ij}.

Then

$$c_{21} = (-1)^{2+1} \times a_{12} = -a_{12}$$

$$c_{22} = (-1)^{2+2} \times a_{11} = a_{11}$$

Now,

$$a_{21}c_{21} + a_{22}c_{22} = a_{21}(-a_{12}) + a_{22}(a_{11})$$

$$= -a_{21}a_{12} + a_{22}a_{11}$$

$$= a_{22}a_{11} - a_{21}a_{12} = -15 \qquad \qquad \text{[Using (i)]}$$

6. (b) 0

Explanation:

$$A^2 = I \qquad \qquad \text{(Given)}$$

$$\begin{bmatrix} \alpha & \beta \\ \gamma & -\alpha \end{bmatrix} \begin{bmatrix} \alpha & \beta \\ \gamma & -\alpha \end{bmatrix} = \begin{bmatrix} 1 & 0 \\ 0 & 1 \end{bmatrix}$$

$$\Rightarrow \quad \begin{bmatrix} \alpha^2 + \beta\gamma & \alpha\beta - \alpha\beta \\ \alpha\gamma - \alpha\gamma & \beta\gamma + \alpha^2 \end{bmatrix} = \begin{bmatrix} 1 & 0 \\ 0 & 1 \end{bmatrix}$$

On comparing the corresponding elements

$$\alpha^2 + \beta\gamma = 1$$

$$1 - \alpha^2 - \beta\gamma = 0$$

7. (c) $\dfrac{8^x}{x^8}\left[\log 8-\dfrac{8}{x}\right]$

Explanation:

$$y = \dfrac{8^x}{x^8}$$

Differentiating w.r.t. x, we get

$$\dfrac{dy}{dx} = \dfrac{x^8(8^x.\log 8)-8^x(8.x^7)}{x^{16}} \qquad \left[\because \dfrac{d}{dx}\left(\dfrac{u}{v}\right)=\dfrac{v.u'-uv'}{v^2}\right]$$

$$= 8^x.x^{-8}\log 8 - 8.8^x.x^{-9} = \dfrac{8^x\log 8}{x^8}-\dfrac{8.8^x}{x^9}$$

$$\Rightarrow \qquad \dfrac{dy}{dx} = \dfrac{8^x}{x^8}\left[\log 8-\dfrac{8}{x}\right]$$

8. (c) 103

Explanation: Given,

$$y = 4x^3 - 5x$$

Differentiating w.r.t. x,

$$\dfrac{dy}{dx} = 12x^2 - 5$$

$$\therefore \qquad \left(\dfrac{dy}{dx}\right)_{(\text{at } x=3)} = 12(3)^2 - 5$$

$$= 108 - 5 = 103.$$

9. (c) $\{-2, -1, 0, 1, 2\}$

Explanation: Given,

$$R = \{(x, y) : x, y \in I, x^2 + y^2 \le 4\}$$

$$= \{(0, 0), (0, -1), (0, 1), (0, -2) \ldots (-2, 0)\}$$

$$\therefore \qquad \text{Domain of } R = \{x : (x, y) \in R = \{-2, -1, 0, 1, 2\}.$$

10. (a) $\dfrac{3}{4}$

Explanation:

$$(\text{L.H.L at } x = 2) = \lim_{x \to 2^-} f(x)$$

$$= \lim_{x \to 2^-} kx^2$$

and

$$f(2) = k(2)^2 = 4k$$

$$(\text{R.H.L at } x = 2) = \lim_{x \to 2^+} f(x) = \lim_{x \to 2^+} 3 = 3$$

$\because f(x)$ is continuous at $x = 2$

$$\lim_{x \to 2^-} f(x) = f(2) = \lim_{x \to 2^+} f(x)$$

$$\Rightarrow \qquad 4k = 3$$

$$\Rightarrow \qquad k = \dfrac{3}{4}$$

11. (c) 8

Explanation: Since $f(x)$ is continuous at $x = 0$

$\therefore$ LHL at $x = 0 = f(0) =$ RHL at $x = 0$

$$\lim_{x \to 0} \frac{1 - \cos 4x}{x^2} = a = \lim_{x \to 0} \frac{\sqrt{x}}{\sqrt{16 + \sqrt{x}} - 4}$$

$$\lim_{x \to 0} \frac{4 \sin 4x}{2x} = a = \lim_{x \to 0} \sqrt{16 + \sqrt{x}} + 4$$

$$\lim_{x \to 0} \frac{4 \sin 4x}{4x} \times \frac{4x}{2x} = a = \lim_{x \to 0} \sqrt{16 + \sqrt{x}} + 4$$

$\therefore \qquad\qquad\qquad\qquad a = 8.$

12. (b) $\dfrac{\pi}{3}$

Explanation: $\tan^{-1}\left[2\sin\left(2\cos^{-1} \dfrac{\sqrt{3}}{2} \right) \right] = \tan^{-1}\left(2\sin\left(2 \times \dfrac{\pi}{6} \right) \right)$ $\qquad\left[\because \cos^{-1} \dfrac{\sqrt{3}}{2} = \dfrac{\pi}{6} \right]$

$$= \tan^{-1}\left(2\sin \frac{\pi}{3} \right)$$

$$= \tan^{-1}\left(2 \times \frac{\sqrt{3}}{2} \right)$$

$$= \tan^{-1}(\sqrt{3}) = \frac{\pi}{3}$$

13. (a) $\left(-\dfrac{\pi}{3}, \dfrac{\pi}{3} \right)$

Explanation: $\qquad\qquad\qquad\qquad f(x) = \tan x - 4x$

$\Rightarrow \qquad\qquad\qquad\qquad f'(x) = \sec^2 x - 4$

When $\qquad\qquad\qquad \dfrac{-\pi}{3} < x < \dfrac{\pi}{3}, 1 < \sec x < 2$

Therefoer, $\qquad\qquad\qquad 1 < \sec^2 x < 4$

$\Rightarrow \qquad\qquad\qquad -3 < (\sec^2 x - 4) < 0$

Thus for $\qquad\qquad \dfrac{-\pi}{3} < x < \dfrac{\pi}{3}, f'(x) < 0$

Hence, f is strictly decreasing on $\left(-\dfrac{\pi}{3}, \dfrac{\pi}{3} \right)$

14. (a) Reflexive

Explanation: R is reflexive, since $(a, a), (b, b), (c, c) \in$ R
R is not symmetric, since $(a, b) \in$ R but $(b, a) \notin$ R
R is not transitive, since $(b, c) \in$ R and $(c, a) \in$ R but $(b, a) \notin$ R.
Thus, R is only reflexive.

15. (d) $\dfrac{\pi}{3}$

Explanation:
$$\sin^{-1}\left(\sin\dfrac{2\pi}{3}\right) = \sin^{-1}\left[\sin\left(\pi - \dfrac{\pi}{3}\right)\right]$$
$$= \sin^{-1}\left(\sin\dfrac{\pi}{3}\right) = \dfrac{\pi}{3} \qquad \left[\because \dfrac{\pi}{3} \in \left[-\dfrac{\pi}{2}, \dfrac{\pi}{2}\right]\right]$$

16. (c) 512

Explanation: Number of elements of 3×3 matrix $= 3 \times 3 = 9$

Number of ways to write 0 or 1 at one place $= 2$

Number of ways to write 0 or 1 at nine places
$$= 2 \times 2 \times 2 \times 2 \times 2 \times 2 \times 2 \times 2 \times 2$$
$$= 2^9 = 512$$

$\therefore$ There are 512 possible matrices.

17. (a) $\dfrac{15}{2}$

Explanation: We have,
$$\Delta = \begin{vmatrix} \log_3 512 & \log_4 3 \\ \log_3 8 & \log_4 9 \end{vmatrix}$$

$\Rightarrow$
$$\Delta = \begin{vmatrix} \log_3 2^9 & \log_{2^2} 3 \\ \log_3 2^3 & \log_{2^2} 3^2 \end{vmatrix}$$

$\Rightarrow$
$$\Delta = \begin{vmatrix} 9\log_3 2 & \dfrac{1}{2}\log_2 3 \\ 3\log_3 2 & \dfrac{2}{2}\log_2 3 \end{vmatrix} \qquad \left[\because \log_{a^p} m^n = \dfrac{n}{p}\log_a m\right]$$

$\Rightarrow \quad \Delta = (9\log_3 2) \times (\log_2 3) - \left(\dfrac{1}{2}\log_2 3\right)(3\log_3 2)$

$\Rightarrow \quad \Delta = 9\,(\log_3 2 \times \log_2 3) - \dfrac{3}{2}\,(\log_2 3 \times \log_3 2)$

$\Rightarrow \quad \Delta = 9 - \dfrac{3}{2}$

$\Rightarrow \quad \Delta = \dfrac{15}{2} \qquad [\because \log_b a \times \log_a b = 1]$

18. (c) $9x^2 - 8x$

Explanation:
$$y = 3x^3 - 4x^2$$
Differentiating w.r.t. x, we get
$$\dfrac{dy}{dx} = 9x^2 - 8x$$

19. (b) decreasing in $\left[0, \dfrac{\pi}{2}\right]$

Explanation: Given, $\qquad f(x) = \log(\cos x)$

Differentiate $f(x)$ w.r.t x, we get

$$f'(x) = \frac{1}{\cos x}(-\sin x) = -\tan x$$

But we know that $\qquad \tan x > 0$ for $\left[0, \dfrac{\pi}{2}\right]$

$\Rightarrow \qquad\qquad f'(x) < 0$ for $x \in \left[0, \dfrac{\pi}{2}\right]$

$\Rightarrow f(x)$ is decreasing in $\left[0, \dfrac{\pi}{2}\right]$.

20. (d) 0

Explanation: We have, $\qquad y = e^{\sin x} \Rightarrow \dfrac{dy}{dx} = e^{\sin x} . \cos x$

$$\therefore \qquad \frac{dy}{dx}\Big|_{x=\frac{\pi}{2}} = \; = e^1 . 0 = 0$$

Section – B

21. (b) $-\cot t$

Explanation: Given, $\qquad x = a \sin^3 t$

$\therefore \qquad\qquad \dfrac{dx}{dt} = 3a \sin^2 t . \cos t$

Also, $\qquad\qquad y = a \cos^3 t$

$\therefore \qquad\qquad \dfrac{dx}{dt} = 3a \cos^2 t \, (-\sin t)$

$\therefore \qquad\qquad \dfrac{dy}{dx} = \dfrac{-3a \cos^2 t . \sin t}{3a \sin^2 t . \cos t} \qquad \left[\because \dfrac{dy}{dx} = \dfrac{dy/dt}{dx/dt}\right]$

$\Rightarrow \qquad\qquad \dfrac{dy}{dx} = -\cot t$

22. (c) {2, 4, 6}

Explanation: Given, $\qquad R = \{(x, y) : x + 2y = 8, x, y \in N\}$

$\therefore \qquad\qquad R = \{(2, 3), (4, 2), (6, 1)\}$

$\therefore \qquad$ Domain of $R = \{x : (x, y) \in R\} = \{2, 4, 6\}$.

23. (d) None of these

Explanation: $R = \{(x, y) : x, y \in N, 2x + y = 41\}$

Reflexive : $(1, 1) \notin R$ as $2.1 + 1 = 3 \neq 41$. R is not reflexive.

Symetric : $(1, 39) \in R$ but $(39, 1) \notin R$. So R is not symmetric.

Transitive : $(20, 1) \in R$ and $(1, 39) \in R$. But $(20, 39) \notin R$, so R is not transitive.

24. (c) $\left\{\dfrac{\pi}{4}, \dfrac{3\pi}{4}\right\}$

Explanation: Given $f(x) = \sin^{-1} x + \tan^{-1} x + \sec^{-1} x$

Domain of $\sin^{-1} x = [-1, 1]$

Domain of $\tan^{-1} x = (-\infty, \infty)$

Domain of $\sec^{-1} x = (-\infty, \infty) - (-1, 1)$

Domain of $f(x) = [-1, 1] \cap [(-\infty, \infty) \cap [(-\infty, \infty)] - (-1, 1)] = \{-1, 1\}$

Now, $f(-1) = \sin^{-1}(-1) + \tan^{-1}(-1) + \sec^{-1}(-1) = -\dfrac{\pi}{2} - \dfrac{\pi}{4} + \pi = \dfrac{\pi}{4}$

and $f(1) = \sin^{-1}(1) + \tan^{-1}(1) + \sec^{-1}(1) = \dfrac{\pi}{2} + \dfrac{\pi}{4} + 0 = \dfrac{3\pi}{4}$

Range of $f(x) = \left\{\dfrac{\pi}{4}, \dfrac{3\pi}{4}\right\}$

25. (b) $\dfrac{59}{36}$

Explanation: $\sin^2\left(\cos^{-1}\dfrac{1}{2}\right) + \cos^2\left(\sin^{-1}\dfrac{1}{3}\right)$

$= 1 - \cos^2\left(\cos^{-1}\dfrac{1}{2}\right) + 1 - \sin^2\left(\sin^{-1}\dfrac{1}{3}\right) = 1 - \left(\dfrac{1}{2}\right)^2 + 1 - \left(\dfrac{1}{3}\right)^2 = 2 - \dfrac{1}{4} - \dfrac{1}{9} = \dfrac{59}{36}$

26. (c) A^T

Explanation:

$$A^T = \begin{bmatrix} 0 & 1 & -2 \\ -1 & 0 & -3 \\ 2 & 3 & 0 \end{bmatrix} = - \begin{bmatrix} 0 & -1 & 2 \\ 1 & 0 & 3 \\ -2 & -3 & 0 \end{bmatrix} = - A$$

So, $A^T = -A$

$\Rightarrow \quad A + A^T = 0$

Hence, $A + 2A^T = A^T$

27. (b) -1

Explanation: We have, $x^y \cdot y^x = 16$

Taking log on both sides, $\log x^y + \log y^x = \log 16$

$y \log x + x \log y = \log 16$

Differentiating both sides, w.r.t. x, we get

$$\dfrac{y}{x} + \log x \dfrac{dy}{dx} + \dfrac{x}{y}\dfrac{dy}{dx} + \log y = 0$$

At $x = 2, y = 2$

$$1 + \log 2 \left(\dfrac{dy}{dx}\right)_{(2,\,2)} + 1\left(\dfrac{dy}{dx}\right)_{(2,\,2)} + \log 2 = 0$$

$$\Rightarrow \qquad \left(\dfrac{dy}{dx}\right)_{(2,\,2)} = \dfrac{-(\log 2 + 1)}{\log 2 + 1} = -1$$

28. (d) None of these

Explanation: $\lim\limits_{x \to 0} \sin\dfrac{1}{x}$ does not exist. Hence, there is no value of k for which the function is continuos at $x = 0$.

29. (b) 3

Explanation: Area of triangle $= \dfrac{1}{2}\begin{vmatrix} -3 & 0 & 1 \\ 3 & 0 & 1 \\ 0 & k & 1 \end{vmatrix} = \pm 9$

$\Rightarrow \qquad -k(-3-3) = \pm 18$

$\Rightarrow \qquad 6k = \pm 18$

$\Rightarrow \qquad k = \pm 3$

30. (c) Intersection

Explanation: A corner point of a feasible region is a point, in the region, which is the intersection of two boundary lines.

31. (c) 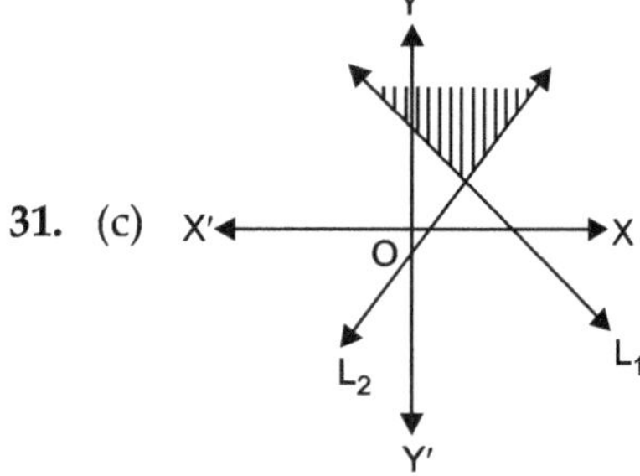

Explanation: The graph of linear equation $x + y = 5$ is drawn in figure. We note that solution of inequality (i) is represented by the shaded region above the line $x + y = 5$, including the points on the line

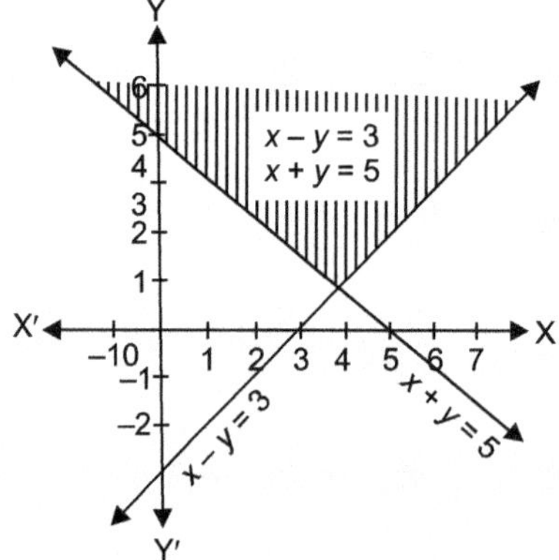

On the same set of axes, we draw the graph of the equation $x - y = 3$ as shown in figure. Then, we note that inequality (ii) represents the shaded region above the line $x - y = 3$, including the points on the line.

Clearly, the double shaded region, common to the above two shaded region is the required solution region of the given system of inequalities.

32. (a) $\quad -4\begin{bmatrix} 1 & 1 \\ 1 & 1 \end{bmatrix}$

Explanation: Given,

$$f(x) = (1 + x)(1 - x)$$
$$= 1 - x^2$$
$$\Rightarrow \quad f(A) = I - A^2 \qquad \text{(Put } x = A)$$
$$\Rightarrow \quad f(A) = \begin{bmatrix} 1 & 0 \\ 0 & 1 \end{bmatrix} - \left\{ \begin{bmatrix} 1 & 2 \\ 2 & 1 \end{bmatrix} \begin{bmatrix} 1 & 2 \\ 2 & 1 \end{bmatrix} \right\}$$
$$= \begin{bmatrix} 1 & 0 \\ 0 & 1 \end{bmatrix} - \begin{bmatrix} 5 & 4 \\ 4 & 5 \end{bmatrix} = \begin{bmatrix} -4 & -4 \\ -4 & -4 \end{bmatrix}$$
$$= -4 \begin{bmatrix} 1 & 1 \\ 1 & 1 \end{bmatrix}$$

33. (d) $x = 0, y = 0$

Explanation:

$$\begin{vmatrix} 6i & -3i & 1 \\ 4 & 3i & -1 \\ 40 & 3 & i \end{vmatrix} = 1(12 - 120i) + 1(18i + 120i) + i(18i^2 + 12i) \qquad (\because i^2 = -1)$$
$$= 12 - 120i + 18i + 120i + i(-18 + 12i)$$
$$= 12 + 18i - 18i - 12 = 0 = 0 + i0$$
$$= x + iy$$

On comparing we get

$$x = y = 0$$

34. (d) $\dfrac{\pi}{2}$

Explanation:

$$\frac{dx}{dt} = -e^t \cdot \sin t + e^t \cos t$$

$$\frac{dy}{dt} = e^t \cos t + e^t \sin t$$

Therefore

$$\left(\frac{dy}{dx} \right)_{t = \frac{\pi}{4}} = \frac{\cos t + \sin t}{\cos t - \sin t} = \frac{1}{-1} = -1$$

35. (a) $\dfrac{1}{7} \begin{bmatrix} 2 & -1 \\ 1 & 3 \end{bmatrix}$

Explanation:

$$|A| = 6 + 1 = 7 \neq 0,$$
$$\therefore \quad A^{-1} \text{ exists.}$$
$$(\text{adj } A) = \begin{bmatrix} 2 & -1 \\ 1 & 3 \end{bmatrix}$$
$$A^{-1} = \frac{1}{7} \begin{bmatrix} 2 & -1 \\ 1 & 3 \end{bmatrix}$$

36. (d) $\sec^2 \theta$

Explanation:

$$\frac{dx}{d\theta} = 3a \cos^2 \theta \, (- \sin \theta)$$

and

$$\frac{dy}{d\theta} = 3a \sin^2 \theta \, (\cos \theta)$$

Now,

$$\frac{dy}{dx} = \frac{3a \sin^2 \theta \cos \theta}{-3a \cos^2 \theta \sin \theta} = - \tan \theta$$

$\therefore$

$$1 + \left(\frac{dy}{dx}\right)^2 = 1 + (- \tan \theta)^2 = 1 + \tan^2 \theta = \sec^2 \theta.$$

37. (d) 20

Explanation: Feasible region is ABCDEA and $Z = x + 2y$

38. (b) $\alpha = a^2 + b^2, \ \beta = 2ab$

Explanation: Given,

$$A = \begin{bmatrix} a & b \\ b & a \end{bmatrix}, A^2 = \begin{bmatrix} \alpha & \beta \\ \beta & \alpha \end{bmatrix}$$

Now,

$$A^2 = A \cdot A = \begin{bmatrix} a & b \\ b & a \end{bmatrix}\begin{bmatrix} a & b \\ b & a \end{bmatrix}$$

$\Rightarrow$

$$\begin{bmatrix} \alpha & \beta \\ \beta & \alpha \end{bmatrix} = \begin{bmatrix} a^2 + b^2 & 2ab \\ 2ab & a^2 + b^2 \end{bmatrix}$$

Now,

$$\alpha = a^2 + b^2; \ \beta = 2ab$$

39. (a) $10x^4 (\sin x^5)(\cos x^5)(\cos x^3) - 3x^2 \sin x^3 \sin^2 x^5$

Explanation: Let $\quad y = \cos x^3 \sin^2 (x^5)$

On differentiating both sides w.r.t. x, we get

$$\frac{dy}{dx} = \frac{d}{dx}\{\cos x^3 \sin^2 (x^5)\}$$

$$= \cos x^3 \frac{d}{dx} \sin^2 (x^5) + \sin^2 (x^5) \frac{d}{dx} (\cos x^3)$$

$$\left[\because \frac{d}{dx}(uv) = u\frac{d}{dx}v + v\frac{d}{dx}u\right]$$

$$= (\cos x^3)(2 \sin x^5)\frac{d}{dx}(\sin x^5) + \sin^2 (x^5)(- \sin x^3)\frac{d}{dx}(x^3)$$

$$\left[\because \frac{d}{dx} f\{g(x)\} = f'\{g(x)\}\frac{d}{dx} g(x)\right]$$

$$= (\cos x^3)(2 \sin x^5)(\cos x^5)\frac{d}{dx}(x^5) + \sin^2 (x^5)(- \sin x^3)(3x)^2$$

[using chain rule]

$$= (\cos x^3)(2 \sin x^5)(\cos x^5)(5x^4) - \sin^2 (x^5)(\sin x^3)(3x^2)$$

$$= 10x^4 (\sin x^5)(\cos x^5)(\cos x^3) - 3x^2 \sin x^3 \sin^2 x^5.$$

40. (b) Finite

Explanation: In a LPP, the maximum value of the objective function $z = ax + by$ is always finite.

Section – C

41. (d) $q = 3p$

Explanation: The maximum value of Z is unique.

It is given that maximum value of Z occurs at two points (3, 4) and (0, 5). Value of Z at (3, 4) = Value of Z at (0, 5).

$$\Rightarrow \qquad p(3) + q(4) = p(0) + q(5)$$
$$3p + 4q = 5q \Rightarrow 3p = q$$

42. (b) -1

Explanation: We have,

$$y = (1 + x^{1/4})(1 + x^{1/2})(1 - x^{1/4})$$
$$= (1 - x^{1/2})(1 + x^{1/2}) = 1 - x$$
$$\therefore \quad \frac{dy}{dx} = -1.$$

43. (d) 5

Explanation: Since, the given points are collinear.

$$\therefore \quad \frac{1}{2}\begin{vmatrix} 3 & -2 & 1 \\ x & 2 & 1 \\ 8 & 8 & 1 \end{vmatrix} = 0$$

$$\Rightarrow \qquad 3(2 - 8) + 2(x - 8) + 1(8x - 16) = 0$$
$$\Rightarrow \qquad -18 + 2x - 16 + 8x - 16 = 0$$
$$\Rightarrow \qquad x = 5$$

44. (b) skew-symmetric matrix

Explanation:
$$A^T = \begin{bmatrix} 0 & -2 & 3 \\ 2 & 0 & 1 \\ -3 & -1 & 0 \end{bmatrix} = -\begin{bmatrix} 0 & 2 & -3 \\ -2 & 0 & -1 \\ 3 & 1 & 0 \end{bmatrix} = -A$$

Since $A^T = -A$, therefore, A is a skew-symmetric matrix.

45. (d) (5, 2)

Explanation:
$$\lim_{x \to 1^-} f(x) = \lim_{h \to 0} f(1-h)^2 + b = a + b$$

Function $f(x)$ is discontinuous at $x = 1$.

$$\lim_{x \to 1^-} f(x) \neq f(1)$$

$$\Rightarrow \qquad a + b \neq 4$$

Checking options , (5, 2) is the correct answer.

46. (a) $\dfrac{440 - 2x}{\pi}$

> **Explanation:** Perimeter of field is 440 m.
>
> $$x = \text{length},\ y = \text{breadth}$$
>
> $$\text{Radius of semicircle} = \frac{y}{2}$$
>
> $\therefore$
> $$P = 2x + 2\pi.\left(\frac{y}{2}\right)$$
>
> $$440 = 2x + \pi y$$
>
> $$\frac{440 - 2x}{\pi} = y$$

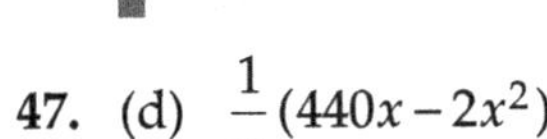

47. (d) $\dfrac{1}{\pi}(440x - 2x^2)$

> **Explanation:** A be the area of rectangular field.
>
> $$A = xy$$
>
> $$A = x\left(\frac{440 - 2x}{\pi}\right) = \frac{1}{\pi}(440x - 2x^2)$$

48. (b) 110 m

> **Explanation:** Differentiate A w.r. to x,
>
> $$\frac{dA}{dx} = \frac{1}{\pi}(440 - 4x)$$
>
> Put
> $$\frac{dA}{dx} = 0$$
>
> $\Rightarrow$
> $$440 - 4x = 0$$
>
> $$440 = 4x$$
>
> $$x = 110\ \text{m}$$

49. (c) 7700 m^2

> **Explanation:** Now, $\dfrac{d^2A}{dx^2} = -4$, $-$ve *i.e.*, area is maximum at $x = 110$
>
> $$\text{Maximum area, } A = xy = 110 \times \frac{220}{\pi} = \frac{24200}{\pi} = \frac{24200}{22} \times 7$$
>
> $$= 7700\ \text{m}^2$$

50. (a) 70 m

> **Explanation:**
> $$y = \frac{440 - 2 \times 110}{\pi} = \frac{440 - 220}{\pi} = \frac{220}{\pi}$$
>
> $$= \frac{220}{22} \times 7 = 70\ \text{m}$$

Sample Paper 2

Section - A

1. (b) 24

Explanation: The total number of injective mappings from the set containing 3 elements into the set containing 4 elements is $^4P_3 = 4! = 24$.

2. (d) $\dfrac{2\pi}{9}$

Explanation:
$$\cos^{-1}[\cos(-680°)] = \cos^{-1}[\cos(680°)]$$
$$= \cos^{-1}[\cos(720° - 40°)]$$
$$= \cos^{-1}[\cos(40°)]$$
$$= \cos^{-1}\left[\cos\left(\dfrac{2\pi}{9}\right)\right] = \dfrac{2\pi}{9}$$

3. (a) 1

Explanation: Given, $\begin{bmatrix} x+y & 4 \\ -5 & 3y \end{bmatrix} = \begin{bmatrix} 3 & 4 \\ -5 & 6 \end{bmatrix}$

Equating the corresponding elements, we get
$$x + y = 3 \text{ and } 3y = 6$$
$$\therefore \qquad 3y = 6$$
$$\Rightarrow \qquad y = 2$$
Putting $y = 2$ in $x + y = 3$, we get
$$x = 1$$

4. (c) $4y = 4x + 33$

Explanation: The equation of given curve is
$$y = -5x^2 + 6x + 7$$
$$\Rightarrow \qquad \dfrac{dy}{dx} = -10x + 6$$
$$\Rightarrow \qquad \left(\dfrac{dy}{dx}\right)_{\left(\frac{1}{2}, \frac{35}{4}\right)} = -10 \times \dfrac{1}{2} + 6 = 1$$

The required equation of tangent at $\left(\dfrac{1}{2}, \dfrac{35}{4}\right)$ is
$$y - \dfrac{35}{4} = \left(x - \dfrac{1}{2}\right)$$
$$\Rightarrow \qquad y = x - \dfrac{1}{2} + \dfrac{35}{4} = x + \dfrac{33}{4}$$
$$\Rightarrow \qquad 4y = 4x + 33$$

5. (a) 0

Explanation: We have
$$y = e^{\sin x}$$
$$\Rightarrow \qquad \frac{dy}{dx} = e^{\sin x}.\cos x$$
$$\therefore \qquad \frac{dy}{dx}\bigg|_{x=\frac{\pi}{2}} = e^1.0 = 0$$

6. (a) 0

Explanation: Given
$$\begin{bmatrix} \cos\alpha & -\sin\alpha \\ \sin\alpha & \cos\alpha \end{bmatrix} = \begin{bmatrix} 1 & 0 \\ 0 & 1 \end{bmatrix}$$
$$\cos\alpha = 1 \cos 0°$$
$$\therefore \qquad \alpha = 0°$$

7. (b) 5×2

Explanation: Given : A is a matrix of order 2×3 and B is a matrix of order 3×5.
$\Rightarrow$ AB is a matrix of order 2×5.
Since, transpose of any matrix is obtained by interchanging rows and columns,
$\therefore$ $(AB)^T$ is a matrix of order 5×2.

8. (c) $(1, 2, 3)$

Explanation: The given relation on N is
$$R = \{(x, y) : x + 2y = 8\}$$
Since both $x, y \in N$, x can take value 2, 4, 6, for all $x, y \in N$.
For $x = 2,$ $\qquad\qquad 2 + 2y = 8$
$\Rightarrow$ $\qquad\qquad\qquad y = 3$
For $x = 4,$ $\qquad\qquad 4 + 2y = 8$
$\Rightarrow$ $\qquad\qquad\qquad y = 2$
For $x = 6,$ $\qquad\qquad 6 + 2y = 8$
$\Rightarrow$ $\qquad\qquad\qquad y = 1$
$$R = \{(2, 3), (4, 2), (6, 1)\}$$
The range of R = Set of second elements
$$= \{1, 2, 3\}$$

9. (a) 1

Explanation: For a singular matrix, $\qquad |A| = 0$
$$\Rightarrow \qquad \begin{vmatrix} 3-2x & x+1 \\ 2 & 4 \end{vmatrix} = 0$$
$$\Rightarrow \qquad 4(3 - 2x) - 2(x + 1) = 0$$
$$\Rightarrow \qquad 12 - 8x - 2x - 2 = 0$$
$$\Rightarrow \qquad x = 1$$

10. (a) $2x \cos x^2 . e^{\sin x^2}$

Explanation: Given :
$$y = e^{\sin x^2}$$
Differentiating both sides w.r.t. x,
$$\frac{dy}{dx} = e^{\sin x^2} . \frac{d}{dx}(\sin x^2)$$
$$= e^{\sin x^2} \cos x^2 \, \frac{d}{dx}(x^2)$$
$$= 2x \cos x^2 . e^{\sin x^2}.$$

11. (d) $-\dfrac{\pi}{4}$

Explanation: We know that principal value of $\tan^{-1}(\theta)$ is $\left(-\dfrac{\pi}{2}, \dfrac{\pi}{2}\right)$.

$$\therefore \qquad \tan^{-1}(-1) = \tan^{-1}\left(-\tan\frac{\pi}{4}\right) \qquad\qquad \left\{\because \tan\frac{\pi}{4} = 1\right\}$$
$$= \tan^{-1}\left(\tan\left(-\frac{\pi}{4}\right)\right) \qquad\qquad [\because -\tan\theta = \tan(-\theta)]$$
$$= -\frac{\pi}{4} \in \left(-\frac{\pi}{2}, \frac{\pi}{2}\right)$$

12. (b) $\dfrac{1}{7}$

Explanation: Given,
$$[1 \ \ x]\begin{bmatrix} 2 & -1 \\ 1 & 2 \end{bmatrix}\begin{bmatrix} 1 \\ 3 \end{bmatrix} = 0$$
$$\Rightarrow \qquad [1 \ \ x]\begin{bmatrix} 2-3 \\ 1+6 \end{bmatrix} = [0]$$
$$\Rightarrow \qquad [1 \ \ x]\begin{bmatrix} -1 \\ 7 \end{bmatrix} = [0]$$
$$\Rightarrow \qquad -1 + 7x = 0$$
$$\Rightarrow \qquad x = \frac{1}{7}$$

13. (a) π

Explanation:
$$\cos^{-1}\left(\cos\frac{2\pi}{3}\right) + \sin^{-1}\left(\sin\frac{2\pi}{3}\right) = \cos^{-1}\left(\cos\frac{2\pi}{3}\right) + \sin^{-1}\left(\sin\left(\pi-\frac{\pi}{3}\right)\right)$$
$$\left[\because \frac{2\pi}{3} \notin \left(-\frac{\pi}{2}, \frac{\pi}{2}\right)\right]$$
$$= \cos^{-1}\left(\cos\frac{2\pi}{3}\right) + \sin^{-1}\left(\sin\frac{\pi}{3}\right)$$

$$= \frac{2\pi}{3} + \frac{\pi}{3}$$

$$= \frac{3\pi}{3} = \pi$$

$$\left[\begin{array}{l}\text{Note : By property of inverse function} \\ \sin^{-1}(\sin x) = x \ \text{if} \ x \in \left[-\dfrac{\pi}{2}, \dfrac{\pi}{2}\right] \\ \text{and} \ \cos^{-1}(\cos x) = x \ \text{if} \ x \in [0, \pi]\end{array}\right]$$

14. (d) $-\dfrac{1}{4}$

Explanation:

$$y = \tan^{-1}\left(\frac{\sqrt{x}-x}{1+x^{3/2}}\right) = \tan^{-1}\left(\frac{\sqrt{x}-x}{1+\sqrt{x}\,.\,x}\right)$$

$$= \tan^{-1}(\sqrt{x}) - \tan^{-1}(x)$$

Differentiating w.r.t. x, we get

$$y' = \frac{1}{1+x}\cdot\frac{1}{2\sqrt{x}} - \frac{1}{1+x^2}$$

$$\Rightarrow \qquad y'(1) = \frac{1}{2}\cdot\frac{1}{2} - \frac{1}{2} = -\frac{1}{4}$$

15. (b) $-\dfrac{1}{1+x^2}$

Explanation: Given :

$$y = \cot^{-1}\left(\frac{a+x}{1-ax}\right)$$

Let

$$a = \tan\alpha$$

$$\Rightarrow \qquad \alpha = \tan^{-1}a$$

and

$$x = \tan\beta$$

$$\Rightarrow \qquad \beta = \tan^{-1}x$$

$$\therefore \qquad y = \cot^{-1}\left[\frac{\tan\alpha + \tan\beta}{1 - \tan\alpha.\tan\beta}\right]$$

$$\Rightarrow \qquad y = \cot^{-1}[\tan(\alpha+\beta)]$$

$$\Rightarrow \qquad y = \cot^{-1}\left[\cot\left(\frac{\pi}{2} - (\alpha+\beta)\right)\right]$$

$$\Rightarrow \qquad y = \frac{\pi}{2} - \alpha - \beta$$

$$\Rightarrow \qquad y = \frac{\pi}{2} - \tan^{-1}a - \tan^{-1}x$$

Differentiating w.r.t. x., we get

$$\frac{dy}{dx} = 0 - 0 - \frac{1}{1+x^2}$$

$$\Rightarrow \qquad \frac{dy}{dx} = -\frac{1}{1+x^2}$$

16. (d) 2

Explanation:
$$[x \ 1]_{1\times 2} \begin{bmatrix} 1 & 0 \\ -2 & 0 \end{bmatrix}_{2\times 2} = 0$$

$\Rightarrow \qquad [(x-2) \ 0 + 0] = [0 \ 0]$

$\Rightarrow \qquad [(x-2) \ 0] = [0 \ 0]$

On comparing, we get

$$x - 2 = 0$$

$\Rightarrow \qquad x = 2$

17. (c) 6

Explanation: Here,
$$A = \begin{bmatrix} 3 & -3 \\ -3 & 3 \end{bmatrix}$$

Given,
$$A^2 = \lambda A$$

$\Rightarrow \qquad \begin{bmatrix} 3 & -3 \\ -3 & 3 \end{bmatrix}\begin{bmatrix} 3 & -3 \\ -3 & 3 \end{bmatrix} = \lambda \begin{bmatrix} 3 & -3 \\ -3 & 3 \end{bmatrix}$

$\Rightarrow \qquad \begin{bmatrix} 18 & -18 \\ -18 & 18 \end{bmatrix} = \lambda \begin{bmatrix} 3 & -3 \\ -3 & 3 \end{bmatrix}$

$\Rightarrow \qquad 6\begin{bmatrix} 3 & -3 \\ -3 & 3 \end{bmatrix} = \lambda \begin{bmatrix} 3 & -3 \\ -3 & 3 \end{bmatrix}$

$\Rightarrow \qquad \lambda = 6$

18. (b) 0

Explanation: We have,
$$f(x) = (x^{a-b})^{a+b}.(x^{b-c})^{b+c}.(x^{c-a})^{c+a}$$

$$= x^{a^2-b^2}.x^{b^2-c^2}.x^{c^2-a^2}$$

$$= x^{a^2-b^2+b^2-c^2+c^2-a^2}$$

$$= x^0$$

$$= 1$$

$\therefore \qquad f'(x) = 0.$

19. (d) $\dfrac{1}{4}, \dfrac{1}{2}$

Explanation:
$$\frac{dy}{dx} = \frac{1}{2y}$$

$\Rightarrow \qquad \tan\dfrac{\pi}{4} = 1$

$\Rightarrow \qquad y = \dfrac{1}{2}$

$\Rightarrow \qquad x = \dfrac{1}{4}$

20. (c) $a + c = -1, b \in R$

Explanation:

$$\text{LHL} = \lim_{x \to 0} \frac{\sin(a+1)x + \sin x}{x} \qquad \left(\frac{0}{0} \text{ form}\right)$$

Using L' Hospital Rule, we get

$$\text{LHL} = \lim_{x \to 0} (a+1)\cos(a+1)x + \cos x = a + 2 \qquad \ldots(i)$$

$$\text{RHL} = \lim_{x \to 0} \frac{\sqrt{x + bx^2} - \sqrt{x}}{bx^{3/2}} = \lim_{x \to 0} \frac{\sqrt{1 + bx} - 1}{bx}$$

$$= \lim_{x \to 0} \frac{1}{\sqrt{1 + bx} + 1} = \frac{1}{2} \qquad \ldots(ii)$$

From eqs. (i) and (ii), we get

$$a + 2 = c = \frac{1}{2}$$

$$\Rightarrow \qquad a = -\frac{3}{2} \text{ and } a + c = -1$$

Section - B

21. (d) 4

Explanation: For singular matrix, $|A| = 0$

$$\therefore \qquad \begin{vmatrix} 1 & 2 & x \\ 1 & 1 & 1 \\ 2 & 1 & -1 \end{vmatrix} = 0$$

$$\Rightarrow \qquad 1(-1-1) - 2(-1-2) + x(1-2) = 0$$

$$\Rightarrow \qquad -2 + 6 - x = 0 \Rightarrow x = 4.$$

22. (b) Symmetric only

Explanation: Given, $\qquad \alpha R \beta \Leftrightarrow \alpha \perp \beta$

$$\therefore \qquad \alpha \perp \beta \Leftrightarrow \beta \perp \alpha \Rightarrow \beta R \alpha$$

Hence, R is symmetric.

23. (b) $\{(1, 2), (2, 4), (3, 6), \ldots\}$

Explanation: $\qquad R = \{(2, 1), (4, 2), (6, 3), \ldots\}$

So, $\qquad R^{-1} = \{(1, 2), (2, 4), (3, 6), \ldots\}$

24. (c) $\dfrac{5\pi}{6}$

Explanation: Let $\qquad \sec^{-1}\left(\dfrac{-2}{\sqrt{3}}\right) = \theta$

$$\Rightarrow \qquad \sec \theta = \frac{-2}{\sqrt{3}} = -\sec \frac{\pi}{6}$$

$$= \sec\left(\pi - \frac{\pi}{6}\right) = \sec\frac{5\pi}{6}$$

$$\Rightarrow \qquad \theta = \frac{5\pi}{6} \in [0, \pi] - \left\{\frac{\pi}{2}\right\}$$

$\therefore$ Principal value of $\sec^{-1}\left(\dfrac{-2}{\sqrt{3}}\right)$ is $\dfrac{5\pi}{6}$

25. (c) 3

Explanation: We know that, $\qquad 0 \le \cos^{-1}x \le \pi$

$\because \qquad \cos^{-1}x + \cos^{-1}y + \cos^{-1}z = 3\pi$

$\therefore \qquad \cos^{-1}x = \cos^{-1}y = \cos^{-1}z = \pi$

$\Rightarrow \qquad x = y = z = -1$

$\therefore \qquad xy + yz + zx = 3$

26. (b) $\dfrac{12}{6 - \sqrt{3}}$

Explanation:

$$P \Rightarrow 3x + 2y = 12$$
$$2y = 12 - 3x$$
$$y = \frac{12 - 3x}{2}$$
$$= 6 - \frac{3}{2}x \qquad \qquad \ldots(i)$$

$$A = xy + \frac{\sqrt{3}}{4}x^2$$

$$A = x\left(6 - \frac{3}{2}x\right) + \frac{\sqrt{3}}{4}x^2 \qquad \text{(Using (i))}$$

$$A = 6x - \frac{3}{2}x^2 + \frac{\sqrt{3}}{4}x^2$$

Differentiating A w.r.t. x,

$$\frac{dA}{dx} = 6 - 3x + \frac{\sqrt{3}}{2}x$$

Put $\dfrac{dA}{dx} = 0$,

$$6 + x\left(\frac{\sqrt{3}}{2} - 3\right) = 0$$

$$x\left(\frac{\sqrt{3}}{2} - 3\right) = -6$$

$$x = \frac{6}{3 - \dfrac{\sqrt{3}}{2}}$$

$$x = \frac{12}{6 - \sqrt{3}}.$$

27. (b) $8x + 3y \leq 100,\ y \geq 0$

> **Explanation:** Consider, $8x + 3y = 100$. We observe that the shaded region and the origin lie on the same side of the line and $(0, 0)$ satisfies $8x + 3y \leq 100$. Therefore, we must have $8x + 3y \leq 100$ as linear inequality corresponding to the line $8x + 3y = 100$. Also, shaded region lies in the first quadrant only, therefore $x \geq 0,\ y \geq 0$. Hence, the linear equalities corresponding to the given solution are $8x + 3y \leq 100,\ x \geq 0,\ y \geq 0$.

28. (b) ± 10

> **Explanation:** $\qquad\qquad \dfrac{dy}{dx} = 0 \Rightarrow 2x + a = 0$
>
> *i.e.* $\qquad\qquad\qquad\qquad x = -\dfrac{a}{2}$
>
> Therefore, $\qquad\qquad \dfrac{a^2}{4} + a\left(-\dfrac{a}{2}\right) + 25 = 0$
>
> $\Rightarrow \qquad\qquad\qquad\qquad a = \pm 10$
>
> Hence, the values of a are ± 10.

29. (b) Two variables

> **Explanation:** LPP of two variable can be solved by graphical method.

30. (c) $\theta = \phi + (2n+1)\dfrac{\pi}{2},\ n = 0, 1, 2, \ldots$

> **Explanation:**
> $$AB = \begin{bmatrix} \cos^2\theta & \sin\theta\,\cos\theta \\ \cos\theta\,\sin\theta & \sin^2\theta \end{bmatrix} \begin{bmatrix} \cos^2\phi & \sin\phi\,\cos\phi \\ \cos\phi\,\sin\phi & \sin^2\phi \end{bmatrix}$$
>
> $$= \begin{bmatrix} \cos^2\theta\cos^2\phi + \sin\theta\cos\phi\cos\theta\sin\phi & \cos^2\theta\sin\phi\cos\phi + \sin^2\phi\sin\theta\cos\theta \\ \cos^2\phi\cos\theta\sin\theta + \sin^2\theta\sin\phi\cos\phi & \cos\theta\sin\theta\sin\phi\cos\phi + \sin^2\theta\sin^2\phi \end{bmatrix}$$
>
> $$= \begin{bmatrix} \cos\theta\cos\phi\cos(\theta-\phi) & \sin\phi\cos\theta\cos(\theta-\phi) \\ \sin\theta\cos\phi\cos(\theta-\phi) & \sin\theta\sin\phi\cos(\theta-\phi) \end{bmatrix}$$
>
> $\because \qquad\qquad AB = 0$
>
> $\Rightarrow \qquad\quad \cos(\theta - \phi) = 0$
>
> $\Rightarrow \qquad\quad \cos(\theta - \phi) = \cos(2n+1)\dfrac{\pi}{2}$
>
> $\Rightarrow \qquad\qquad \theta = (2n+1)\dfrac{\pi}{2} = \phi, \qquad\qquad\qquad\qquad\qquad \text{where } n = 0, 1, 2, \ldots$

31. (c) 5 square unit

> **Explanation:** $\qquad$ Area of triangle $= \dfrac{1}{2}\begin{vmatrix} 6 & 0 & 1 \\ 4 & 3 & 1 \\ 2 & 1 & 1 \end{vmatrix} = \dfrac{1}{2}\{6(3-1) - 0 + 1(4-6)\}$
>
> $$= \dfrac{1}{2}\{12 - 2\} = \dfrac{1}{2} \times 10 = 5 \text{ sq. unit}$$

32. (d) Construct the following table of values of objective function:

Explanation:

Corner Points	Value of $Z = 4x + 3y$	
(0, 0)	$4 \times 0 + 6 \times 2 = 12$	} ← Minimum
(3, 0)	$4 \times 3 + 6 \times 0 = 12$	
(6, 0)	$4 \times 6 + 6 \times 0 = 24$	
(6, 8)	$4 \times 6 + 6 \times 8 = 72$	← Maximum
(0, 5)	$4 \times 0 + 6 \times 5 = 30$	

Since the minimum value (F) = 12 occurs at two distinct corner points, it occurs at every point of the segment joining these two points

33. (b) $\dfrac{\sin^2 (a+y)}{\sin a}$

Explanation: Given

$$\sin y = x \sin (a + y)$$

$$\Rightarrow \quad x = \frac{\sin y}{\sin (a + y)}$$

On differentiating w.r.t. x, we get

$$\frac{dx}{dy} = \frac{\sin (a + y) \cos y - \sin y \cos (a + y)}{\sin^2 (a + y)} = \frac{\sin a}{\sin^2 (a + y)}$$

$$\Rightarrow \quad \frac{dy}{dx} = \frac{\sin^2 (a + y)}{\sin a}$$

34. (a) 0

Explanation: We have

$$AB = \begin{bmatrix} 1 & 2 & x \\ 0 & 1 & 0 \\ 0 & 0 & 1 \end{bmatrix} \begin{bmatrix} 1 & -2 & y \\ 0 & 1 & 0 \\ 0 & 0 & 1 \end{bmatrix} = \begin{bmatrix} 1 & 0 & x+y \\ 0 & 1 & 0 \\ 0 & 0 & 1 \end{bmatrix}$$

Now, $$AB = I_3 \hspace{4cm} \text{(Given)}$$

$$\Rightarrow \quad \begin{bmatrix} 1 & 0 & x+y \\ 0 & 1 & 0 \\ 0 & 0 & 1 \end{bmatrix} = \begin{bmatrix} 1 & 0 & 0 \\ 0 & 1 & 0 \\ 0 & 0 & 1 \end{bmatrix}$$

$$\therefore \quad x + y = 0.$$

35. (c) 15. sq. units

Explanation: Required area = $\left| \dfrac{1}{2} \begin{vmatrix} -2 & -3 & 1 \\ 3 & 2 & 1 \\ -1 & -8 & 1 \end{vmatrix} \right| = \left| \dfrac{1}{2} [-2(2+8) + 3(3+1) + 1(-24+2)] \right|$

$$= \left| \frac{1}{2} (-20 + 12 - 22) \right| = \left| \frac{1}{2} (-30) \right| = 15 \text{ sq. units}$$

36. (b) $(2, 5)$

Explanation:

Corner points	Value of Z = $4x + 3y$	
$(0, 8)$	$4 \times 0 + 3 \times 8 = 24$	
$(2, 5)$	$4 \times 2 + 3 \times 5 = 23$	$\rightarrow$ Minimum
$(4, 3)$	$4 \times 4 + 3 \times 3 = 25$	
$(9, 0)$	$4 \times 9 + 3 \times 0 = 36$	

37. (b) $\dfrac{\cos x - 2}{3}$

Explanation: Given $\qquad\qquad\qquad 2x + 3y = \sin x$

Differentiate both sdies w.r.t. x, $\qquad 2 \times 1 + 3\dfrac{dy}{dx} = \cos x$

$\Rightarrow \qquad\qquad\qquad\qquad 3\dfrac{dy}{dx} = \cos x - 2 \Rightarrow \dfrac{dy}{dx} = \dfrac{\cos x - 2}{3}$

38. (a) 0

Explanation: $\qquad\qquad M_{31} = \begin{vmatrix} -3 & 5 \\ 0 & 4 \end{vmatrix} = -12 - 0 = -12$

$\Rightarrow \qquad\qquad\qquad A_{31} = M_{31} = -12$

$$M_{32} = \begin{vmatrix} 2 & 5 \\ 6 & 4 \end{vmatrix} = 8 - 30 = -22$$

$\Rightarrow \qquad\qquad\qquad A_{32} = -M_{32} = 22$

$$M_{33} = \begin{vmatrix} 2 & -3 \\ 6 & 0 \end{vmatrix} = 0 + 18 = 18 \Rightarrow A_{33} = M_{33} = 18$$

$\therefore \qquad a_{11}A_{31} + a_{12}A_{32} + a_{13}A_{33} = (2)(-12) + (-3)(22) + (5)(18)$
$$= -24 - 66 + 90 = -90 + 90 = 0$$

39. (c) 10

Explanation: Given that, the function f is continuous at $x = 0$.

$\therefore \qquad\qquad\qquad\qquad \lim_{x \to 0} f(x) = f(0)$

$\Rightarrow \qquad\qquad\qquad \lim_{x \to 0} \dfrac{\sin(10x)}{x} = f(0)$

$\Rightarrow \qquad\qquad\quad \lim_{x \to 0} 10 \cdot \dfrac{\sin(10x)}{(10x)} = f(0)$

$\Rightarrow \qquad\qquad 10 \cdot \lim_{x \to 0} \dfrac{\sin(10x)}{(10x)} = f(0) \qquad\qquad \left[\because \lim_{x \to 0} \dfrac{\sin \theta}{\theta} = 1 \right]$

$\Rightarrow \qquad\qquad\qquad\qquad 10 \times 1 = f(0)$

$\therefore \qquad\qquad\qquad\qquad\quad f(0) = 10$

Hence, if f is continuos at $x = 0$, then the value of $f(0)$ will be 10.

40. (a) first quadrant

Explanation: Region represented by $x \geq 0, y \geq 0$ is first quadrant.

Section - C

41. (c) -2

Explanation: Expanding the two determinants, we get
$$(1 - 3x^2 + 2x^3) + (3x^2 - x^3) = 0 \Rightarrow x^3 + 1 = 0$$
$$\Rightarrow \qquad x = -\omega, -\omega^2, -1$$
$$x^{2007} + x^{-2007} = -1 - 1 = -2$$

42. (a) 0

Explanation: Functions which satisfy the relation $x^2 + y^2 = 4$ are $y(x) = \sqrt{4 - x^2}$ and $y(x) = -\sqrt{4 - x^2}$
And both functions are continuous in $[-2, 2]$.

43. (c) Skew symmetric matrix

Explanation: Let
$$A = \begin{bmatrix} 0 & -5 & 8 \\ 5 & 0 & 12 \\ -8 & -12 & 0 \end{bmatrix}$$
$$A^T = \begin{bmatrix} 0 & 5 & -8 \\ -5 & 0 & -12 \\ 8 & 12 & 0 \end{bmatrix} = -\begin{bmatrix} 0 & -5 & 8 \\ 5 & 0 & 12 \\ -8 & -12 & 0 \end{bmatrix} = -A$$

Since $\qquad A^T = -A$
$\therefore$ A is a skew symmetric matrix.

44. (a) $\dfrac{x}{\sqrt{1+x^2}}$

Explanation: Let
$$y = \sec(\tan^{-1} x)$$
$$\frac{dy}{dx} = \frac{d}{dx}[\sec(\sec^{-1}\sqrt{1+x^2})] = \frac{d}{dx}(\sqrt{1+x^2})$$
$$= \frac{1}{2\sqrt{1+x^2}} \times 2x = \frac{x}{\sqrt{1+x^2}}$$

45. (d) None of these

Explanation: Given, $\qquad f(x) = x^{100} + \sin x - 1$
$$\Rightarrow \qquad f'(x) = 100x^{99} + \cos x$$
(a) In the interval $(0, 1)$, $\cos x > 0$ and $100x^{99} > 0$.

$\therefore \qquad f'(x) > 0 \qquad \left[\begin{array}{l} \text{in } \left(0, \dfrac{\pi}{2}\right), \cos x > 0, \text{ i.e., } (0, 1.57), \cos x > 0 \\ \therefore \text{ in } (0, 1), \cos x > 0 \end{array}\right]$

Thus, function f is strictly increasing in the interval $(0, 1)$.

(b) In the interval $\left(\dfrac{\pi}{2}, \pi\right)$, $\cos x < 0$ and $100x^{99} > 0$.

Also, $\qquad\qquad\qquad\qquad 100x^{99} > 1$

$\therefore \qquad\qquad\qquad\qquad f'(x) > 0 \text{ in } \left(\dfrac{\pi}{2}, \pi\right)$

Thus, function f is strictly increasing in the interval $\left(\dfrac{\pi}{2}, \pi\right)$

(c) In the interval $\left(0, \dfrac{\pi}{2}\right)$, $\cos x > 0$ and $100x^{99} > 0$.

$\therefore \qquad\qquad\qquad 100x^{99} + \cos x > 0$

$\Rightarrow \qquad\qquad\qquad f'(x) > 0 \text{ in } \left(0, \dfrac{\pi}{2}\right)$

Thus, f is strictly increasing in the interval $\left(0, \dfrac{\pi}{2}\right)$.

Hence, function f is not strictly decreasing in the given intervals.

46. (a) $\dfrac{1}{8}$

Explanation: Given equation of curve is $\qquad y = x^3 - 11x + 5$

$$\dfrac{dy}{dx} = 3x^2 - 11 \text{ at } (1, -5)$$

$$\dfrac{dy}{dx} = 3(1)^2 - 11 = -8$$

Slope of normal to the curve is $\dfrac{1}{8}$.

47. (d) $8y - x + 41 = 0$

Explanation: Equation of normal is $\qquad y - y_1 = \dfrac{-1}{\dfrac{dy}{dx}}(x - x_1)$

$$y + 5 = \dfrac{1}{8}(x - 1)$$

$$8y + 40 = x - 1$$
$$8y - x + 41 = 0.$$

48. (a) $\pm\sqrt{\dfrac{11}{3}}$

Explanation: For curve parallel to X-axis, slope *i.e.,* $\dfrac{dy}{dx} = 0$.

$$3x^2 - 11 = 0$$

$$x^2 = \dfrac{11}{3}$$

$$x = \pm\sqrt{\dfrac{11}{3}}$$

49. (b) 1

Explanation: Slope of tangent is
$$y = x - 11$$
$$\frac{dy}{dx} = 1.$$

50. (b) $(2, -9)$

Explanation:
$$\text{Slope of tangent} = \text{Slope of curve}$$
$$3x^2 - 11 = 1$$
$$3x^2 = 12$$
$$x^2 = 4$$
$$x = \pm 2$$

If $x = 2$, $y = -9$, if $x = -2$, $y = -19$

But $(-2, -19)$ does not lie on the tangent.

Sample Paper 3

Section - A

1. (d) $[0, \pi] - \left\{\dfrac{\pi}{2}\right\}$

Explanation: By definition, the range of the principal value branch of $y = \sec^{-1} x$ is $[0, \pi] - \left\{\dfrac{\pi}{2}\right\}$

2. (b) Symmetric

Explanation: Given, A = [1, 2, 3]

A relation R on A is defined as R = {(1, 2), (2, 1)}

Here, $(1, 2) \in R$ and $(2, 1) \in R$

So, R is symmetric.

3. (a) $\begin{bmatrix} -5 & -2 & -2 \\ -12 & -4 & -7 \end{bmatrix}$

Explanation: We have,
$$x + y + z = 0$$
$$\Rightarrow \quad z = -[x + y]$$
$$= -\left\{\begin{bmatrix} 3 & 1 & 1 \\ 5 & 2 & 3 \end{bmatrix} + \begin{bmatrix} 2 & 1 & 1 \\ 7 & 2 & 4 \end{bmatrix}\right\}$$
$$\Rightarrow \quad = -\begin{bmatrix} 5 & 2 & 2 \\ 12 & 4 & 7 \end{bmatrix} = \begin{bmatrix} -5 & -2 & -2 \\ -12 & -4 & -7 \end{bmatrix}$$

4. (b) 10

> **Explanation:** Given :
> $$A = [1 \;\; -3 \;\; 0]$$
> So,
> $$AA' = [1 \;\; -3 \;\; 0]\,[1 \;\; -3 \;\; 0]'$$
> $$= [1 \;\; -3 \;\; 0]\begin{bmatrix} 1 \\ -3 \\ 0 \end{bmatrix} = (1 + 9 + 0) = 10$$
>
> $$\therefore \qquad AA' = 10.$$

5. (a) 2

> **Explanation:** A will be skew-symmetric if $A = -A'$
>
> $$\Rightarrow \quad \begin{bmatrix} 0 & 1 & -2 \\ -1 & 0 & 3 \\ x & -3 & 0 \end{bmatrix} = -\begin{bmatrix} 0 & -1 & x \\ 1 & 0 & -3 \\ -2 & 3 & 0 \end{bmatrix}$$
>
> $$\Rightarrow \quad \begin{bmatrix} 0 & 1 & -2 \\ -1 & 0 & 3 \\ x & -3 & 0 \end{bmatrix} = \begin{bmatrix} 0 & 1 & -x \\ -1 & 0 & 3 \\ 2 & -3 & 0 \end{bmatrix}$$
>
> Equating the corresponding elements we get, $x = 2$

6. (c) $\dfrac{x}{\sqrt{1+x^2}}$

> **Explanation:** Let
> $$y = \sec(\tan^{-1} x)$$
> Differentiating w.r.t. x, we get
>
> $$\frac{dy}{dx} = \sec(\tan^{-1} x) \times \tan(\tan^{-1} x) \times \frac{d(\tan^{-1} x)}{dx}$$
>
> $$= \sec(\tan^{-1} x) \times \tan(\tan^{-1} x) \times \frac{1}{1+x^2}$$
>
> $$= \sec\left(\sec^{-1} \frac{\sqrt{1+x^2}}{1}\right) \times \tan(\tan^{-1} x) \times \frac{1}{1+x^2}$$
>
> $$= \sqrt{1+x^2} \times x \times \frac{1}{1+x^2}$$
>
> $$= \frac{x}{\sqrt{1+x^2}}$$

7. (b) Perpendicular

> **Explanation:** From first equation of the curve, we have
>
> $$3x^2 - 3y^2 - 6xy\,\frac{dy}{dx} = 0$$
>
> $$\Rightarrow \qquad \frac{dy}{dx} = \frac{x^2 - y^2}{2xy} = m_1 \text{ (say)} \qquad\qquad ...(i)$$

and second equation of the curve gives

$$6xy + 3x^2 \frac{dy}{dx} - 3y^2 \frac{dy}{dx} = 0$$

$$\Rightarrow \qquad \frac{dy}{dx} = \frac{-2xy}{x^2 - y^2} = m_2 \text{ (say)} \qquad \qquad ...(ii)$$

From (i) and (ii), $\qquad m_1 . m_2 = -1.$

8. (c) 6

Explanation: Number of elements in matrix $= 12$

$\therefore$ All possible pairs of natural numbers whose product is 12 are (1, 12), (2, 6), (3, 4), (4, 3), (6, 2), (12, 1)

So, $\qquad\qquad$ Possible orders $= 1 \times 12, 2 \times 6, 3 \times 4, 4 \times 3, 6 \times 2, 12 \times 1.$

So total no of passible orders are 6.

9. (b) $\dfrac{-\pi}{3}$

Explanation: $\qquad \sin^{-1}\left(\dfrac{-\sqrt{3}}{2}\right) = \sin^{-1}\left(-\sin\dfrac{\pi}{3}\right)$

$$= -\sin^{-1}\left(\sin\dfrac{\pi}{3}\right) = -\dfrac{\pi}{3}$$

10. (b) $48x^5 - 12x^2$

Explanation: We have, $\qquad y = 8x^6 - 4x^3$

$$\frac{dy}{dx} = 8(6)\, x^{6-1} - 4(3)\, x^{3-1} \qquad \left[\because \frac{d(x^n)}{dx} = nx^{n-1}\right]$$

$$= 48x^5 - 12x^2$$

11. (c) 4

Explanation: $(1 \times 8), (8 \times 1), (2 \times 4), (4 \times 2)$ are the possible orders of a matrix having 8 elements.

12. (b) $\left[-1, -\dfrac{1}{2}\right]$

Explanation: $\because$ $\qquad\qquad\qquad y = f(x)$

$$= \sin^{-1}(4x + 3)$$

or $\qquad\qquad\qquad\qquad \sin y = 4x + 3$

We know that,

$$-1 \le \sin y \le 1$$

$$\Rightarrow \qquad -1 \le 4x + 3 \le 1$$

$$\Rightarrow \qquad -1 - 3 \le 4x \le 1 - 3$$

$$\Rightarrow \qquad\qquad -4 \le 4x \le -2$$

$$\Rightarrow \qquad\qquad -1 \le x \le -\frac{1}{2}$$

Hence, domain of $f = \left[-1, -\frac{1}{2}\right]$.

13. (b) $\dfrac{1}{4}$

Explanation:
$$f(0) = \lim_{x \to 0} f(x) = \lim_{x \to 0} \frac{\sqrt{4+x} - 2}{x}$$

$$= \lim_{x \to 0} \left(\frac{\sqrt{4+x} - 2}{x} \times \frac{\sqrt{4+x} + 2}{\sqrt{4+x} + 2} \right)$$

$$= \lim_{x \to 0} \frac{4 + x - 4}{x(\sqrt{4+x} + 2)} = \lim_{x \to 0} \frac{x}{x(\sqrt{4+x} + 2)}$$

$$= \lim_{x \to 0} \frac{1}{\sqrt{4+x} + 2} = \frac{1}{2+2} = \frac{1}{4}$$

14. (c) $x + y = 0$

Explanation: Given :
$$y = \sin x$$

$$\therefore \qquad\qquad \frac{dy}{dx} = \cos x$$

$$\therefore \qquad \text{Slope of normal} = \left(\frac{-1}{\cos x} \right)_{x=0} = -1$$

Hence, the equation of normal is
$$y - 0 = -1(x - 0)$$

or
$$x + y = 0$$

15. (d) $6(3x^2 - 9x + 5)(2x - 3)$

Explanation: Let
$$y = (3x^2 - 9x + 5)^2$$

Differentiating w.r.t. x,

$$\Rightarrow \qquad \frac{dy}{dx} = 2(3x^2 - 9x + 5). \frac{d}{dx}(3x^2 - 9x + 5)$$

$$= 2(3x^2 - 9x + 5). (6x - 9)$$

$$= 6(3x^2 - 9x + 5)(2x - 3)$$

16. (d) $n!$

Explanation: Given
$$\text{set} = \{1, 2, 3, \dots, n\}$$

$$\Rightarrow \qquad \text{number of elements} = n$$

$\therefore$ Total number of one-one functions from the set $\{1, 2, 3, \dots n\}$ to itself

$$= {}^nc_n \, n! = 1 \times n!$$

$$= n!$$

17. (d) Neither one-one nor onto

> **Explanation:** Since, $f(x) = f(-x)$
> $\therefore f$ is not one-one.

18. (a) $\dfrac{\pi}{3}$

> **Explanation:** $\sin^{-1}\sin\left(-600\times\dfrac{\pi}{180}\right) = \sin^{-1}\sin\left(\dfrac{-10\pi}{3}\right)$
>
> $$= \sin^{-1}\left[-\sin\left(4\pi-\dfrac{2\pi}{3}\right)\right] = \sin^{-1}\left(\sin\dfrac{2\pi}{3}\right)$$
>
> $$= \sin^{-1}\left(\sin\left(\pi-\dfrac{\pi}{3}\right)\right) = \sin^{-1}\left(\sin\dfrac{\pi}{3}\right) = \dfrac{\pi}{3}$$

19. (a) $\pm\dfrac{3}{\sqrt{5}}$

> **Explanation:** We know, $\tan(\sec^{-1}x) = \sin\left(\cos^{-1}\dfrac{1}{\sqrt{5}}\right)$
>
> $\Rightarrow \qquad \sqrt{\sec^2(\sec^{-1}x)-1} = \sqrt{1-\cos^2\left(\cos^{-1}\dfrac{1}{\sqrt{5}}\right)}$
>
> $\Rightarrow \qquad \sqrt{x^2-1} = \sqrt{1-\dfrac{1}{5}}$
>
> $\Rightarrow \qquad x^2-1 = \dfrac{4}{5}$
>
> $\Rightarrow \qquad x = \pm\dfrac{3}{\sqrt{5}}$

20. (d) [20]

> **Explanation:** $UV = \begin{bmatrix}2 & -3 & 4\end{bmatrix}\begin{bmatrix}3\\2\\1\end{bmatrix}$
>
> $$= [6-6+4]$$
> $$= [4]$$
>
> and $XY = \begin{bmatrix}0 & 2 & 3\end{bmatrix}\begin{bmatrix}2\\2\\4\end{bmatrix}$
>
> $$= [0+4+12]$$
> $$= [16]$$
>
> $\therefore \qquad UV + XY = [4] + [16]$
> $$= [20]$$

Section - B

21. (c) a bijection

> **Explanation:** Given, $\qquad f(x) = x^3 - 1$
> Let $\qquad x_1, x_2 \in R$
> Now $\qquad f(x_1) = f(x_2)$
> $\Rightarrow \qquad x_1^3 - 1 = x_2^3 - 1 \Rightarrow x_1 = x_2$
> $\therefore f(x)$ is one-one. Also, it is onto. Hence, it is a bijection.

22. (b) $225x - \dfrac{x^2}{2}$

> **Explanation:** $\qquad$ Total energy = rate × no. of passenger
> $$\text{TE} = 225x - \frac{x^2}{2}$$

23. (a) ₹ 4,95,000

> **Explanation:** The people will get the maximum income of ₹ 4,95,000.

24. (a) Continuous at $x = 0$ as well as at $x = 1$

> **Explanation:** Given that, $\qquad f(x) = |x| + |x - 1|$
> $$f(x) = \begin{cases} -x - (x-1) & \text{when } x \le 0 \\ x - (x-1) & \text{when } 0 \le x < 1 \\ x + (x-1) & \text{when } x \ge 1 \end{cases}$$
> $$f(x) = \begin{cases} 1 - 2x & x \le 0 \\ 1 & 0 \le x < 1 \\ 2x - 1 & x \ge 1 \end{cases}$$
> At $\qquad x = 0$
> $$\lim_{x \to 0} f(x) = \lim_{x \to 0} 1 - 2x = 1$$
> $$\lim_{x \to 0^+} f(x) = \lim_{x \to 0} f(x) = \lim_{x \to 0} 1 = 1$$
> $\therefore$ It is continuous at 0.
> At $x = 1$
> $$\lim_{x \to 1^-} f(x) = \lim_{x \to 1^-} 1 = 1$$
> $$\lim_{x \to 1^+} f(x) = \lim_{x \to 1} f(x) = \lim_{x \to 1^-} f(x) = \lim_{x \to 1} 2x - 1 = 1$$
> $\therefore$ Continous at $x = 1$

25. (a) Null matrix

> **Explanation:** Given. $\qquad A = \begin{bmatrix} 4 & 2i \\ i & 1 \end{bmatrix}$
> $\therefore \qquad (A - 2I)(A - 3I) = \begin{bmatrix} 2 & 2i \\ i & -1 \end{bmatrix} \begin{bmatrix} 1 & 2i \\ i & -2 \end{bmatrix} = \begin{bmatrix} 0 & 0 \\ 0 & 0 \end{bmatrix}$

26. (b) 12

Explanation: We have,

$$\lim_{x \to 3} f(x) = \lim_{x \to 3} \frac{(x+3)^2 - 36}{x-3} = \lim_{x \to 3} \frac{(x+3)^2 - (6)^2}{x-3}$$

$$= \lim_{x \to 3} \frac{(x+3)^2 - (6)^2}{x-3}$$

$$= \lim_{x \to 3} \frac{(x+3+6)(x+3-6)}{x-3} \qquad [\because a^2 - b^2 = (a+b)(a-b)]$$

$$= \lim_{x \to 3} \frac{(x+9)(x-3)}{(x-3)}$$

$$= \lim_{x \to 3} (x+9) = 3+9 = 12$$

But given that, $f(x)$ is continous at $x = 3$.

27. (c) $\dfrac{5}{4}$

Explanation: Given, $[1 \;\; x \;\; 1] \begin{bmatrix} 1 & 2 & 3 \\ 0 & 5 & 1 \\ 0 & 3 & 2 \end{bmatrix} \begin{bmatrix} x \\ 1 \\ -2 \end{bmatrix} = 0$

$$\Rightarrow \qquad [1 \; x \; 1] \begin{bmatrix} x+2-6 \\ 0+5-2 \\ 0+3-4 \end{bmatrix} = 0$$

$$\Rightarrow \qquad [1 \; x \; 1] \begin{bmatrix} x-4 \\ 3 \\ -1 \end{bmatrix} = 0$$

$$\Rightarrow \qquad [x - 4 + 3x - 1] = 0$$

$$\Rightarrow \qquad 4x - 5 = 0$$

$$\Rightarrow \qquad x = \frac{5}{4}$$

28. (a) $-6 \cot^2 2x \cdot \operatorname{cosec}^2 2x$

Explanation: Let $\qquad y = \cot^3 2x$

Differentiate w.r.t., x

$$\frac{dy}{dx} = 3 \cot^2 (2x) \frac{d}{dx} \cot 2x$$

$$= 3 \cot^2 2x \, (-\operatorname{cosec}^2 2x) \frac{d}{dx}(2x)$$

$$\therefore \qquad \frac{dy}{dx} = 3 \cot^2 2x \, (-\operatorname{cosec}^2 2x) \cdot 2$$

$$= -6 \cot^2 2x \cdot \operatorname{cosec}^2 2x$$

29. (c) a^9

Explanation: $|A| = a^3, |\text{adj } A| = (a^3)^2$

$\Rightarrow \qquad |A| \, |\text{adj } A| = a^9$

$\Rightarrow \qquad$ Product of $|A| \, |\text{adj } A| = a^9$.

30. (a) 0

Explanation: Construct the following table of values of the objective function F :

Corner Points	Value of F = $3x - 4y$	
(0, 0)	$3 \times 0 - 4 \times 0 = 0$	$\leftarrow$ Maximum
(6, 12)	$3 \times 6 - 4 \times 12 = -30$	
(6, 16)	$3 \times 6 - 4 \times 12 = -46$	$\leftarrow$ Minimum
(0, 4)	$3 \times 0 - 4 \times 4 = -16$	

Hence, maximum of F = 0

31. (b) 28

Explanation: Given, $\qquad y = (1+x)(1+x^2)(1+x^4)$

On differentiating w.r.t. x, we get

$$\frac{dy}{dx} = (1+x)(1+x^2)\frac{d}{dx}(1+x^4)+(1+x)(1+x^4)\cdot\frac{d}{dx}(1+x^2)+(1+x^2)(1+x^4)\frac{d}{dx}(1+x)$$

$$= (1+x)(1+x^2)(4x^3) + (1+x)(1+x^4)(2x) + (1+x^2)(1+x^4)$$

$$\therefore \quad \left[\frac{dy}{dx}\right]_{x=1} = (1+1)(1+1)^2(4\times 1^3) + (1+1)(1+1^4)(2\times 1) + (1+1^2)(1+1^4)$$

$$= 2\times 2\times 4 + 2\times 2\times 2 + 2\times 2$$
$$= 16 + 8 + 4 = 28$$

32. (a) 2

Explanation: Let $\qquad y = \cos^{-1}(2x^2-1) = 2\cos^{-1}x$

Differentiating w.r.t. $\cos^{-1}x$, we get

$$\frac{dy}{d(\cos^{-1}x)} = \frac{2d(\cos^{-1}x)}{d(\cos^{-1}x)} = 2$$

33. (d) $q = 3p$

Explanation: Value of $Z = px + qy$ at (15, 15) is $15p + 15q$ and that at (0, 20) is $20q$. According to given condition, we must have

$$15p + 15q = 20q$$
$$\Rightarrow \qquad 15p = 5q$$
$$\Rightarrow \qquad q = 3p$$

34. (b) Zero or positive

Explanation: The values of variables of objective function of the LPP can never take negative values, therefore these variables are zero or positive.

35. (c) $\dfrac{-1+2m^3}{3m^2}$

> **Explanation:** Given,
>
> $$x = \dfrac{a}{1+m^3}$$
>
> $$\dfrac{dx}{dm} = \dfrac{a \times -1 \times (3m^2)}{(1+m^3)^2} = \dfrac{-3am^2}{(1+m^3)^2}$$
>
> Also,
>
> $$y = \dfrac{am}{1+m^3}$$
>
> $$\dfrac{dy}{dm} = a \times \dfrac{(1+m^3) \times 1 - m(3m^2)}{(1+m^3)^2}$$
>
> $$= a \times \left[\dfrac{1+m^3-3m^3}{(1+m^3)^2} \right]$$
>
> $$= a \left[\dfrac{1-2m^3}{(1+m^3)^2} \right]$$
>
> Now,
>
> $$\dfrac{dy}{dx} = \dfrac{dy}{dm} \times \dfrac{dm}{dx} = \dfrac{a(1-2m^3)}{(1+m^3)^2} \times \dfrac{(1+m^3)^2}{-3am^2}$$
>
> $$= \dfrac{1-2m^3}{-3m^2} = \dfrac{2m^3-1}{3m^2}$$

36. (c) $(1, \infty)$

> **Explanation:**
>
> $$y = x^4 - \dfrac{4x^3}{3}$$
>
> $$\Rightarrow \quad \dfrac{dy}{dx} = 4x^3 - 4x^2$$
>
> $$= 4x^2(x-1)$$
>
> Now,
>
> $$\dfrac{dy}{dx} = 0$$
>
> $$\Rightarrow \quad x = 0, x = 1$$
>
> Since $f'(x) < 0 \;\forall\; x \in (-\infty, 0) \cup (0, 1)$ and f is continuous in $(-\infty, 0)$ and $(0, 1)$.
>
> Therefore f is decreasing in $(-\infty, 1)$ and f is increasing in $[1, \infty)$.

37. (b) $\left(\dfrac{1}{4}, \dfrac{1}{2} \right)$

> **Explanation:**
>
> $$\dfrac{dy}{dx} = \dfrac{1}{2y} = \tan\dfrac{\pi}{4} = 1$$
>
> $$\Rightarrow \quad y = \dfrac{1}{2}$$
>
> $$\Rightarrow \quad x = \dfrac{1}{4}$$

38. (b) $\dfrac{\pi}{3}$

Explanation: We have, $\qquad\qquad y = 2 \sin^2 x \qquad\qquad\qquad$ ...(i)

and $\qquad\qquad\qquad\qquad\qquad y = \cos 2x \qquad\qquad\qquad\qquad$ ...(ii)

On differentiating eq. (i) w.r.t. x, we get

$$\frac{dy}{dx} = 4 \sin x \cos x$$

$$\Rightarrow \qquad \left[\frac{dy}{dx}\right]_{x=\frac{\pi}{6}} = 4 \cdot \left(\frac{1}{2}\right) \cdot \frac{\sqrt{3}}{2} = \sqrt{3} = m_1 \qquad\qquad \text{(say)}$$

On differentiating eq. (ii), w.r.t. x, we get

$$\frac{dy}{dx} = -2 \sin 2x$$

$$\Rightarrow \qquad \left[\frac{dy}{dx}\right]_{x=\frac{\pi}{6}} = -2 \sin \frac{\pi}{3} = -\sqrt{3} = m_2 \qquad\qquad \text{(say)}$$

Hence, angle between two curves is

$$\theta = \pm \tan^{-1}\left(\frac{m_1 - m_2}{1 + m_1 m_2}\right) = \pm \tan^{-1} \sqrt{3}$$

$$= \frac{\pi}{3} \text{ or } \frac{2\pi}{3}$$

39. (b) $\sqrt{2}$

Explanation: Let $\qquad\qquad\qquad y = \sin x + \cos x$

Then, $\qquad\qquad\qquad\qquad \dfrac{dy}{dx} = \cos x - \sin x$

and $\qquad\qquad\qquad\qquad \dfrac{d^2y}{dx^2} = -\sin x - \cos x$

Now, for maximum or minimum value of y, $\dfrac{dy}{dx} = 0$

$$\Rightarrow \qquad\qquad \cos x - \sin x = 0$$
$$\Rightarrow \qquad\qquad\qquad \sin x = \cos x$$
$$\Rightarrow \qquad\qquad\qquad \frac{\sin x}{\cos x} = 1$$
$$\Rightarrow \qquad\qquad\qquad \tan x = \tan \frac{\pi}{4}$$
$$\Rightarrow \qquad\qquad\qquad\qquad x = \frac{\pi}{4}$$

$$\therefore \qquad \left[\frac{d^2y}{dx^2}\right]_{x=\frac{\pi}{4}} = -\sin \frac{\pi}{4} - \cos \frac{\pi}{4}$$

$$= -\frac{1}{\sqrt{2}} - \frac{1}{\sqrt{2}} = -\frac{2}{\sqrt{2}} = -\sqrt{2}$$

We see that at $x = \dfrac{\pi}{4}$, the value of $\dfrac{d^2y}{dx^2}$ is negative.

So, at $x = \dfrac{\pi}{4}$, y or given function is maximum.

So, put $x = \dfrac{\pi}{4}$ in $(\sin x + \cos x)$,

$$\text{Maximum value of function} = \sin\dfrac{\pi}{4} + \cos\dfrac{\pi}{4} = \dfrac{1}{\sqrt{2}} + \dfrac{1}{\sqrt{2}}$$

$$= \dfrac{2}{\sqrt{2}} = \sqrt{2}$$

40. (c) If an LPP has two optimal solutions, then it has infinitely many solutions

Explanation: If optimal solution is obtained at two distinct points A and B (corners of the feasible region), then optimal solution is obtained at every point of segment [AB].

Section - C

41. (a) $2, -\dfrac{1}{2}$

Explanation: Given, $\qquad\qquad y = a \log x + bx^2 + x$

$\therefore \qquad\qquad \dfrac{dy}{dx} = \dfrac{a}{x} + 2bx + 1$

If the value of y is maximum or minimum at $x = -1$, then

$$\left[\dfrac{dy}{dx}\right]_{x=-1} = 0 \ i.e., \ \dfrac{a}{(-1)} + 2b\times(-1) + 1 = 0$$

or $\qquad\qquad -a - 2b + 1 = 0 \qquad\qquad\qquad\qquad\qquad …(i)$

If the value of y is maximum or minimum at $x = 2$

$$\left[\dfrac{dy}{dx}\right]_{x=2} = 0 \ i.e., \ \dfrac{a}{2} + 2b\times2 + 1 = 0$$

or $\qquad\qquad a + 8b + 2 = 0 \qquad\qquad\qquad\qquad\qquad …(ii)$

Adding eqs. (i) and (ii), we get

$$6b + 3 = 0$$

$\Rightarrow \qquad\qquad b = -\dfrac{3}{6}$

$$= -\dfrac{1}{2}$$

From eqn. (i),

$$a = 1 - 2b$$

$$= 1 - 2\times\left(-\dfrac{1}{2}\right) = 2$$

Hence, $\qquad\qquad a = 2,$

$$b = -\dfrac{1}{2}$$

42. (a) one-one

> **Explanation:** We have $f(x) = 4x + 7, x \in R$
> Let $x_1, x_2 \in R$, such that
> $$f(x_1) = f(x_2)$$
> $$\Rightarrow \quad 4x_1 + 7 = 4x_2 + 7$$
> $$\Rightarrow \quad 4x_1 = 4x_2 \Rightarrow x_1 = x_2$$
> So, f is one-one.

43. (a) 200 m

> **Explanation:** We have, $x = 100t - \dfrac{25}{2}t^2$
>
> On differentiating both sides w.r.t. t, we get
> $$\frac{dx}{dt} = 100 - \frac{25}{2} \cdot (2t) = 100 - 25t$$
>
> At maximum height, velocity $\dfrac{dx}{dt} = 0$
>
> $$\Rightarrow \quad 100 - 25t = 0$$
> $$\Rightarrow \quad t = 4$$
> $$\therefore \quad x = 100 \times 4 - \frac{25 \times 16}{2} = 200\ \text{m}$$

44. (b) $x = 45, y = 15$

> **Explanation:** We have, $x + y = 60 \Rightarrow y = 60 - x$
> $$\Rightarrow \quad x^3 y = (60 - x)(x^3); x \in (0, 60)$$
> Let $f(x) = x^3 (60 - x)$
> $$\Rightarrow \quad f'(x) = 3x^2 (60 - x) - x^3$$
> For maxima or minima, put $f'(x) = 0$
> $$\therefore \quad 3x^2(60 - x) - x^3 = 0$$
> $$\Rightarrow \quad x^2(180 - 3x - x) = 0$$
> $$\Rightarrow \quad x = 45 \qquad\qquad [\because x \neq 0]$$
> $$\therefore \quad f'(45^+) < 0 \text{ and } f'(45^-) > 0$$
> Hence, total maxima is at $x = 45$.
> So, $x = 45$ and $y = 15$

45. (d) 1

> **Explanation:** Let α and β be the roots of the given equation, so that
> $$\alpha + \beta = a - 2 \text{ and } \alpha\beta = -(a - 1)$$
> Let $S = \alpha^2 + \beta^2$
> Then, $S = (\alpha + \beta)^2 - 2\alpha\beta = (a - 2)^2 + 2(a - 1) = a^2 - 2a + 2$
> $$\therefore \quad \frac{dS}{da} = 2a - 2$$
> Now, $\dfrac{dS}{da} = 0 \Rightarrow 2a - 2 = 0 \Rightarrow a = 1$

Also, $\qquad \dfrac{d^2S}{da^2} = 2 > 0, \forall\, a$

Hence, S is minimum when $a = 1$

46. (b) 4000

Explanation: Let x and y be the number of seats in section A and section B respectively.

$\therefore \qquad\qquad\qquad x + y = 4000$

47. (a) 18,000

Explanation: $\qquad\qquad 50x + 40y = 1,80,000$

$\qquad\qquad\qquad\qquad 5x + 4y = 18,000$

48. (a) $A = \begin{bmatrix} 1 & 1 \\ 5 & 4 \end{bmatrix}, B = \begin{bmatrix} 4000 \\ 18000 \end{bmatrix}$

Explanation: Writing these equation in matrix form $AX = B$

where $\qquad\qquad \begin{bmatrix} 1 & 1 \\ 5 & 4 \end{bmatrix}\begin{bmatrix} x \\ y \end{bmatrix} = \begin{bmatrix} 4000 \\ 18000 \end{bmatrix}$

So, $\qquad\qquad A = \begin{bmatrix} 1 & 1 \\ 5 & 4 \end{bmatrix}, X = \begin{bmatrix} x \\ y \end{bmatrix}, B = \begin{bmatrix} 4000 \\ 18000 \end{bmatrix}$

49. (b) $\begin{bmatrix} -4 & 1 \\ 5 & -1 \end{bmatrix}$

Explanation: $\qquad\qquad X = A^{-1}B$

$\because \qquad\qquad\qquad A^{-1} = \dfrac{\text{adj } A}{|A|}$

$\qquad\qquad |A| = \begin{bmatrix} 1 & 1 \\ 5 & 4 \end{bmatrix} = 4 - 5 = -1$

$\therefore \qquad\qquad \text{adj } A = \begin{bmatrix} 4 & -1 \\ -5 & 1 \end{bmatrix}$

So, $\qquad A^{-1} = \dfrac{1}{-1}\begin{bmatrix} 4 & -1 \\ -5 & 1 \end{bmatrix} = \begin{bmatrix} -4 & 1 \\ 5 & -1 \end{bmatrix}$

50. (c) 2000, 2000

Explanation: $\qquad X = \begin{bmatrix} -4 & 1 \\ 5 & -1 \end{bmatrix}\begin{bmatrix} 4000 \\ 18000 \end{bmatrix}$

$\qquad\qquad\qquad = \begin{bmatrix} 16000 + 18000 \\ 20000 - 18000 \end{bmatrix} = \begin{bmatrix} 2000 \\ 2000 \end{bmatrix}$

$\therefore \qquad\qquad x = 2000$ seats in Sec. A

$\qquad\qquad\qquad y = 2000$ seats in Sec. B.

Sample Paper 4

Section - A

1. (a) $\sqrt{\dfrac{2}{3}}$

Explanation: $\sin\left[\cot^{-1}\left(\cos\dfrac{\pi}{4}\right)\right] = \sin\left[\cot^{-1}\dfrac{1}{\sqrt{2}}\right] = \sin\left[\sin^{-1}\sqrt{\dfrac{2}{3}}\right] = \sqrt{\dfrac{2}{3}}$

2. (a) 4

Explanation: Given,
$$\begin{bmatrix} a+b & 2 \\ 5 & b \end{bmatrix} = \begin{bmatrix} 6 & 2 \\ 5 & 2 \end{bmatrix}$$

$\Rightarrow \qquad a+b = 6$

and $\qquad b = 2$

$\Rightarrow \qquad a = 4$

3. (d) 252

Explanation: Given,
$$y = x^4 - 4x$$

$\therefore \qquad \dfrac{dy}{dx} = 4x^3 - 4 = 4(x^3 - 1)$

$\therefore \qquad \left(\dfrac{dy}{dx}\right)_{(\text{at } x = 4)} = 4[(4)^3 - 1]$

$$= 4(64 - 1)$$
$$= 4 \times 63$$
$$= 252$$

4. (b) 2

Explanation: $\because \qquad g(x) = \dfrac{x}{2} + \dfrac{2}{x}$

$\therefore \qquad g'(x) = \dfrac{1}{2} - \dfrac{2}{x^2}$

For maxima and minima,

$$g'(x) = 0$$

$\Rightarrow \qquad \dfrac{1}{2} - \dfrac{2}{x^2} = 0$

$\Rightarrow \qquad x = \pm 2$

Now, $\qquad g''(x) = \dfrac{4}{x^3}$

and $\qquad g''(x) > 0$ for $x = 2$

$\therefore \qquad x = 2$ is point of minima

5. (b) m^2y

> **Explanation:** Given,
> $$y = ae^{mx} + be^{-mx} \qquad \text{...(i)}$$
> $$\Rightarrow \quad \frac{dy}{dx} = ame^{mx} - bme^{-mx}$$
> $$\Rightarrow \quad \frac{d^2y}{dx^2} = am^2e^{mx} + bm^2e^{-mx}$$
> $$\Rightarrow \quad \frac{d^2y}{dx^2} = m^2(ae^{mx} + be^{-mx})$$
> $$\Rightarrow \quad \frac{d^2y}{dx^2} = m^2y \qquad \text{[From eq. (i)]}$$

6. (c) Objective function.

> **Explanation:** The LPP objective function either has maximum value or minimim value or has no solution. A convex set is a region such that for every pair of points within the region every point on the like segment must be within the region.

7. (b) Feasible

> **Explanation:** Feasible region or feasible solution.

8. (a) $\begin{bmatrix} -3 & -2 & 1 \\ -4 & -1 & -6 \end{bmatrix}$

> **Explanation:** Additive inverse of matrix, A is $-$ A
> $$\therefore \quad -A = -\begin{bmatrix} 3 & 2 & -1 \\ 4 & 1 & 6 \end{bmatrix}$$
> $$= \begin{bmatrix} -3 & -2 & 1 \\ -4 & -1 & -6 \end{bmatrix}$$

9. (c) $\begin{bmatrix} 9 & -6 \\ -1 & -4 \end{bmatrix}$

> **Explanation:** Here, numbers of columns of A = number of rows of B = 2, so AB is defined.
> $$AB = \begin{bmatrix} 3 & 2 \\ 2 & -1 \end{bmatrix}\begin{bmatrix} 1 & -2 \\ 3 & 0 \end{bmatrix}$$
> $$= \begin{bmatrix} 3\times1+2\times3 & 3\times(-2)+2\times0 \\ 2\times1+(-1)\times3 & 2\times(-2)+(-1)\times0 \end{bmatrix}$$
> $$= \begin{bmatrix} 3+6 & -6+0 \\ 2-3 & -4+0 \end{bmatrix}$$
> $$= \begin{bmatrix} 9 & -6 \\ -1 & -4 \end{bmatrix}$$

10. (b)   Open half plane not containing the origin.

> **Explanation:** The graph of the inequation $2x + y > 5$ represents open half plane not containing the origin.

11. (c) $[-1, 1]$

> **Explanation:** We know that
> $$0 \le \cos x \le 1,\ \forall\ x \in R \Rightarrow 0 \le \cos^2 x \le 1$$
> $$\Rightarrow \qquad 0 \le 2 \cos^2 x \le 2$$
> $$\Rightarrow \qquad 0 - 1 \le 2 \cos^2 x - 1 \le 2 - 1$$
> $$\Rightarrow \qquad -1 \le \cos 2x \le 1$$
> Hence, range of the function is $[-1, 1]$.

12. (a) $\sin^2 x\,(3 \cos^2 x - \sin^2 x)$

> **Explanation:** Differentiating w.r.t. x, we get
> $$\frac{dy}{dx} = (3 \sin^2 x \cos x) \cos x + \sin^3 x\,(-\sin x)$$
> $$= 3 \sin^2 x \cos^2 x - \sin^4 x = \sin^2 x\,(3 \cos^2 x - \sin^2 x)$$

13. (a) $\dfrac{\pi}{6}, \dfrac{5\pi}{6}, \dfrac{13\pi}{6}, \dfrac{8\pi}{3}$

> **Explanation:** $\because\qquad 2 \sin^2 x + 5 \sin x - 3 = 0$
> $$\Rightarrow \qquad \sin x = \frac{-5 \pm \sqrt{(5)^2 - 4 \times 2 \times (-3)}}{2 \times 2}$$
> $$= \frac{-5 \pm \sqrt{25 + 24}}{4} = \frac{-5 \pm 7}{4} = -3, \frac{1}{2}$$
> $$\because \qquad \sin x \in [-1, 1]$$
> $$\therefore \qquad \sin x = \frac{1}{2}$$
> Now, $\qquad x \in [0, 3\pi]$
> $$\therefore \qquad x = \frac{\pi}{6}, \frac{5\pi}{6}, \frac{13\pi}{6}, \frac{8\pi}{3}$$

14. (b) -1

> **Explanation:** Given :
> $$f(x) = \begin{cases} 5x - 4, & 0 < x < 1 \\ 4x^2 + 3bx, & 1 < x < 2 \end{cases}$$
> $\because f(x)$ is continuous at $x = 1$
> $$\therefore \qquad \lim_{x \to 1^+} f(x) = \lim_{x \to 1} f(x)$$
> $$\Rightarrow \qquad \lim_{x \to 1^+} (4x^2 + 3bx) = \lim_{x \to 1}(5x - 4)$$
> $$\Rightarrow \qquad \lim_{x \to 0}(4(1+h)^2 + 3b(1+h)) = 5(1) - 4$$
> $$\Rightarrow \qquad \lim_{x \to 0}(4 + 8h + 4h^2 + 3b + 3bh) = 1$$
> $$\Rightarrow \qquad 3b + 4 = 1 \Rightarrow b = -1$$

15. (a) $e^x \left[\tan^{-1} x + \dfrac{1}{1+x^2} \right]$

> **Explanation:**
> $$y = e^x \tan^{-1} x$$
> $$\frac{dy}{dx} = e^x \left(\frac{1}{1+x^2} \right) + \tan^{-1} x \cdot e^x$$
> $$\frac{dy}{dx} = e^x \left[\tan^{-1} x + \frac{1}{1+x^2} \right]$$

16. (b) Bounded

> **Explanation:** A feasible region of a system of linear inqualities is said to be bounded it can be enclosed within a circle.

17. (b) $a+b$

> **Explanation:**
> $$f(0) = \lim_{x \to 0} f(x) = \lim_{x \to 0} \frac{\ln (1+ax) - \ln (1-bx)}{x} \qquad \left(\frac{0}{0} \text{ form} \right)$$
> $$= \lim_{x \to 0} \left[\frac{a}{1+ax} + \frac{b}{1-bx} \right] \qquad \text{(Using L' Hospital Rule)}$$
> $$= a+b$$

18. (b) $\dfrac{\pi}{4}$

> **Explanation:** $\tan^{-1}\left[2\cos\left(2\sin^{-1}\dfrac{1}{2} \right) \right] = \tan^{-1}\left[2\cos\left\{ 2\sin^{-1}\left(\sin\dfrac{\pi}{6} \right) \right\} \right] \qquad \left[\because \sin\dfrac{\pi}{6} = \dfrac{1}{2} \right]$
> $$= \tan^{-1}\left[2\cos\left(2\times\frac{\pi}{6} \right) \right] = \tan^{-1}\left[2\cos\frac{\pi}{3} \right]$$
> $$= \tan^{-1}\left[2\times\frac{1}{2} \right] = \tan^{-1}(1) \qquad \left[\because \cot\frac{\pi}{3} = \frac{1}{2} \right]$$
> $$= \tan^{-1}\left(\tan\frac{\pi}{4} \right) = \frac{\pi}{4}$$

19. (d) 0

> **Explanation:** $\cos^{-1}\left(\cos\left(\dfrac{5\pi}{3} \right) \right) + \sin^{-1}\left(\sin\dfrac{5\pi}{3} \right) = \cos^{-1}\left\{ \cos\left(2\pi - \dfrac{\pi}{3} \right) \right\} + \sin^{-1}\left\{ \sin\left(2\pi - \dfrac{\pi}{3} \right) \right\}$
> $$= \cos^{-1}\left\{ \cos\frac{\pi}{3} \right\} + \sin^{-1}\left(-\sin\frac{\pi}{3} \right) = \frac{\pi}{3} - \frac{\pi}{3} = 0$$

20. (a) $A+B$

> **Explanation:** We have, $AB = A$ and $BA = B$, so that
> $$ABA = A^2 \Rightarrow A(BA) = A^2$$
> $\Rightarrow \qquad A \cdot B = A^2 \qquad\qquad\qquad \text{or } A = A^2$
> Also, $\qquad BA = B \qquad\qquad\qquad \Rightarrow BAB = B^2$
> or $\qquad\quad B(A) = B^2 \qquad\qquad\qquad \Rightarrow BA = B^2$
> $\Rightarrow \qquad\quad B = B^2$
> $\therefore \qquad A^2 + B^2 = A + B$

Section - B

21. (c) An equivalence relation

> **Explanation:** Given, any element a in A, both a and a must be either odd or even, so that $(a, a) \in$ R.
> Further, $(a, b) \in$ R $\Rightarrow$ both a and b must be either odd or even
> $\Rightarrow (b, a) \in$ R. Similarly, $(a, b) \in$ R and $(b, c) \in$ R
> $\Rightarrow$ All elements a, b, c must be either even or odd simultaneously.
> $\Rightarrow (a, c) \in$ R. Hence, R is an equivalence relation.

22. (b) Unbounded

> **Explanation:** Given, constraints are $3y + x \geq 3$, $x \geq 0$, $y \geq 0$.

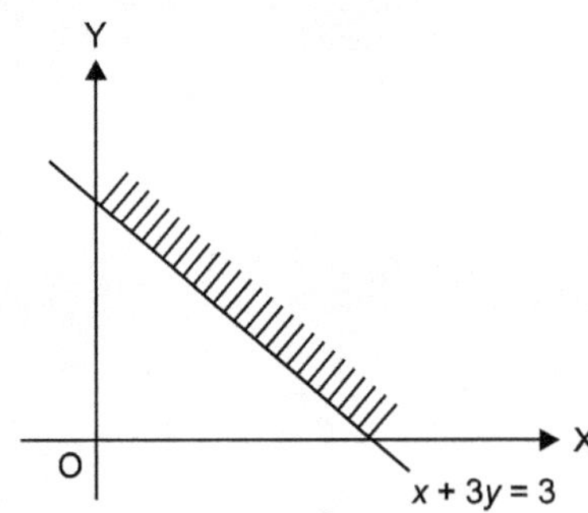

> It is clear from the graph that, it is bounded.

23. (b) $0, -1, 2$

> **Explanation:**
> $$f(x) = 3x^4 - 4x^3 - 12x^2 + 5$$
> $$f'(x) = 12x^3 - 12x^2 - 24x + 0$$
> $$= 12x(x^2 - x - 2)$$
> $$= 12x(x^2 - 2x + x - 2)$$
> $$= 12x[x(x - 2) + 1(x - 2)] = 12x(x + 1)(x - 2)$$
> For critical points put $f'(x) = 0 \Rightarrow x = 0, x = -1, x = 2$
> $\therefore$ Critical points are $(0, -1, +2)$.

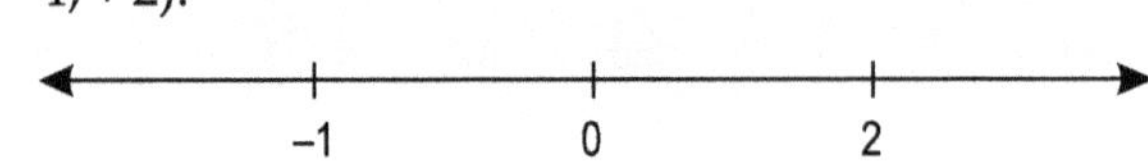

24. (d) $\begin{bmatrix} 3,55,000 \\ 3,40,000 \end{bmatrix}$

> **Explanation:**
> $$Q = \begin{bmatrix} 20 & 15 & 35 \\ 10 & 20 & 30 \end{bmatrix}$$
>
> $$S = \begin{matrix} \text{LG} \\ \text{IP} \\ \text{Samsung} \end{matrix} \begin{bmatrix} 20,000 \\ 50,000 \\ 15,000 \end{bmatrix}$$
>
> $$C = \text{Total Cost} = \begin{matrix} \text{LG} \\ \text{IP} \\ \text{Samsung} \end{matrix} \begin{bmatrix} 15,000 \\ 40,000 \\ 12,000 \end{bmatrix}$$
>
> $$P = \text{Profit Matrix} = S - C$$

$$P = \begin{bmatrix} 20,000 \\ 50,000 \\ 15,000 \end{bmatrix} - \begin{bmatrix} 15,000 \\ 40,000 \\ 12,000 \end{bmatrix} = \begin{bmatrix} 5,000 \\ 10,000 \\ 3,000 \end{bmatrix}$$

Total profit in each mall $= QP$

$$= \begin{bmatrix} 20 & 15 & 35 \\ 10 & 20 & 30 \end{bmatrix} \begin{bmatrix} 5,000 \\ 10,000 \\ 3,000 \end{bmatrix}$$

$$= \begin{bmatrix} 1,00,000+1,50,000+1,05,000 \\ 50,000+2,00,000+90,000 \end{bmatrix} = \begin{bmatrix} 3,55,000 \\ 3,40,000 \end{bmatrix}$$

25. (b) $\begin{bmatrix} 0 & -1/3 & -1/2 \\ 1/3 & 0 & -1/5 \\ 1/2 & 1/5 & 0 \\ 3/5 & 1/3 & 1/7 \end{bmatrix}$

Explanation: Given, $A = [a_{ij}]_{4 \times 3}$ and $a_{ij} = \dfrac{i-j}{i+j}$

$\therefore$

$$A = \begin{bmatrix} a_{11} & a_{12} & a_{13} \\ a_{21} & a_{22} & a_{23} \\ a_{31} & a_{32} & a_{33} \\ a_{41} & a_{42} & a_{43} \end{bmatrix} = \begin{bmatrix} \frac{1-1}{1+1} & \frac{1-2}{1+2} & \frac{1-3}{1+3} \\ \frac{2-1}{2+1} & \frac{2-2}{2+2} & \frac{2-1}{2+3} \\ \frac{3-1}{3+1} & \frac{3-2}{3+2} & \frac{3-3}{3+3} \\ \frac{4-1}{4+1} & \frac{4-2}{4+2} & \frac{4-3}{4+3} \end{bmatrix} = \begin{bmatrix} 0 & \frac{-1}{3} & \frac{-1}{2} \\ \frac{1}{3} & 0 & \frac{-1}{4} \\ \frac{1}{2} & \frac{1}{4} & 0 \\ \frac{3}{5} & \frac{1}{3} & \frac{1}{7} \end{bmatrix}$$

26. (a) 0

Explanation: We have, $\begin{vmatrix} \cos 15° & \sin 15° \\ \sin 75° & \cos 75° \end{vmatrix} = \cos 75° \cos 15° - \sin 75° \sin 15°$

$$= \cos(75° + 15°) = \cos 90° = 0$$

27. (c) continuous at non-integer points only

Explanation: It is evident from the graph of $f(x)$ that it is discontinuous at integer points and is continuous at non-integer points only.

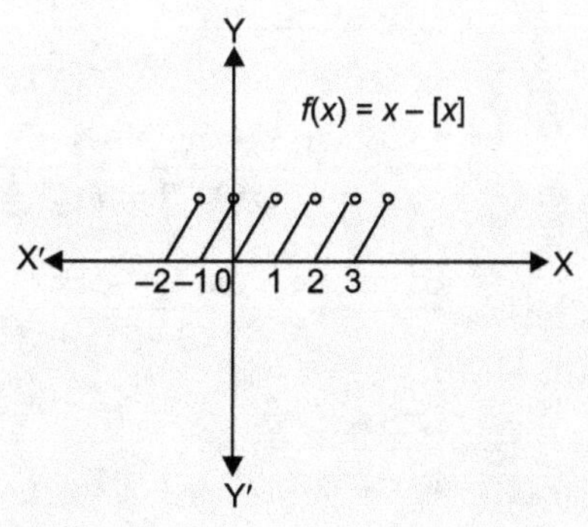

28. (a) -3

Explanation: We have
$$f(0) = 3$$
$$\text{LHL} = \lim_{x \to 0^-} f(x) = \lim_{h \to 0} f(0-h) = \lim_{h \to 0} \frac{k(0-h)}{|0-h|}$$
$$= \lim_{h \to 0} \frac{-kh}{h} = -k$$
$$\text{RHL} = \lim_{x \to 0+} f(x) = \lim_{h \to 0} f(0+h) = \lim_{h \to 0} 3 = 3$$

$\therefore$ The given function is continuous at $x = 0$.

$\therefore$
$$\text{LHL} = \text{RHL} = f(0)$$
$$\Rightarrow \qquad -k = 3 \text{ or } k = -3$$

29. (c) 0

Explanation: Given,
$$A = \begin{bmatrix} -3 & 5 & -8 \\ x & 5 & 5 \\ 0 & y & 4 \end{bmatrix}$$

Since A is upper triangular matrix.

$\therefore$
$$x = y = 0$$
So,
$$x + y = 0 + 0 = 0$$

30. (b) 0

Explanation: We have,
$$f(x) = (x^{a-b})^{a+b} \cdot (x^{b-c})^{b+c} \cdot (x^{c-a})^{c+a}$$
$$= x^{a^2-b^2} \cdot x^{b^2-c^2} \cdot x^{c^2-a^2}$$
$$= x^{a^2-b^2 + b^2-c^2 + c^2-a^2}$$
$$= x^0 = 1$$
$$\therefore \qquad f'(x) = 0$$

31. (d) $\dfrac{3\sec^2 x}{(3+2\tan x)^2}$

Explanation: Let
$$y = \frac{\tan x}{3+2\tan x}$$

Differentiate both sides w.r.t. x, we get

$$\frac{dy}{dx} = \frac{(3+2\tan x)\dfrac{d}{dx}\tan x - \tan x \dfrac{d}{dx}(3+2\tan x)}{(3+2\tan x)^2}$$

$$= \frac{(3+2\tan x)(\sec^2 x) - \tan x (2\sec^2 x)}{(3+2\tan x)^2}$$

$$= \frac{3\sec^2 x + 2\tan x - \sec^2 x - 2\tan x . \sec^2 x}{(3+2\tan x)^2}$$

$$\therefore \qquad \frac{dy}{dx} = \frac{3\sec^2 x}{(3+2\tan x)^2}$$

32. (b) $\det A + \det B \neq 0$

Explanation: Let $A = \begin{bmatrix} 1 & -1 \\ 1 & 0 \end{bmatrix}$ and $B = \begin{bmatrix} -1 & 1 \\ -1 & 0 \end{bmatrix}$

$\Rightarrow \qquad A + B = \begin{bmatrix} 0 & 0 \\ 0 & 0 \end{bmatrix}$

$\therefore \qquad \det (A + B) = 0$

But $\qquad \det A = 1, \det B = 1$

$\therefore \qquad \det A \neq 0, \det B \neq 0$

and $\det (A + B) \neq \det A + \det B \Rightarrow \det A + \det B \neq 0$

33. (a) 7

Explanation: The given relation is R = {(1, 2), (2, 3)} in the set A = {1, 2, 3}.

Now, $\qquad$ R is reflexive, if (1, 1), (2, 2), (3, 3) $\in$ R

$\qquad$ R is symmetric, if (2, 1), (3, 2) $\in$ R

$\qquad$ R is transitive, if (1, 3) and (3, 1) $\in$ R

Thus, the minimum number of ordered pairs which are to be added, so that R becomes an equivalence relation is 7.

34. (b) 35 sq. units

Explanation: Let Δ be the area of the triangle PQR, then

$$\Delta = \frac{1}{2} \begin{vmatrix} 4 & 5 & 1 \\ 4 & -2 & 1 \\ -6 & 2 & 1 \end{vmatrix}$$

Applying $R_1 \to R_1 - R_2, R_2 \to R_2 - R_3$, we get

$$\Delta = \frac{1}{2} \begin{vmatrix} 0 & 7 & 0 \\ 10 & -4 & 0 \\ -6 & 2 & 1 \end{vmatrix}$$

Expanding along R_1, we get $\qquad \Delta = \frac{1}{2} |[-7(10-0)]|$

$$= \frac{1}{2} |-70| = 35 \text{ sq. units}$$

35. (d) $\dfrac{2\pi}{3}$

Explanation: Let $\qquad \cos^{-1}\left(\dfrac{1}{2}\right) = \theta$

$\Rightarrow \qquad \cos \theta = \dfrac{1}{2} = \cos \dfrac{\pi}{3}$

$\Rightarrow \qquad \theta = \dfrac{\pi}{3} \in [0, \pi]$

$\therefore$ Principal value of $\cos^{-1} \dfrac{1}{2}$ is $\dfrac{\pi}{3}$

Let
$$\sin^{-1}\left(\frac{1}{2}\right) = \phi$$

$\Rightarrow$
$$\sin \phi = \frac{1}{2} = \sin \frac{\pi}{6}$$

$\Rightarrow$
$$\phi = \frac{\pi}{6} \in \left[\frac{-\pi}{2}, \frac{\pi}{2}\right]$$

$\therefore$ Principal value of $\sin^{-1} \dfrac{1}{2}$ is $\dfrac{\pi}{6}$

So, the value of $\cos^{-1}\left(\dfrac{1}{2}\right) + 2\sin^{-1}\left(\dfrac{1}{2}\right) = \dfrac{\pi}{3} + 2 \times \dfrac{\pi}{6} = \dfrac{\pi}{3} + \dfrac{\pi}{3} = \dfrac{2\pi}{3}$

36. (b) $[1, \infty)$

Explanation:
$$f(x) = x^2 - 4x + 5$$
Let
$$y = x^2 - 4x + 5$$
$\Rightarrow$
$$y = (x-2)^2 + 1$$
$\Rightarrow$
$$(x-2)^2 = y - 1$$
$\Rightarrow$
$$x - 2 = \sqrt{y-1}$$
$\Rightarrow$
$$x = \sqrt{y-1} + 2$$

For range $y - 1 \geq 0$

$\Rightarrow$
$$y \geq 1$$

$\therefore$ Range is $[1, \infty)$.

37. (b) 1

Explanation: We have, $\quad xe^{xy} - y = \sin^2 x$

On putting $x = 0$, we get
$$0 \cdot e^0 - y = 0 \Rightarrow y = 0$$

Differentiating both sides w.r.t. x,
$$xe^{xy}\left(\frac{x\,dy}{dx} + y\right) + e^{xy} - \frac{dy}{dx} = 2\sin x . \cos x$$

On putting $x = 0$, $y = 0$, we get
$$0(0+0) + e^0 - \frac{dy}{dx} = 2\sin 0 . \cos 0$$

$$1 - \frac{dy}{dx} = 0$$

$$\frac{dy}{dx} = 1$$

38. (a) 3

Explanation: Given
$$\begin{bmatrix} x \\ y \\ z \end{bmatrix} = \frac{1}{40}\begin{bmatrix} 5 & 10 & -5 \\ -5 & -2 & 13 \\ 10 & -4 & 6 \end{bmatrix}\begin{bmatrix} 5 \\ 0 \\ 5 \end{bmatrix}$$

$$= \frac{1}{40}\begin{bmatrix} 50+0-25 \\ -25+0+65 \\ 50+0+30 \end{bmatrix} = \frac{1}{40}\begin{bmatrix} 0 \\ 40 \\ 80 \end{bmatrix} = \begin{bmatrix} 0 \\ 1 \\ 2 \end{bmatrix}$$

$\Rightarrow \qquad x = 0, y = 1 \text{ and } z = 2$

$\therefore \qquad x + y + z = 0 + 1 + 2 = 3$

39. (b) $(2, 3)$

Explanation: Clearly, $f(x)$ is defined for all $x > 2$.

We have
$$f(x) = 2 \log (x - 2) - x^2 + 4x + 1$$

$\Rightarrow \qquad f'(x) = \dfrac{2}{x-2} - 2x + 4$

$\Rightarrow \qquad f'(x) = 2\left\{\dfrac{1-(x-2)^2}{x-2}\right\} = \dfrac{-2(x-1)(x-3)}{x-2}$

$\Rightarrow \qquad f'(x) = \dfrac{2(x-1)(x-3)(x-2)}{(x-2)^2}$

$\therefore \qquad f'(x) > 0$

$\Rightarrow \qquad -2(x-1)(x-3)(x-2) > 0$

$\Rightarrow \qquad (x-1)(x-2)(x-3) < 0$

$\Rightarrow \qquad x \in (-\infty, 1) \cup (2, 3)$

Clearly, domain of $f(x)$ is $(2, \infty)$.

Thus, $f(x)$ is increasing on $(2, 3)$.

40. (d) None of these

Explanation: We have,
$$5x^2 + y^2 = 1$$

$\Rightarrow \qquad 10x + 2y\dfrac{dy}{dx} = 0$

$\Rightarrow \qquad \dfrac{dy}{dx} = -\dfrac{5x}{y}$

$\therefore \qquad \left[\dfrac{dy}{dx}\right]_{\left(\frac{1}{3}, -\frac{2}{3}\right)} = \dfrac{-5\left(\frac{1}{3}\right)}{\left(-\frac{2}{3}\right)} = \dfrac{5}{2}$

Hence, the equation of the tangent at $\left(\dfrac{1}{3}, -\dfrac{2}{3}\right)$ is

$$y + \dfrac{2}{3} = \dfrac{5}{2}\left(x - \dfrac{1}{3}\right)$$

$\Rightarrow \qquad 5x - 2y - 3 = 0$

which clearly passes through the point $(1, 1)$.

Section – C

41. (c) town A

Explanation: Given that, $AB = 60$

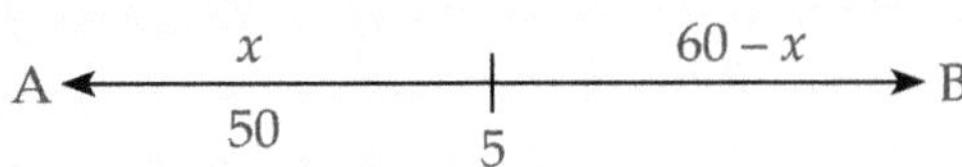

Let the school be at a distance x from A (with 150 students), then the distance travelled by 200 students is

$$D = 150x + 50(60 - x)$$
$$= 100x + 3000$$

D will be least and equal to 3000, if $x = 0$, *i.e.*, school is built at A.

42. (a) $0, 2, -2\sin\theta$

Explanation:

$$M_{12} = \begin{vmatrix} -\sin\theta & \sin\theta \\ -1 & 1 \end{vmatrix}$$
$$= -\sin\theta + \sin\theta = 0$$

$\Rightarrow \qquad c_{12} = -M_{12} = 0$

$$M_{22} = \begin{vmatrix} 1 & 1 \\ -1 & 1 \end{vmatrix}$$
$$= 1 + 1 = 2$$

$\Rightarrow \qquad c_{22} = M_{22} = 0$

$$M_{32} = \begin{vmatrix} 1 & 1 \\ -\sin\theta & \sin\theta \end{vmatrix}$$
$$= \sin\theta + \sin\theta$$
$$= 2\sin\theta$$

$\Rightarrow \qquad c_{32} = -M_{32} = -2\sin\theta$

43. (b) $[0, \pi] - \left\{\dfrac{\pi}{2}\right\}$

Explanation: The principal value branch of $y = \sec^{-1} x$ is $[0, \pi] - \left\{\dfrac{\pi}{2}\right\}$

44. (b) 2

Explanation: Given $A = \{a, b\}$

$\Rightarrow \qquad n(A) = 2$

$\therefore$ Total number of one-one functions from A to A $= {}^2C_2\, 2!$
$$= 1 \times 2 \times 1$$
$$= 2$$

45. (a) $\dfrac{1}{2}\begin{bmatrix} 2 & 4 \\ 3 & -5 \end{bmatrix}$

Explanation: Let

$$X = \begin{bmatrix} a & b \\ c & d \end{bmatrix}$$

Since,

$$A = BX$$

$$\therefore \quad \begin{bmatrix} 1 & 2 \\ 3 & -5 \end{bmatrix} = \begin{bmatrix} 1 & 0 \\ 0 & 2 \end{bmatrix} \begin{bmatrix} a & b \\ c & d \end{bmatrix} = \begin{bmatrix} a & b \\ 2c & 2d \end{bmatrix}$$

Here,

$$a = 1, b = 2, c = \frac{3}{2}$$

and

$$d = -\frac{5}{2}$$

$$\therefore \quad X = \begin{bmatrix} 1 & 2 \\ 3/2 & -5/2 \end{bmatrix} = \frac{1}{2} \begin{bmatrix} 2 & 4 \\ 3 & -5 \end{bmatrix}$$

46. (b) $3x^2 - \dfrac{3}{x^4}$

Explanation:

$$f(x) = x^3 + \frac{1}{x^3}$$

$$\text{Slope} = f'(x) = 3x^2 - \frac{3}{x^4}.$$

47. (a) ± 1

Explanation: For critical values put $f'(x) = 0$

$$3x^2 - \frac{3}{x^4} = 0$$

$$3x^2 = \frac{3}{x^4}$$

$$x^6 = 1$$

$$x = \pm 1$$

48. (a) $(-\infty, -1) \cup (1, \infty)$

Explanation:

$$(-\infty, -1) \Rightarrow f'(x) = +\text{ve}$$
$$(-1, 1) \Rightarrow f'(x) = -\text{ve}$$
$$(1, \infty) \Rightarrow f'(x) = +\text{ve}$$

$\therefore f(x)$ is increasing in $(-\infty, -1) \cup (1, \infty)$.

49. (c) $(-1, 1)$

Explanation: $f(x)$ is decreasing in $(-1, 1)$.

50. (a) $(-\infty, \infty)$.

Explanation: In $(-\infty, \infty)$ interval function is neither increasing nor decreasing.

Sample Paper 5

Section - A

1. (a) $\left(-\dfrac{\pi}{2}, \dfrac{\pi}{2}\right)$

   Explanation: The range of principal value brance of $\tan^{-1} x \left(\dfrac{-\pi}{2}, \dfrac{\pi}{2}\right)$ and $\tan\left(\dfrac{\pi}{4}\right) = 1$.

2. (c) Square maxtrix

   Explanation: Sqare matrix is a matrix with equal number of rows and columns.

3. (d) None of the intervals

   Explanation: We have $\qquad\qquad f(x) = x^{100} + \sin x - 1$

   $\therefore \qquad\qquad\qquad\qquad f'(x) = 100\, x^{99} + \cos x$

   In interval $(0, 1)$, $\cos x > 0$ and $100\, x^{99} > 0$.

   $\therefore \qquad\qquad\qquad\qquad\qquad f'(x) > 0.$

   Thus, function f is strictly increasing in interval $(0, 1)$.

   In interval $\left(\dfrac{\pi}{2}, \pi\right)$, $\cos x < 0$ and $100\, x^{90} > 0$. Also, $100\, x^{99} > \cos x$.

   $\therefore \qquad\qquad\qquad\qquad\qquad f'(x) > 0$

   Thus, function f is strictly increasing in interval $\left(\dfrac{\pi}{2}, \pi\right)$

   In interval $\left(0, \dfrac{\pi}{2}\right)$, $\cos x > 0$ and $100\, x^{99} > 0$.

   $\therefore \qquad\qquad\qquad 100\, x^{99} + \cos x > 0 \Rightarrow f'(x) > 0$

   $\therefore f$ is strictly increasing in interval $\left(0, \dfrac{\pi}{2}\right)$.

   Hence, function f is strictly decreasing in none of the intervals.

4. (b) Feasible solution

   Explanation: A feasible solution is a set of values for the decision varibles that satisfies all the constraints in an optimization problem.

5. (b) Optimization technique

   Explanation: Linear programming is an optimization technique for a system of linear constraints and a linear objective function.

6. (a) $\dfrac{-1}{3}$

Explanation:

$$y = 2x^2 + 3\sin x$$

$$\frac{dy}{dx} = 4x + 3\cos x$$

$$\text{Slope of normal} = \frac{-1}{4x + 3\cos x}$$

At $x = 0$, $\quad\quad\quad$ Slope of normal $= \dfrac{-1}{3}$

7. (a) (1, 2)

Explanation:

$$\text{For } y^2 = 4x$$

$$\frac{dy}{dx} = \frac{2}{y}$$

Slope of given line $y = x + 1$ is 1

$\therefore \quad\quad$ Slope of tangent = Slope of line

$$\Rightarrow \quad\quad\quad \frac{2}{y} = 1$$

$$\Rightarrow \quad\quad\quad y = 2$$

Substituting $y = 2$ in $y^2 = 4x$, we get

$$x = 1$$

Thus, the required point (1, 2)

8. (a) $\dfrac{2\pi}{5}$

Explanation: We know that $\dfrac{-\pi}{2} \le \sin^{-1} x \le \dfrac{\pi}{2}$

$$\therefore \quad \sin^{-1}\left(\sin\frac{3\pi}{5}\right) = \sin^{-1}\left[\sin\left(\pi - \frac{3\pi}{5}\right)\right]$$

$$= \sin^{-1}\left(\sin\frac{2\pi}{5}\right)$$

$$= \frac{2\pi}{5}$$

9. (c) $3, \dfrac{13}{4}$

Explanation: Given,
$$\begin{bmatrix} 3 & -2 \\ -1/6 & 4 \end{bmatrix}\begin{bmatrix} 2x \\ 1 \end{bmatrix} + 2\begin{bmatrix} -4 \\ 5 \end{bmatrix} = 4\begin{bmatrix} 2 \\ y \end{bmatrix}$$

$$\Rightarrow \begin{bmatrix} 3 \times 2x + (-2) \times 1 \\ -1/6 \times 2x + 4 \times 1 \end{bmatrix} + \begin{bmatrix} -8 \\ 10 \end{bmatrix} = \begin{bmatrix} 8 \\ 4y \end{bmatrix}$$

$$\Rightarrow \begin{bmatrix} 6x - 2 \\ -x/3 + 4 \end{bmatrix} + \begin{bmatrix} -8 \\ 10 \end{bmatrix} = \begin{bmatrix} 8 \\ 4y \end{bmatrix}$$

$$\Rightarrow \qquad \begin{bmatrix} 6x - 10 \\ -x/3 + 14 \end{bmatrix} = \begin{bmatrix} 8 \\ 4y \end{bmatrix}$$

$$\Rightarrow \qquad 6x - 10 = 8$$

$$\Rightarrow \qquad x = 3$$

and

$$\frac{-x}{3} + 14 = 4y$$

$$\Rightarrow \qquad y = \frac{13}{4}$$

10. (b) (1.5, 4)

> **Explanation:** We have, minimise $Z = 8x + 10y$
>
> Subject to $2x + y \geq 7,\ 2x + 3y \geq 15,\ y \geq 2,\ x \geq 0,\ y \geq 0$
>
> Let $l_1 : 2x + y = 7,\ l_2 : 2x + 3y = 15,\ l_3 : y = 2,\ l_4 : x = 0,\ l_5 : y = 0$
>
> 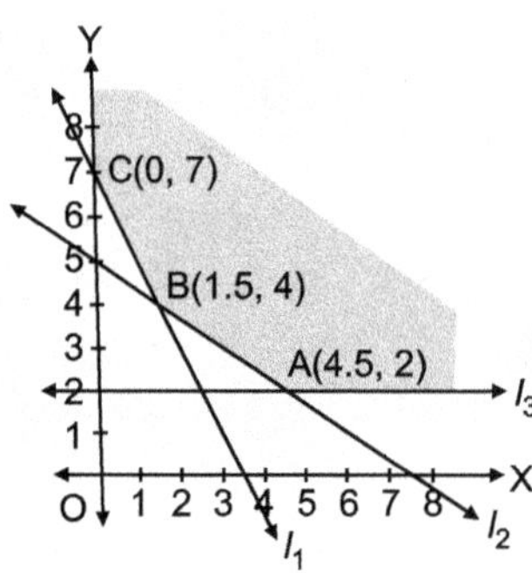
>
>
> **For A :** Solving l_2 and l_3, we get A(4.5, 2)
>
> **For B :** Solving l_1 and l_2, we get B(1.5, 4)
>
> Shaded portion is the feasible region, where A(4.5, 2), B(1.5, 4), (C(0, 7)
>
> Now, minimise $Z = 8x + 10y$
>
> $$Z \text{ at A(4.5, 2)} = 8(4.5) + 10(2) = 56$$
>
> $$Z \text{ at B(1.5, 4)} = 8(1.5) + 10(4) = 52$$
>
> $$Z \text{ at C(0, 7)} = 8(0) + 10(07) = 70$$
>
> Thus, Z is minimised at B(1.5, 4) and its minimum value is 52.

11. (b) $\begin{bmatrix} 2 & 2 \\ 2 & 0 \end{bmatrix}$

> **Explanation:** $A = \begin{bmatrix} 2 & 3 \\ 1 & 0 \end{bmatrix}$
>
> $\therefore$ $A' = \begin{bmatrix} 2 & 1 \\ 3 & 0 \end{bmatrix}$
>
> Now, $P = \dfrac{1}{2}(A + A')$
>
> $\Rightarrow$ $P = \dfrac{1}{2}\begin{bmatrix} 2+2 & 3+1 \\ 1+3 & 0+0 \end{bmatrix}$

$$\Rightarrow \qquad P = \frac{1}{2}\begin{bmatrix} 4 & 4 \\ 4 & 0 \end{bmatrix}$$

$$\Rightarrow \qquad P = \begin{bmatrix} 2 & 2 \\ 2 & 0 \end{bmatrix}$$

12. (a) $x = 7, y = -1$

Explanation:
$$\begin{bmatrix} x+3y & y \\ 7-x & 4 \end{bmatrix} = \begin{bmatrix} 4 & -1 \\ 0 & 4 \end{bmatrix}$$

Equating the corresponding elements, we get
$$x + 3y = 4, \; y = -1, \; 7 - x = 0$$
$$\Rightarrow \qquad x = 7, \; y = -1$$

13. (b) $|A| = 8$

Explanation: We know that, $\qquad A(\text{adj. } A) = |A| \, I$
$$\Rightarrow \qquad |A| I = A(\text{adj. } A)$$
$$|A| \begin{bmatrix} 1 & 0 \\ 0 & 1 \end{bmatrix} = \begin{bmatrix} 8 & 0 \\ 0 & 8 \end{bmatrix}$$
$$|A| \begin{bmatrix} 1 & 0 \\ 0 & 1 \end{bmatrix} = 8 \begin{bmatrix} 1 & 0 \\ 0 & 1 \end{bmatrix}$$
$$\therefore \qquad |A| = 8$$

14. (c) Objective function

Explanation: In a LPP, linear function $Z = ax + by$ is called objective function.

15. (a) 11

Explanation:
$$\tan^2(\sec^{-1} 2) + \cot^2(\operatorname{cosec}^{-1} 3) = \sec^2(\sec^{-1} 2) - 1 + \operatorname{cosec}^2(\operatorname{cosec}^{-1} 3) - 1$$
$$= 2^2 + 3^2 - 2$$
$$= 11$$

16. (a) $\dfrac{dy}{dx} = e^{-x}[-6a \sin ax + 5b \cos bx - 6 \cos ax - 5 \sin bx]$

Explanation: Given : $\qquad y = e^{-x}(6 \cos ax + 5 \sin bx)$
Differentiating w.r.t. x
$$\Rightarrow \qquad \frac{dy}{dx} = e^{-x} \frac{d}{dx}(6 \cos ax + 5 \sin bx) + (6 \cos ax + 5 \sin bx)\frac{d}{dx} e^{-x}$$
$$\Rightarrow \qquad \frac{dy}{dx} = e^{-x}[a(-6 \sin ax) + b(5 \cos bx)] + (6 \cos ax + 5 \sin bx)e^{-x}(-1)$$
$$\Rightarrow \qquad \frac{dy}{dx} = e^{-x}[-6a \sin ax + 5b \cos bx - 6 \cos ax - 5 \sin bx]$$

17. (c) $\dfrac{1}{\sqrt{1-x^2}-2\sqrt{x(1-x)}}$

Explanation: Let

$$y = \frac{d}{dx}[\sin^{-1}(x\sqrt{1-x}-\sqrt{x}\,\sqrt{1-x^2})]$$

$$= \frac{d}{dx}[\sin^{-1}(x\sqrt{1-(\sqrt{x})^2}-\sqrt{x}\,\sqrt{1-x^2})]$$

$$= \frac{d}{dx}[\sin^{-1}x - \sin^{-1}\sqrt{x}]$$

$$= \frac{1}{\sqrt{1-x^2}} - \frac{1}{2\sqrt{x}\,\sqrt{1-x}}$$

$$= \frac{1}{\sqrt{1-x^2}} - \frac{1}{2\sqrt{x(1-x)}}$$

18. (b) $\sqrt{2}$

Explanation: We know that

$$\cos A \cos 2A \cos 2^2 A \ldots \cos 2^{n-1} A = \frac{\sin(2^n A)}{2^n \sin A}$$

$$\therefore \qquad \cos x \cos 2x \cos 4x \cos 8x \cos 16x = \frac{\sin 32x}{32 \sin x}$$

$$\Rightarrow \qquad f(x) = \frac{1}{32}\cdot\frac{\sin 32x}{\sin x}$$

$$\therefore \qquad f'(x) = \frac{1}{32}\times\frac{\sin x\,(32\cos 32x)-\sin 32x\cdot\cos x}{\sin^2 x}$$

$$\therefore \qquad f'\left(\frac{\pi}{4}\right) = \sqrt{2}$$

19. (a) $-\dfrac{\pi}{3}$

Explanation: Let $\quad \mathrm{cosec}^{-1}\left(\dfrac{-2}{\sqrt{3}}\right) = \theta$

$$\Rightarrow \qquad \mathrm{cosec}\,\theta = \frac{-2}{\sqrt{3}} = -\mathrm{cosec}\,\frac{\pi}{3} = \mathrm{cosec}\left(\frac{-\pi}{3}\right)$$

$$\Rightarrow \qquad \theta = \frac{-\pi}{3} \in \left[\frac{-\pi}{2},\frac{\pi}{2}\right] - \{0\}$$

$\therefore$ Principal value of $\mathrm{cosec}^{-1}\left(\dfrac{-2}{\sqrt{3}}\right)$ is $\left(\dfrac{-\pi}{3}\right)$

20. (c) $\{2, 4, 6\}$

Explanation: Given, $\qquad R = \{(x, y) : x + 2y = 8,\ x, y \in N\}$

$\therefore \qquad R = \{(2, 3), (4, 2), (6, 1)\}$

$\therefore \qquad$ Domain of $R = \{x : (x, y) \in R\} = \{2, 4, 6\}$

Section - B

21. (d) 512

> **Explanation:** As order of 3×3 matrix contains 9 elements. Each element can be selected in 2 ways (it can be either 0 or 1). Hence, all the nine entries can be chosen in $2^9 = 512$ ways.
>
> (By the multiplication principle)
>
> Required number of matrices is 512.

22. (b) $f(x) = x + 2$

> **Explanation:**
> $$f(x) = x^3 \text{ cannot be onto as range of}$$
> $$f = \{\ldots, -27, -8, -1, 0, 1, 8, 27, \ldots\} \neq Z$$
> $$f(x) = 2x + 1 \text{ is also not onto as}$$
> $$Rf = \{\ldots, -3, -1, 1, 3, \ldots\} \neq Z$$
> $$f(x) = x^2 + 1 \text{ is not one-one as } f(x) = f(-x) = x^2 + 1$$
>
> And $\qquad f(x) = x + 2$ is one-one as $f(x_1) = f(x_2) \Rightarrow x_1 = x_2$
>
> and it is onto also $\hfill [\because R_f = Z]$
>
> Hence, $\qquad f(x) = (x + 2)$ is bijective.

23. (c) 30

> **Explanation:** The points in the feasible region are $(0, 0)$, $(0, 10)$, $\left(\dfrac{20}{3}, \dfrac{10}{3}\right)$ and $(10, 0)$.
>
> 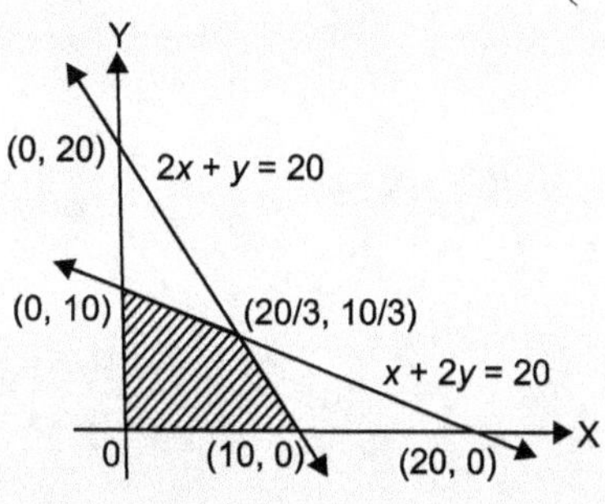
>
>
> Objective function P $\qquad = x + 3y$
>
> $$P_{(10, 0)} = 10$$
> $$P_{(0, 10)} = P_{\left(\frac{20}{3}, \frac{10}{3}\right)} = \frac{50}{3}$$
>
> $\therefore$ Maximum value of P is 30 at $(0, 10)$.

24. (a) 150

> **Explanation:**
> $$x = \text{length of garden}$$
> $$y = \text{breadth of garden}$$
> $$4y + 2x = 600$$
> $$4y = 600 - 2x$$
> $$y = 150 - \frac{1}{2}x$$
> $$A = l \times b$$
> $$A = x\left(150 - \frac{1}{2}x\right)$$

$$A = 150x - \frac{1}{2}x^2$$

Differentiating A, w.r.t. x

$$\frac{dA}{dx} = 150 - x$$

Put

$$\frac{dA}{dx} = 0 \Rightarrow x = 150$$

25. (b) $x + y + z = 18,\ x + 2z = 21,\ 3x + y + z = 36$

Explanation: According to the conditions given.

26. (a) Corresponding elements

Explanation: Two matrices of same order are said to be equal if the corresponding elements of the matrices are equal.

27. (a) $R = \{(2, 2), (3, 5), (4, 10), (5, 17), (6, 26)\}$

Explanation: $\qquad R = \{(2, 2), (3, 5), (4, 10), (5, 17), (6, 26)\}$

Domain of $R = \{x : (x, y) \in R\} = \{2, 3, 4, 5, 6\}$

and $\qquad$ range of $R = \{y : (x, y) \in R\} = \{2, 5, 10, 17, 26\}$

28. (c) 7

Explanation: Given $\qquad f(2) = k$

Now, $\qquad \lim\limits_{x \to 2} f(x) = \lim\limits_{x \to 2^+} f(x)$

$$= \lim\limits_{x \to 2} \frac{x^3 + x^2 - 16x + 20}{(x-2)^2}$$

$$= \lim\limits_{x \to 2} \frac{(x+5)(x-2)^2}{(x-2)^2}$$

$$= \lim\limits_{x \to 2} (x+5) = 7$$

As f is continuous at $x = 2$, we have

$$\lim\limits_{x \to 2} f(x) = f(2)$$

$\Rightarrow \qquad\qquad k = 7.$

29. (d) $[-\sqrt{5}, -\sqrt{3}] \cup [\sqrt{3}, \sqrt{5}]$

Explanation: $\qquad y = \cos^{-1}(x^2 - 4)$

$\Rightarrow \qquad \cos y = x^2 - 4$

i.e., $\qquad -1 \leq x^2 - 4 \leq 1 \qquad\qquad$ (since $-1 \leq \cos y \leq 1$)

$\Rightarrow \qquad 3 \leq x^2 \leq 5$

$\Rightarrow \qquad \sqrt{3} \leq |x| \leq \sqrt{5}$

$\Rightarrow \qquad x \in [-\sqrt{5}, -\sqrt{3}] \cup [\sqrt{3}, \sqrt{5}]$

30. (c) f and g both are discontinous

> **Explanation:** Consider, $\qquad h(x) = f(x) + g(x)$
>
> If $f(x)$ is continuous and $g(x)$ is discontinuous, then let us assume that $h(x)$ is continuous.
>
> Now, $\qquad\qquad\qquad g(x) = \underbrace{h(x)}_{\text{Continous function}} - \underbrace{f(x)}_{\text{Continous function}}$
>
> $\Rightarrow g(x)$ is a continuous function.
>
> Which is contradictory to the given fact that $g(x)$ is a discontinuous function.
>
> Hence, our assumption that $h(x)$ is continuous is wrong, i.e., if f is continuous and g is discontinuos, then $f + g$ cannot be a continuous function.
>
> i.e., choice (a) is wrong.
>
> Similarly, choice (b) is wrong.
>
> From choice (c), we wake
>
> $$f(x) = x - [x], \text{ i.e., discontinuous function}$$
> $$g(x) = x + [x], \text{ i.e., discontinuous function}$$
> $$(f + g)(x) = (x - [x]) + (x + [x])$$
> $$= 2x, \text{ i.e., continuous fucntion.}$$

31. (c) Determinant is a number associated to a square matrix

> **Explanation:** We know that for every square matrix, $A = [a_{ij}]$ of order n, where $a_{ij} = (i, j)^{\text{th}}$ element of A. We can associate a number called the determinant of square matrix A.
>
> Thus, the determinant is a number associated to a square matrix.

32. (d) 125Δ

> **Explanation:** Given $\qquad\qquad$ $|\,A\,|_{3 \times 3} = \Delta$
>
> $\therefore \qquad\qquad$ $|\,5A\,|_{3 \times 3} = (5)^3\,|\,A\,|_{3 \times 3} = 125\,\Delta$

33. (b) $\dfrac{1}{4\sqrt{x}} (\sec \sqrt{x})^{3/2} . \sin \sqrt{x}$

> **Explanation:** Let $\qquad\qquad$ $y = \sqrt{\sec \sqrt{x}}$
>
> Differentiating w.r.t. x, we get
>
> $$\frac{dy}{dx} = \frac{1}{2\sqrt{\sec \sqrt{x}}} . \sec \sqrt{x} . \tan \sqrt{x} . \frac{1}{2\sqrt{x}}$$
>
> $$= \frac{1}{4\sqrt{x}} (\sec \sqrt{x})^{1/2} \frac{\sin \sqrt{x}}{\cos \sqrt{x}} = \frac{1}{4\sqrt{x}} (\sec \sqrt{x})^{3/2} . \sin \sqrt{x}$$

34. (c) $\begin{bmatrix} 5 & 14 \\ 7 & 16 \end{bmatrix}$

> **Explanation:** Given, $\qquad$ $A_{ij} = |2i + 3j^2|$
>
> $\therefore \qquad\qquad a_{11} = |2 \times 1 + 3 \times 1| = 5$
>
> $\qquad\qquad\quad a_{12} = |2 \times 1 + 3 \times 4| = 14$
>
> $\qquad\qquad\quad a_{21} = |2 \times 2 + 3 \times 1| = 7$
>
> and $\qquad\qquad a_{22} = |2 \times 2 + 3 \times 4| = 16$
>
> $\therefore \qquad\qquad A_{22} = \begin{bmatrix} a_{11} & a_{12} \\ a_{21} & a_{22} \end{bmatrix} = \begin{bmatrix} 5 & 14 \\ 7 & 16 \end{bmatrix}$

35. (b) Symmetric

Explanation: Given R and R' are not disjoint, so there is atleast one ordered pair, say $(a, b) \in R \cap R'$.

$\Rightarrow$ $\qquad\qquad\qquad (a, b) \in R$ and $(a, b) \in R'$

As R and R' are symmetric relations, we get

$\qquad\qquad\qquad (b, a) \in R$ and $(b, a) \in R'$

$\Rightarrow$ $\qquad\qquad\qquad (b, a) \in R \cap R'$

Hence, $R \cap R'$ is symmetric.

36. (d) $x^{3e^{3x}} \cdot 3e^{3x}\left(3\log x + \dfrac{1}{x}\right)$

Explanation: Consider $\qquad\qquad y = x^{3e^{3x}}$

Applying log on both sides, we get

$$\log y = 3e^{3x} \log x$$

Differentiating both sides w.r.t. x, we get

$$\frac{1}{y}\frac{dy}{dx} = \frac{d}{dx}(3e^{3x})\log x + \frac{d}{dx}(\log x)3e^{3x}$$

$$\frac{1}{y}\frac{dy}{dx} = 3e^{3x}\cdot 3.\log x + \frac{1}{x}3e^{3x}$$

$$\frac{dy}{dx} = y\left(3e^{3x}\cdot 3.\log x + \frac{1}{x}3e^{3x}\right)$$

$$\frac{dy}{dx} = x^{3e^{3x}}\cdot 3e^{3x}\left(3\log x + \frac{1}{x}\right)$$

37. (a) $y = 2x$

Explanation: Let $Q(x, y)$ be any point on the line joining A(1, 2) and B(3, 6). Then, area of $\triangle ABQ = 0$.

$\Rightarrow$
$$\frac{1}{2}\begin{vmatrix} 1 & 2 & 1 \\ 3 & 6 & 1 \\ x & y & 1 \end{vmatrix} = 0$$

$\Rightarrow$ $\qquad 1(6 - y) - 2(3 - x) + 1(3y - 6x) = 0$

$\Rightarrow$ $\qquad\qquad 6 - y - 6 + 2x + 3y - 6x = 0$

$\Rightarrow$ $\qquad\qquad\qquad\qquad -4x = -2y$

$\Rightarrow$ $\qquad\qquad\qquad\qquad\quad 2 = y$

38. (c) $x + y = 0$

Explanation: $\qquad\qquad \dfrac{dy}{dx} = \cos x$

Therefore, $\qquad$ slope of normal $= \left(\dfrac{-1}{\cos x}\right)_{x=0} = -1$

Hence, the equation of normal is $y - 0 = -1(x - 0)$ or $x + y = 0$

39. (c) 0

> **Explanation:** As A contains 5 elements.
>
> $\therefore$ For any one-one onto mapping $f : A \to B$, $f(A)$ also contains 5 elements but B contains 6 elements.
>
> $\therefore$ $$f(A) \neq B$$
>
> So, no one-one mapping from A to B can be onto.

40. (c) $\dfrac{2a}{125}$

> **Explanation:** We have,
> $$\begin{bmatrix} 1/25 & 0 \\ x & 1/25 \end{bmatrix} = \begin{bmatrix} 5 & 0 \\ -a & 5 \end{bmatrix}^{-2}$$
>
> Pre-multiply both sides by $\begin{bmatrix} 5 & 0 \\ -a & 5 \end{bmatrix}$, we get
> $$\begin{bmatrix} 1/5 & 0 \\ -a/25 + 5x & 1/5 \end{bmatrix} = \begin{bmatrix} 5 & 0 \\ -a & 5 \end{bmatrix}^{-1}$$
>
> Again pre-multiply by $\begin{bmatrix} 5 & 0 \\ -a & 5 \end{bmatrix}$
>
> So that $$-\frac{2a}{5} + 25x = 0$$
>
> $\Rightarrow$ $$x = \frac{2a}{125}$$

Section - C

41. (b) $a^2 - b^2 = 0$

> **Explanation:** Let the curves intersect at (x_1, y_1). Thereore,
> $$\frac{x^2}{a^2} - \frac{y^2}{b^2} = 1$$
>
> $\Rightarrow$ $$\frac{2x}{a^2} - \frac{2y}{b^2}\frac{dy}{dx} = 0$$
>
> $\Rightarrow$ $$\frac{dy}{dx} = \frac{b^2 x}{a^2 y}$$
>
> $\Rightarrow$ Slope of tangent at the point of intersection $(m_1) = \dfrac{b^2 x_1}{a^2 y_1}$
>
> Again $$xy = c^2 \Rightarrow x\frac{dy}{dx} + y = 0$$
>
> $\Rightarrow$ $$\frac{dy}{dx} = \frac{-y}{x} \Rightarrow m_2 = \frac{-y_1}{x_1}$$
>
> For orthogonality, $$m_1 \times m_2 = -1$$
>
> $\Rightarrow$ $$\frac{b^2}{a^2} = 1 \text{ or } a^2 - b^2 = 0$$

42. (c) $\dfrac{\pi}{3}$

Explanation: Let ABC be a right angled triangle in which side

$$BC = x \text{ (say) and hypotenuse } AC = y \qquad \text{(say)}$$

Given, $\qquad x + y = k \qquad$ (constant)

$\Rightarrow \qquad y = k - x$

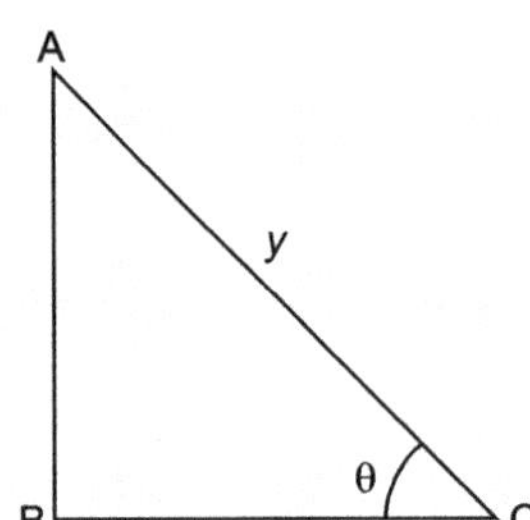

Now, the area of $\triangle ABC$ is given by

$$A = \frac{1}{2} \cdot BC \cdot AB = \frac{1}{x} x\sqrt{(y^2 - x^2)}$$

$$= \frac{1}{2} x\sqrt{[(k-x)^2 - x^2]}$$

Let $\qquad u = A^2 = \dfrac{1}{4} x^2 (k^2 - 2kx)$

$\Rightarrow \qquad \dfrac{du}{dx} = \dfrac{1}{2} k(kx - 3x^2) \text{ and } \dfrac{d^2u}{dx^2} = \dfrac{1}{2} k(k - 6x)$

For maximum or minimum of u, put $\dfrac{du}{dx} = 0$.

$\Rightarrow \qquad x = \dfrac{k}{3} \qquad\qquad [\because x \neq 0]$

When $\qquad x = \dfrac{k}{3} \cdot \dfrac{d^2u}{dx^2} = \dfrac{1}{2} k\left(k - 6 \times \dfrac{1}{3} k\right) = -\dfrac{1}{2} k^2 (-ve)$

$\Rightarrow u$, *i.e.*, A is maximum when $x = \dfrac{k}{3}$

and when $\qquad y = k - x = \dfrac{2k}{3}$

Now, $\qquad \cos\theta = \dfrac{BC}{AC} = \dfrac{x}{y} = \dfrac{1}{2} \Rightarrow \theta = \dfrac{\pi}{3}$

Hence, the requried angle is $\dfrac{\pi}{3}$

43. (d) $\sqrt{\dfrac{2}{3}}$

Explanation: $\quad \sin\left[\cot^{-1}\left(\cos\dfrac{\pi}{4}\right)\right] = \sin\left[\cot^{-1}\dfrac{1}{\sqrt{2}}\right] = \sin\left[\sin^{-1}\sqrt{\dfrac{2}{3}}\right] = \sqrt{\dfrac{2}{3}}$

44. (c) $\dfrac{1}{e^2}$

> **Explanation:** Given,
> $$f(x) = x^2 e^{-2x}$$
> $$\therefore \quad f'(x) = 2xe^{-2x} - 2x^2 e^{-2x}$$
> $$= 2x(1-x)e^{-2x}$$
> For maxima and minima, put $f'(x) = 0$
> $$2x(1-x)e^{-2x} = 0$$
> $$\Rightarrow \quad x = 0, 1$$
> Now,
> $$f''(x) = 2x(-1)e^{-2x} + 2(1-x)e^{-2x} - 2 \cdot 2x(1-x)e^{-2x}$$
> $$f''(0) = 0 + 2e^0 = 2 > 0 \qquad \text{[minima]}$$
> and
> $$f''(1) = -2e^{-2} + 0 - 0 = -\frac{2}{e^2} < 0 \qquad \text{[maxima]}$$
> Thus, maximum value is
> $$f(1) = 1 \cdot e^{-2} = \frac{1}{e^2}$$

45. (a) $-\dfrac{1}{1+x^2}$

> **Explanation:**
> $$\frac{d}{dx}\left[\tan^{-1}\left(\frac{a-x}{1+ax} \right) \right] = \frac{d}{dx}[\tan^{-1} a - \tan^{-1} x]$$
> $$= 0 - \frac{1}{1+x^2} = -\frac{1}{1+x^2}$$

46. (a) $h = \dfrac{300}{\pi r^2}$

> **Explanation:** Given,
> $$h = \text{Height of cylinder}$$
> $$r = \text{Radius}$$
> $$V = \text{Volume}$$
> We know,
> $$V = \pi r^2 h$$
> $$300 = \pi r^2 h$$
> $$\therefore \quad h = \frac{300}{\pi r^2} \qquad \qquad \text{...(i)}$$

47. (a) $\dfrac{3000}{r} + 20\pi r^2$

> **Explanation:** Let C be the cost function
> $$C = 5 \times (\text{curved surface area of tin}) + 10(\text{cost of top and bottom})$$
> $$= 5 \times 2\pi rh + 10 \times 2.\pi r^2$$
> $$C = 10\pi r. \frac{300}{\pi r^2} + 20.\pi r^2 \qquad \text{[From (i)]}$$
> $$C = \frac{3000}{r} + 20\pi r^2$$

Differentiating C with respect to r, we get

$$\frac{dC}{dr} = \frac{-3000}{r^2} + 40\pi r$$

48. (a) $r = \left(\dfrac{75}{\pi}\right)^{1/3}$

Put, $\dfrac{dC}{dr} = 0$

$$\frac{3000}{r^2} = 40\pi r$$

$$\frac{3000}{40\pi} = r^3$$

$$r^3 = \frac{75}{\pi}$$

$$r = \left(\frac{75}{\pi}\right)^{1/3}$$

49. (a) $\dfrac{300\pi^{-1/3}}{(75)^{2/3}}$

Explanation:

$$h = \frac{300}{\pi r^2} = \frac{300}{\pi\left(\dfrac{75}{\pi}\right)^{2/3}}$$

$$= \frac{300}{\pi^{1/3}(75)^{2/3}}$$

$$= \frac{300\pi^{-1/3}}{(75)^{2/3}}.$$

50. (b) $4500\left(\dfrac{75}{\pi}\right)^{-1/3}$

Explanation:

$$\text{Cost} = \frac{3000 + 20\pi r^3}{r}$$

$$= \frac{3000 + 20\pi \times \dfrac{75}{\pi}}{r}$$

$$= \frac{3000 + 1500}{r}$$

$$= \frac{4500}{\left(\dfrac{75}{\pi}\right)^{1/3}}$$

$$= 4500\left(\frac{75}{\pi}\right)^{-1/3}$$

Sample Paper 6

Section - A

1. (b) ± 3

Explanation: $\because$
$$\begin{vmatrix} 2 & 5 \\ 8 & x^2 \end{vmatrix} = \begin{vmatrix} 6 & 5 \\ 8 & 3 \end{vmatrix}$$

$$\Rightarrow \qquad 2x^2 - 40 = 18 - 40$$
$$\Rightarrow \qquad 2x^2 = 18$$
$$\Rightarrow \qquad x^2 = 9$$
$$\Rightarrow \qquad x = \pm 3$$

2. (a) $\dfrac{\pi}{6}$

Explanation: Let $\qquad \operatorname{cosec}^{-1}(2) = x$
$$\therefore \qquad \operatorname{cosec} x = 2$$
$$= \operatorname{cosec} \dfrac{\pi}{6}$$

Range of the principal value of $\operatorname{cosec} x$ is $\left\{ \dfrac{-\pi}{2}, \dfrac{\pi}{2} \right\} - \{0\}$.

Hence, $\qquad \operatorname{cosec}^{-1}(2) = \dfrac{\pi}{6}$

3. (d) 0

Explanation:
$$\lim_{x \to 0} \frac{f(a+h) - f(a)}{h} = \lim_{x \to 0} \frac{|0+h|^3 - |0|^3}{h}$$
$$= \lim_{x \to 0} h^2 = 0$$

4. (a) 15

Explanation: Here, $\qquad y = -x^3 + 3x^2 + 12x - 5$
$$\therefore \qquad \frac{dy}{dx} = -3x^2 + 6x + 12$$
$$= -3(x^2 - 2x - 4)$$
$$= -3[(x-1)^2 - 5]$$
$$= 15 - 3(x-1)^2$$

To get maximum value of $\dfrac{dy}{dx}$, put $3(x-1)^2 = 0$

$$\Rightarrow \qquad x = 1$$

Hence, maximum value of slope at $x = 1$ is 15.

5. (b) Skew symmetric matrix

Explanation:
$$(AB' - BA')' = (AB')' - (BA')'$$
$$= (BA' - AB')$$
$$= -(AB' - BA')$$

6. (a) $\dfrac{-\pi}{10}$

Explanation:
$$\sin^{-1}\left(\cos\frac{43\pi}{5}\right) = \sin^{-1}\left(\cos\frac{40\pi + 3\pi}{5}\right)$$
$$= \sin^{-1}\left(\cos\left(8\pi + \frac{3\pi}{5}\right)\right)$$
$$= \sin^{-1}\left(\cos\frac{3\pi}{5}\right)$$
$$= \sin^{-1}\left(\sin\left(\frac{\pi}{2} - \frac{3\pi}{5}\right)\right)$$
$$= \sin^{-1}\left(\sin\left(-\frac{\pi}{10}\right)\right)$$
$$= -\frac{\pi}{10}$$

7. (a) $\begin{bmatrix} 1 & 18 & 7 \\ 7 & 33 & 16 \\ 19 & -30 & 1 \end{bmatrix}$

Explanation:
$$AB = \begin{bmatrix} 5 & -3 & 2 \\ -3 & 8 & 1 \end{bmatrix}\begin{bmatrix} 2 & 3 \\ 5 & 6 \\ 2 & -3 \end{bmatrix}$$
$$= \begin{bmatrix} 10-15+4 & 15-18-6 \\ -6+40+2 & -9+48-3 \end{bmatrix}$$
$$= \begin{bmatrix} -1 & -19 \\ 36 & 36 \end{bmatrix}$$

and
$$BA = \begin{bmatrix} 2 & 3 \\ 5 & 6 \\ 2 & -3 \end{bmatrix}\begin{bmatrix} 5 & -3 & 2 \\ -3 & 8 & 1 \end{bmatrix}$$
$$= \begin{bmatrix} 10-9 & -6+24 & 4+3 \\ 25-18 & -15+48 & 10+6 \\ 10+9 & -6-24 & 4-3 \end{bmatrix}$$
$$= \begin{bmatrix} 1 & 18 & 7 \\ 7 & 33 & 16 \\ 19 & -30 & 1 \end{bmatrix}$$

8. (c) -16

Explanation: Here $f(x) = x^3 - 12x$

Then,
$$f'(x) = 3x^2 - 12$$
$$= 3(x - 2)(x + 2)$$
$$f'(x) = 0$$
$$\Rightarrow \qquad 3(x - 2)(x + 2) = 0$$
$$\Rightarrow \qquad x = 2, -2$$

Now, find the values of $f(0), f(3), f(2)$ and $f(-2)$ $f(0) = 0, f(3) = -9, f(2) = -16$ and $f(-2) = 16$.

Thus, absolute minimum value is -16.

9. (a) $1, 2$

Explanation: For $y^2 = 4x$, $\qquad \dfrac{dy}{dx} = \dfrac{2}{y}$

Slope of given line $y = x + 1$ is 1

$\therefore \qquad$ Slope of tangent = Slope of line

$$\Rightarrow \qquad \dfrac{2}{y} = 1 \Rightarrow y = 2$$

Put $y = 2$ in $y^2 = 4x$, we get $x = 1$

Thus, required point is $1, 2$.

10. (c) 5 sq. units

Explanation: Area of triangle is given by :

$$\Delta = \dfrac{1}{2} \begin{vmatrix} 0 & 0 & 1 \\ 2 & 3 & 1 \\ 0 & 5 & 1 \end{vmatrix}$$

$$= \dfrac{1}{2} 1(10 - 0) = 5 \text{ sq. units}$$

11. (c) $\dfrac{-1}{2} \le x \le \dfrac{1}{2}$

Explanation: Let $\qquad \sin^{-1} 2x = \theta$

Then, $\qquad 2x = \sin \theta.$

$$\Rightarrow \qquad x = \dfrac{\sin \theta}{2}$$

We know that, $\qquad -1 \le \sin \theta \le 1$

$$\dfrac{-1}{2} \le \dfrac{\sin \theta}{2} \le \dfrac{1}{2}$$

$$\dfrac{-1}{2} \le x \le \dfrac{1}{2}$$

12. (c) 3×3

Explanation: Order is 3×3 because it is product of two matrices having order 3×1 and 1×3.

13. (b) $\dfrac{7\pi}{12}$

Explanation:
$$\sec^{-1}(2) + \sin^{-1}\left(\dfrac{1}{\sqrt{2}}\right) = \sec^{-1}\left(\sec\dfrac{\pi}{3}\right) + \sin^{-1}\left(\sin\dfrac{\pi}{4}\right)$$
$$= \dfrac{\pi}{3} + \dfrac{\pi}{4}$$
$$= \dfrac{4\pi + 3\pi}{12} = \dfrac{7\pi}{12}.$$

14. (b) $\dfrac{1}{2}$

Explanation: Let
$$f(x) = \sin x \cdot \cos x$$
$$= \dfrac{1}{2}\sin 2x$$

The value of $f(x)$ is maximum when $\sin 2x = 1$

$\therefore$ Maximum value of $f(x) = \dfrac{1}{2}$

15. (d) $2\cos 2x$

Explanation: Given $\qquad y = \sin^2 x$
On differentiating 'y' twice w.r.t. x, we get
$$\dfrac{dy}{dx} = 2\sin x \cos x$$
$$\dfrac{dy}{dx} = \sin 2x$$
$$\dfrac{d^2y}{dx^2} = 2\cos 2x$$

16. (b) 28

Explanation:
$$\begin{vmatrix} 8 & 4 \\ 5 & 6 \end{vmatrix} = (8 \times 6 - 5 \times 4)$$
$$= 48 - 20$$
$$= 28.$$

17. (c) $\{(2, 8), (3, 27), (5, 125), (7, 343)\}$

Explanation: Here, prime numbers less than 10 are 2, 3, 5 and 7.
$\therefore$ Relation in the roster form is $\{(2, 8), (3, 27), (5, 125), (7, 343)\}$

18. (a) {(3, 3), (3, 1), (5, 2)}

> **Explanation:**
> $$R = \{(1, 3), (2, 5), (3, 3)\}$$
> $$\therefore \quad R^{-1} = \{(3, 1), (5, 2), (3, 3)\}$$

19. (d) $-\dfrac{\pi}{4}$

> **Explanation:**
> $$\tan^{-1}\left\{\sin\left(-\frac{\pi}{2}\right)\right\} = \tan^{-1}\left\{-\sin\frac{\pi}{2}\right\}$$
> $$= -\tan^{-1}(-1) = -\tan^{-1}(1) = -\tan^{-1}\tan\frac{\pi}{4} = -\frac{\pi}{4}$$

20. (d) $-\dfrac{24}{25}$

> **Explanation:**
> $$\sin\left\{2\cos^{-1}\left(-\frac{3}{5}\right)\right\} = 2\sin\left\{\cos^{-1}\left(-\frac{3}{5}\right)\right\}\cos\left\{\cos^{-1}\left(-\frac{3}{5}\right)\right\}$$
> $$= 2\sin\left\{\pi - \cos^{-1}\frac{3}{5}\right\}\times\left(-\frac{3}{5}\right) = -\frac{6}{5}\sin\left\{\cos^{-1}\frac{3}{5}\right\}$$
> $$= -\frac{6}{5}\sin\left(\sin^{-1}\sqrt{1-\frac{9}{25}}\right) = -\frac{6}{5}\times\frac{4}{5} = -\frac{24}{25}$$

Section - B

21. (c) $c = 0,\ d = a$

> **Explanation:** Since, matrix $\begin{bmatrix} a & b \\ c & d \end{bmatrix}$ is commutative with the matrix $\begin{bmatrix} 1 & 1 \\ 0 & 1 \end{bmatrix}$
> $$\therefore \quad \begin{bmatrix} a & b \\ c & d \end{bmatrix}\begin{bmatrix} 1 & 1 \\ 0 & 1 \end{bmatrix} = \begin{bmatrix} 1 & 1 \\ 0 & 1 \end{bmatrix}\begin{bmatrix} a & b \\ c & d \end{bmatrix}$$
> $$\Rightarrow \quad \begin{bmatrix} a & a+b \\ c & c+d \end{bmatrix} = \begin{bmatrix} a+c & b+d \\ c & d \end{bmatrix}$$
> $$\Rightarrow \quad a = a + c,\ a + b = b + d$$
> $$\Rightarrow \quad c = 0,\ a = d$$

22. (a) 10

> **Explanation:** Since $f(x)$ is continuos at $x = 5$
> $$\therefore \quad \lim_{x \to 5} f(x) = f(5)$$
> $$\Rightarrow \quad k = \lim_{x \to 5}\frac{x^2 - 25}{x - 5} = \lim_{x \to 5}\frac{(x-5)(x+5)}{x-5}$$
> $$= \lim_{x \to 5}(x + 5) \Rightarrow k = 10$$

23. (a) Ordered pairs

Explanation: A relation is a set of all ordered pairs.

24. (c) 3, 8

Explanation: Since, AB is defined.

$\therefore$ Number of columns in A = Number of rows in B

$\Rightarrow$ $x + 5 = y$ or $x - y = -5$ ...(i)

Also, BA is defined.

$\therefore$ Number of columns in B = Number of rows in A

$\Rightarrow$ $x = 11 - y$ or $x + y = 11$ ...(ii)

Froms eqs. (i) and (ii), we get,

$$x = 3, \ y = 8.$$

25. (c) Bounded in first quadrant

Explanation: The region represented by the inequation system $x, y \geq 0, \ y \leq 6, \ x + y \leq 3$ is bounded in first quadrant.

26. (c) 7

Explanation: Given $f(2) = k$

Now,

$$\lim_{x \to 2} f(x) = \lim_{x \to 2^+} f(x) = \lim_{x \to 2} \frac{x^3 + x^2 - 16x + 20}{(x-2)^2}$$

$$= \lim_{x \to 2} \frac{(x+5)(x-2)^2}{(x-2)^2} = \lim_{x \to 2} (x+5) = 7$$

As f is continuous at $x = 2$, we have

$$\lim_{x \to 2} f(x) = f(2)$$

$\Rightarrow$ $k = 7.$

27. (b) $(-\infty, \infty) - \{2\}$

Explanation: Since, $| x - 2 |$ is not differentiable at $x = 2$, therefore $f(x) = | x - 2 | \cos x$ is not differentiable at $x = 2$. Hence, $f(x)$ is differentiable in $(-\infty, \infty) - \{2\}$.

28. (a) $4A - 3I$

Explanation: We have,

$$A^2 = \begin{bmatrix} 2 & -1 \\ -1 & 2 \end{bmatrix} \begin{bmatrix} 2 & -1 \\ -1 & 2 \end{bmatrix}$$

$$= \begin{bmatrix} 4+1 & -2-2 \\ -2-2 & 1+4 \end{bmatrix} = \begin{bmatrix} 5 & -4 \\ -4 & 5 \end{bmatrix}$$

Now,

$$4A - 3I = \begin{bmatrix} 2 & -1 \\ -1 & 2 \end{bmatrix} - \begin{bmatrix} 3 & 0 \\ 0 & 3 \end{bmatrix}$$

$$= \begin{bmatrix} 5 & -4 \\ -4 & 5 \end{bmatrix} = A^2$$

29. (a) $4a$

Explanation: We have, $y = ax^2 + b \Rightarrow \dfrac{dy}{dx} = 2ax$

$$\left[\dfrac{dy}{dx}\right]_{x=2} = 2a \times 2 = 4a$$

30. (c) Given by corner points of the feasible region

Explanation: The optimal value of the objective function is attained at the points given by corner points of the feasible region.

31. (b) $\dfrac{1}{4\sqrt{x}}(\sec\sqrt{x})^{3/2}.\sin\sqrt{x}$

Explanation: Let $y = \sqrt{\sec\sqrt{x}}$

Differentiating w.r.t. x, we get

$$\dfrac{dy}{dx} = \dfrac{1}{2\sqrt{\sec\sqrt{x}}}.\sec\sqrt{x}.\tan\sqrt{x}.\dfrac{1}{2\sqrt{x}}$$

$$= \dfrac{1}{4\sqrt{x}}(\sec\sqrt{x})^{1/2}\dfrac{\sin\sqrt{x}}{\cos\sqrt{x}} = \dfrac{1}{4\sqrt{x}}(\sec\sqrt{x})^{3/2}.\sin\sqrt{x}$$

32. (b) $(I - A)^{-1}$

Explanation: $\qquad\qquad I - A^3 = I$

$\Rightarrow \qquad\qquad (I - A)(I + A + A^2) = I$

$\therefore \qquad\qquad I + A + A^2 = (I - A)^{-1}$

33. (c) $\dfrac{1}{2\sqrt{1-x^2}}$

Explanation: Let $y = \tan^{-1}\left(\dfrac{\sqrt{1+x}-\sqrt{1-x}}{\sqrt{1+x}+\sqrt{1-x}}\right)$

Put $x = \cos 2\theta \Rightarrow \theta = \dfrac{1}{2}\cos^{-1}x$

$\therefore \qquad y = \tan^{-1}\left(\dfrac{\sqrt{1+\cos 2\theta}-\sqrt{1-\cos 2\theta}}{\sqrt{1+\cos 2\theta}+\sqrt{1-\cos 2\theta}}\right)$

$\Rightarrow \qquad y = \tan^{-1}\left(\dfrac{\cos\theta-\sin\theta}{\cos\theta+\sin\theta}\right)$

$\Rightarrow \qquad y = \tan^{-1}\left(\dfrac{1-\tan\theta}{1+\tan\theta}\right)$

$\Rightarrow \qquad y = \tan^{-1}\left(\tan\left(\dfrac{\pi}{4}-\theta\right)\right)$

$\Rightarrow \qquad y = \dfrac{\pi}{4}-\theta \Rightarrow y = \dfrac{\pi}{4}-\dfrac{1}{2}\cos^{-1}x$

Differentiatng w.r.t. x, we get

$$\frac{dy}{dx} = -\frac{1}{2}\left(\frac{-1}{\sqrt{1-x^2}}\right) = \frac{1}{2\sqrt{1-x^2}}$$

34. (c) $4e^{2x^2}(4x^2+1)$

Explanation: Given that, $y = e^{2x^2}$

$$\frac{dy}{dx} = e^{2x^2}.4x$$

By using $u \times v$ rule, we get $\dfrac{d^2y}{dx^2} = \dfrac{d}{dx}(e^{2x^2}).4x + \dfrac{d}{dx}(4x).e^{2x^2} = 16x^2e^{2x^2} + 4e^{2x^2} = 4e^{2x^2}(4x^2+1)$

35. (d)   Unbounded solutions

Explanation: If the value of the objective function Z of a LPP can be increased or decreased indefinitely such solutions are called unbounded solutions.

36. (a)   1

Explanation: $\begin{vmatrix} x & x+1 \\ x-1 & x \end{vmatrix} = x^2 - (x^2-1) = x^2 - x^2 + 1 = 1$

37. (c) $x + y = 0$

Explanation: $\dfrac{dy}{dx} = \cos x$. Therefore, slope of nromal $= \left(\dfrac{-1}{\cos x}\right)_{x=0} = -1$

Hence, the equation of normal is $y - 0 = -1(x-0)$ or $x + y = 0$.

38. (d) $\dfrac{40}{7}$

Explanation: The given points are collinear.

$\therefore$ $\dfrac{1}{2}\begin{vmatrix} 2 & -3 & 1 \\ k & -1 & 1 \\ 0 & 4 & 1 \end{vmatrix} = 0$

Applying $R_2 \to R_2 - R_1$ and $R_3 \to R_3 - R_1$, we get

$\begin{vmatrix} 2 & -3 & 1 \\ k-2 & 2 & 0 \\ -2 & 7 & 0 \end{vmatrix} = 0$

Expanding along C_3, we get

$$(k-2)7 + 4 = 0$$

$\Rightarrow$ $k = \dfrac{10}{7}$

$\therefore$ $4k = \dfrac{40}{7}$

39. (a) $2x + y - 3\sqrt{3} = 0$

Explanation: On putting $y = x$ in $y = \sqrt{9 - 2x^2}$, we get

$$x = \sqrt{9 - 2x^2} \Rightarrow x^2 = 9 - 2x^2$$

$$\Rightarrow \qquad x = \sqrt{3}, -\sqrt{3}$$

Since, $y > 0$, therefore the point is $(\sqrt{3}, \sqrt{3})$

Now, we have, $\qquad y^2 = 9 - 2x^2$

On differentiating w.r.t. x, we get

$$2y\frac{dy}{dx} = -4x \Rightarrow \frac{dy}{dx} = -\frac{2x}{y}$$

$$\therefore \qquad \left[\frac{dy}{dx}\right]_{(\sqrt{3}, \sqrt{3})} = -\frac{2\sqrt{3}}{\sqrt{3}} = -2$$

So, the equation of tangent at $(\sqrt{3}, \sqrt{3})$ is

$$(y - \sqrt{3}) = -2(x - \sqrt{3}) \Rightarrow 2x + y - 3\sqrt{3} = 0$$

40. (b) $|A| = |A'|$

Explanation: $|A| = |A'|$ for all square matrix A

Section - C

41. (c) $1 - \alpha^2 - \beta\gamma = 0$

Explanation: Given, $\qquad A^2 = I$

$\therefore \qquad AA = I$

$$\Rightarrow \quad \begin{bmatrix} \alpha & \beta \\ \gamma & -\alpha \end{bmatrix}\begin{bmatrix} \alpha & \beta \\ \gamma & -\alpha \end{bmatrix} = \begin{bmatrix} 1 & 0 \\ 0 & 1 \end{bmatrix} \Rightarrow \begin{bmatrix} \alpha^2 + \beta\gamma & \alpha\beta - \alpha\beta \\ \alpha\gamma - \gamma\alpha & \gamma\beta + \alpha^2 \end{bmatrix} = \begin{bmatrix} 1 & 0 \\ 0 & 1 \end{bmatrix}$$

On comparing the corresponding elements, we have

$$\alpha^2 + \beta\gamma = 1 \Rightarrow \alpha^2 + \beta\gamma - 1 = 0$$

$$\Rightarrow \qquad 1 - \alpha^2 - \beta\gamma = 0$$

42. (c) (2, 0)

Explanation: Graph of inequality $x + y \le 2$, $x, y \ge 0$ is shown in the figure.

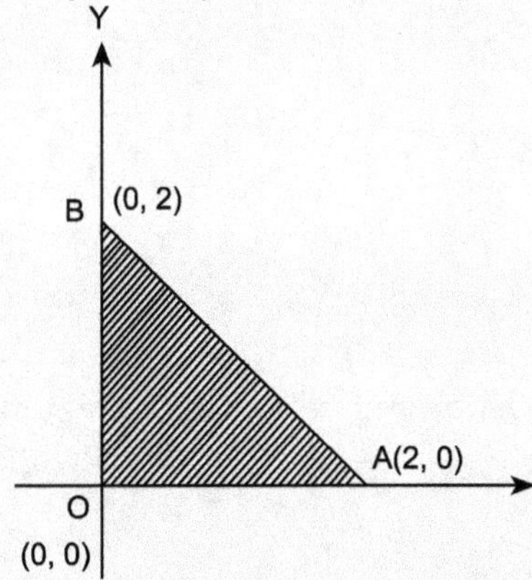

The corner points are O(0, 0), A(2, 0) and B(0, 2).

Here, the objective function is $Z = 3x + 2y$ and at (0, 0), (2, 0) and (0, 2), its values are 0, 6 and 4.

So, requried point is (2, 0) at which maximum value is attained.

43. (c) 1, 2

Explanation: We have,
$$y = \frac{ax}{b-x}$$

$$\Rightarrow \qquad \frac{dy}{dx} = \frac{(b-x)a - ax \cdot (-1)}{(b-x)^2} = \frac{ab}{(b-x)^2}$$

$$\therefore \qquad \left[\frac{dy}{dx}\right]_{(1,1)} = \frac{ab}{(b-1)^2} = 2 \text{ [given]} \qquad \qquad \text{...(i)}$$

Since, the curve passes through the point (1, 1), therefore

$$1 = \frac{a}{b-1} \Rightarrow a = b - 1 \qquad \qquad \text{...(ii)}$$

On putting $a = b - 1$ in eq. (i), we get

$$\frac{(b-1)b}{(b-1)^2} = 2 \Rightarrow b = 2 \text{ and } b \neq 1$$

$$\therefore \qquad a = 2 - 1 = 1$$

Hence, $\qquad a = 1, b = 2$

44. (a) e

Explanation: Let
$$f(x) = \frac{x}{\log x}$$

$$\Rightarrow \qquad f'(x) = \frac{\log x - 1}{(\log x)^2}$$

For maximum or minimum, $f'(x) = 0$

$$\Rightarrow \qquad \log x = 1 \Rightarrow x = e$$

Now, $\qquad f''(x) = \dfrac{\dfrac{1}{x} \cdot (\log x)^2 - (\log x - 1) \cdot \dfrac{2\log x}{x}}{(\log x)^4}$

$$\Rightarrow \qquad f''(x)_{x=e} = \frac{\dfrac{1}{e} - 0}{1} = \frac{1}{e} > 0$$

So, $f(x)$ is minimum at $x = e$.

$\therefore$ Minimum value of $f(x) = f(e) = \dfrac{e}{1} = e$.

45. (c) 4

Explanation: If x tables and y chairs are purchased for maximum profit.

Then, $x + y \leq 60$, $5x + \dfrac{6y}{5} \leq 100$, $x \geq 0$, $y \geq 0$.

So, number of constraints are four.

46. (c) $y = 4000 - 2x$

Explanation: Given,
$$x = \text{length}$$
$$y = \text{breadth of the plot}$$
$$\text{Total length of fencing} = 4000 \text{ m}$$
$$2x + y = 4000$$
$$y = 4000 - 2x$$

47. (a) $A = x(4000 - 2x)$

Explanation:
$$A = l \times b = xy$$
$$A = x(4000 - 2x) = 4000x - 2x^2$$

48. (c) 1000

Explanation:
$$\frac{dA}{dx} = 4000 - 4x$$

Put
$$\frac{dA}{dx} = 0$$
$$4000 - 4x = 0$$
$$4000 = 4x$$
$$x = 1000$$

49. (b) 2 km^2

Explanation:
$$\frac{d^2A}{dx^2} = -4 < 0$$

$\therefore$ Area is maximum at $x = 1000$ m
$$y = 4000 - 2 \times 1000 = 2000 \text{ m}$$
$$\text{Maximum Area } A = 1000(2000) = 2000000 \text{ m}^2 = 2 \text{ km}^2 \quad [\because 1 \text{ km} = 1000 \text{ m}]$$

50. (b) $2 \text{ km} \times 1 \text{ km}$

Explanation: Dimensions of floor = 2000 m × 1000 m or 2 km × 1 km.

Sample Paper 7

Section - A

1. (a) $\dfrac{\pi}{8}$

Explanation:
$$\tan^{-1}\left(\tan\frac{9\pi}{8}\right) = \tan^{-1}\left[\tan\left(\pi + \frac{\pi}{8}\right)\right] \qquad \left[\because \frac{\pi}{8} \in \left(\frac{-\pi}{2}, \frac{\pi}{2}\right)\right]$$
$$= \tan^{-1}\left(\tan\frac{\pi}{8}\right) = \frac{\pi}{8}$$

2. (c) $\begin{bmatrix} 1 & 0 \\ 9 & 4 \end{bmatrix}$

Explanation: Let A be a matrix of order 2×2.

$$A = [a_{ij}]_{2 \times 2} = \begin{bmatrix} a_{11} & a_{12} \\ a_{21} & a_{22} \end{bmatrix}$$

Given, $a_{ij} = (2i - j)^2$

For 2×2 order matrix,

$$i = 1, 2 \text{ and } j = 1, 2$$

$\therefore$
$$a_{11} = [2(1) - 1]^2 = 1, \ a_{12} = [2(1) - 2]^2 = 0$$
$$a_{21} = [2(2) - 1]^2 = 9, \ a_{22} = [2(2) - 2]^2 = 4$$

$\Rightarrow$
$$A = \begin{bmatrix} 1 & 0 \\ 9 & 4 \end{bmatrix}$$

3. (b) $\dfrac{3}{4t}$

Explanation: Here,
$$x = t^2$$
$$\frac{dx}{dt} = 2t \qquad \qquad \text{...(i)}$$

and
$$y = t^3$$

$\therefore$
$$\frac{dy}{dt} = 3t^2$$

$$\frac{dy}{dx} = \frac{3t^2}{2t} = \frac{3}{2}t$$

$$\frac{d^2y}{dx^2} = \frac{3}{2}\frac{dt}{dx} = \frac{3}{2} \times \frac{1}{2t} \qquad \qquad \text{(from (i))}$$

$$= \frac{3}{4t}$$

4. (b) 3

Explanation: $\because$
$$\begin{bmatrix} 2x + y & 3y \\ 0 & 4 \end{bmatrix} = \begin{bmatrix} 6 & 0 \\ 0 & 4 \end{bmatrix}$$

$\therefore$
$$2x + y = 6 \text{ and } 3y = 0$$
$$y = 0$$

$\Rightarrow$
$$2x = 6$$

$\Rightarrow$
$$x = 3$$

5. (a) 1

Explanation: Let
$$u = \sin^{-1} x$$
$$\frac{du}{dx} = \frac{1}{\sqrt{1 - x^2}}$$

and
$$v = \cos^{-1}\sqrt{1-x^2}$$

$$\frac{dv}{dx} = \frac{2}{\sqrt{1-(\sqrt{1-x^2})^2}} = \frac{x}{\sqrt{1-x^2}} \times \frac{1}{\sqrt{x^2}} = \frac{1}{\sqrt{1-x^2}}$$

$$\therefore \quad \frac{du}{dv} = 1$$

6. (c) $[0, 1]$

Explanation: Given, $\cos^{-1}(2x-1)$

$\Rightarrow \qquad -1 \le 2x - 1 \le 1 \qquad\qquad [\because x \in [-1, 1]$

$\Rightarrow \qquad -1 + 1 \le 2x \le 1 + 1$

$\Rightarrow \qquad 0 \le 2x \le 2 \Rightarrow 0 \le x \le 1$

Hence, $x \in [0, 1]$.

7. (b) $\dfrac{1}{K} A^{-1}$

Explanation: $(K.A)^{-1} = \dfrac{1}{K} A^{-1}$

8. (a) -62

Explanation: $\begin{vmatrix} -8 & 6 \\ 5 & 4 \end{vmatrix} = -8 \times 4 - 5 \times 6 = -32 - 30 = -62$

9. (b) $\dfrac{2}{1+4x^2}$

Explanation: Let $t = 2x,\ y = \tan^{-1} t$

$\therefore \qquad \dfrac{dy}{dx} = \dfrac{dy}{dt} \times \dfrac{dt}{dx} \qquad\qquad \text{...(i)}$

Here, $\qquad \dfrac{dy}{dt} = \dfrac{1}{1+t^2}$ and $\dfrac{dt}{dx} = 2$

$$\dfrac{dy}{dx} = \dfrac{1}{1+4x^2} \times 2 \ \ i.e.,\ \ \dfrac{2}{1+4x^2}$$

10. (c) $-\dfrac{1}{2}$

Explanation: $f\left(\dfrac{\pi}{4}\right) = \lim\limits_{x \to \frac{\pi}{4}} \dfrac{1-\tan x}{4x - \pi} \qquad \left(\dfrac{0}{0}\ \text{form}\right)$

Using L' Hospital Rule we get

$$\lim\limits_{x \to \frac{\pi}{4}} \dfrac{-\sec^2 x}{4} = -\dfrac{1}{2}$$

11. (c) 9

> **Explanation:** Given, A is a matrix of order 3×3
> $\therefore$ Number of minors in determinant of A $= 3 \times 3 = 9$.

12. (a) $2x \sec (x^2 + 2) \tan (x^2 + 2)$

> **Explanation:** Given, $\qquad y = \sec (x^2 + 2)$
> On differentiating w.r.t x we get
> $$\frac{dy}{dx} = \sec (x^2 + 2) \tan (x^2 + 2) \frac{d}{dx} (x^2 + 2)$$
> $$= 2x \sec (x^2 + 2) \tan (x^2 + 2)$$

13. (c) 1

> **Explanation:** $\quad \sin\left[\dfrac{\pi}{3} - \sin^{-1}\left(\dfrac{-1}{2}\right)\right] = \sin\left[\dfrac{\pi}{3} + \sin^{-1}\left(\dfrac{1}{2}\right)\right]$ $\qquad [\because \sin^{-1}(-x) = -\sin^{-1}x]$
> $$= \sin\left[\dfrac{\pi}{3} + \dfrac{\pi}{6}\right] = \sin\left(\dfrac{\pi}{2}\right) = 1$$

14. (b) 120

> **Explanation:** Let, $\qquad\qquad f(x) = x^4 - 62x^2 + ax + 9$
> On differentiating w.r.t x, we get
> $$f(x) = 4x^3 - 124x + a$$
> Since, it is given that $f(x)$ is maximum at $x = 1$
> $\therefore \qquad\qquad\qquad\qquad f'(1) = 0$
> $\Rightarrow \qquad\qquad 4(1)^3 - 124\,(1) + a = 0$
> $\Rightarrow \qquad\qquad\qquad 4 - 124 + a = 0$
> $\Rightarrow \qquad\qquad\qquad\qquad a = 120$

15. (a) $\dfrac{\sqrt{1-x^2}}{x}$

> **Explanation:** Let $\qquad\qquad \sin^{-1} x = \theta,$
> then $\qquad\qquad\qquad\qquad \sin \theta = x$
> $\Rightarrow \qquad\qquad \operatorname{cosec} \theta = \dfrac{1}{x} \Rightarrow \operatorname{cosec}^2 \theta = \dfrac{1}{x^2}$
> $\Rightarrow \qquad\qquad\qquad 1 + \cot^2 \theta = \dfrac{1}{x^2}$
> $\Rightarrow \qquad\qquad\qquad\qquad \cot^2 \theta = \dfrac{1}{x^2} - 1$
> $\Rightarrow \qquad\qquad\qquad\qquad \cot \theta = \dfrac{\sqrt{1-x^2}}{x}$
> $\Rightarrow \qquad\qquad \cot (\sin^{-1} x) = \dfrac{\sqrt{1-x^2}}{x}$

16. (c) $\dfrac{1}{\sqrt{2}}$

> **Explanation:** When $\dfrac{\pi}{2} < x < \pi$, $\cos x < 0$ so that $|\cos x| = -\cos x$
>
> *i.e.,* $$f(x) = -\cos x \Rightarrow f'(x) = \sin x$$
>
> Hence, $$f'\left(\dfrac{3\pi}{4}\right) = \sin\left(\dfrac{3\pi}{4}\right) = \dfrac{1}{\sqrt{2}}$$

17. (a) 0

> **Explanation:** $\tan^{-1}\left(\tan\dfrac{5\pi}{6}\right) + \cos^{-1}\left(\cos\dfrac{13\pi}{6}\right) = \tan^{-1}\left(\tan\left(\pi - \dfrac{\pi}{6}\right)\right) + \cos^{-1}\left(\cos\left(2\pi + \dfrac{\pi}{6}\right)\right)$
>
> $$= \tan^{-1}\left(-\tan\dfrac{\pi}{6}\right) + \cos^{-1}\left(\cos\dfrac{\pi}{6}\right)$$
>
> $$= \tan^{-1}\left(\tan\left(-\dfrac{\pi}{6}\right)\right) + \dfrac{\pi}{6}$$
>
> $$= -\dfrac{\pi}{6} + \dfrac{\pi}{6} = 0$$

18. (b) $R - \left\{\dfrac{1}{2}\right\}$

> **Explanation:**
> $$f(x) = |\,2x - 1\,|\sin x$$
> $$f(x) = \begin{cases} -(2x-1)\sin x, & x < 1/2 \\ (2x-1)\sin x, & x \geq 1/2 \end{cases}$$
>
> $$Lf'\left(\dfrac{1}{2}\right) = \lim_{h \to 0^-} \dfrac{f(1/2 + h) - f(1/2)}{h}$$
>
> $$= \lim_{h \to 0^-} \dfrac{-[2(1/2 + h) - 1]\sin(1/2 + h) - 0}{h}$$
>
> $$= \lim_{h \to 0^-} \dfrac{-2h\sin(1/2 + h)}{h} = -2\sin(1/2)$$
>
> $$Rf'(1/2) = \lim_{h \to 0^+} \dfrac{f(1/2 + h) - f(1/2)}{h}$$
>
> $$= \lim_{h \to 0^+} \dfrac{[2(1/2 + h) - 1]\sin(1/2 + h) - 0}{h}$$
>
> $$= \lim_{h \to 0^+} \dfrac{2h\sin(1/2 + h)}{h} = 2\sin(1/2)$$
>
> $$Lf'(1/2) \neq Rf'(1/2)$$
> So, $f(x)$ is not differentiable at $x = 1/2$
>
> Hence $f(x)$ is differentiable $\forall\, x \in R - \left\{\dfrac{1}{2}\right\}$

19. (d) f is not defined

> **Explanation:** Since, $\dfrac{1}{x}$ is not defined for $x = 0$
>
> $\therefore f : R \to R$ cannot be defined.

20. (c) 6

> **Explanation:** $\cos^{-1}\alpha + \cos^{-1}\beta + \cos^{-1}\gamma = 3\pi$
>
> $\because \qquad\qquad 0 \le \cos^{-1} x \le \pi$
>
> $\Rightarrow \qquad\qquad \cos^{-1}\alpha = \cos^{-1}\beta$
>
> $\qquad\qquad\qquad = \cos^{-1}\gamma = \pi$
>
> $\Rightarrow \qquad\qquad \alpha = \beta = \gamma = -1$
>
> $\therefore \quad \alpha(\beta+\gamma) + \beta(\gamma+\alpha) + \gamma(\alpha+\beta) = -1(-1-1) + (-1)(-1-1) + (-1)(-1-1)$
>
> $\qquad\qquad\qquad\qquad = 2 + 2 + 2$
>
> $\qquad\qquad\qquad\qquad = 6$

21. (b) Symmetric matrix

> **Explanation:**
> $$A = \begin{bmatrix} 1 & 0 & 0 \\ 0 & 2 & 0 \\ 0 & 0 & 0 \end{bmatrix}$$
>
> $\Rightarrow$
> $$A^{T} = \begin{bmatrix} 1 & 0 & 0 \\ 0 & 2 & 0 \\ 0 & 0 & 0 \end{bmatrix} = A$$
>
> $\therefore$ A is a symmetric matrix.

22. (c) $(106)!$

> **Explanation:** The toal number of bijections from a set containing n elements to itself is $n!$
>
> Hence, required number $= (106)!$

23. (b) 2

> **Explanation:**
> $$\lim_{x \to 0} f(x) = \lim_{x \to 0}\left(\frac{\sin x}{x} + \cos x\right)$$
>
> $$= \lim_{x \to 0}\left(\frac{\sin x}{x}\right) + \lim_{x \to 0}\cos x$$
>
> $$= 1 + 1$$
>
> $$= 2$$
>
> It is given that, $f(x)$ is continuous at $x = 0$
>
> $\therefore \qquad\qquad \lim_{x \to 0} f(x) = f(0)$
>
> $\Rightarrow \qquad\qquad k = 2$

24. (d) any point on the line segment joining the points (0, 2) and (3, 0)

Explanation: Construct the following table of values of objective function:

Corner Points	Value of Z = 4x + 3y
(0, 0)	4 × 0 + 6 × 2 = 12
(3, 0)	4 × 3 + 6 × 0 = 12
(6, 0)	4 × 6 + 6 × 0 = 24
(6, 8)	4 × 6 + 6 × 8 = 72
(0, 5)	4 × 0 + 6 × 5 = 30

$\}$ ← Minimum (for (0,0) and (3,0))

← Maximum (for (6, 8))

Since the minimum value (F) = 12 occurs at two distinct corner points, it occurs at every point of the segment joining these two points.

25. (c) 1

Explanation: It is given that the function f is continuous at $x = 0$.

$$\therefore \quad \lim_{x \to 0} f(x) = f(0)$$

$$\Rightarrow \quad \lim_{x \to 0} \frac{1 - \cos 4x}{8x^2} = k \qquad [\because \cos 4\theta = 1 - 2\sin^2 2\theta]$$

$$\Rightarrow \quad \lim_{x \to 0} \frac{2\sin^2 2x}{8x^2} = k$$

$$\Rightarrow \quad \lim_{x \to 0} \left(\frac{\sin 2x}{2x}\right)^2 = k$$

$$\Rightarrow \quad k = (1)^2 \qquad \left[\because \lim_{\theta \to 0} \frac{\sin \theta}{\theta} = 1\right]$$

Hence, $k = 1$

26. (b) 2, 3

Explanation:
$$\begin{bmatrix} 2x + y & 4x \\ 5x - 7 & 4x \end{bmatrix} = \begin{bmatrix} 7 & 7y - 13 \\ y & x + 6 \end{bmatrix}$$

On comparing, we get

$$4x = x + 6$$

$$\Rightarrow \quad x = 2 \text{ and } 2x + y = 7$$

$$\Rightarrow \quad y = 7 - 4 = 3$$

27. (c) I + 15A

Explanation: Here,
$$(I + A)^4 = (I + A)^2 (I + A)^2$$
$$= (I + IA + AI + A^2)^2$$
$$= (I + 2A + A^2)^2 = (I + 2A + A)^2 = (I + 3A)^2$$
$$= I + 3IA + 3AI + 9A^2 = I + 6A + 9A$$
$$= I + 15A$$

28. (a) Corresponding elements

Explanation: Two matrices of same order are said to be equal if the corresponding elements of the two matrices are equal.

29. (c) which are corner points of the feasible region

Explanation: When we solve an LPP graphically, the optimal (or optimum) value of the objective function is attained at corner points of the feasible region.

30. (d) 3×3

Explanation: When a 3×2 matrix is post multiplied by a 2×3 matrix, the product is a 3×3 matrix.

31. (b) $-\cosec^2 (x + y)$

Explanation: Given $\qquad\qquad y = \tan (x + y)$
Differentiating both sides w.r.t. x, we get

$$\frac{dy}{dx} = \sec^2 (x+y) \, \frac{d}{dx}(x+y) = \sec^2 (x+y) \left(1 + \frac{dy}{dx}\right)$$

or $\qquad\qquad [1 - \sec^2 (x+y)]\frac{dy}{dx} = \sec^2 (x+y)$

Therefore, $\qquad\qquad \frac{dy}{dx} = \frac{\sec^2 (x+y)}{1 - \sec^2 (x+y)} = -\cosec^2 (x+y).$

32. (c) $\dfrac{\pi}{3}$

Explanation: Let ABC be a right angled triangle in which side
$\qquad\qquad$ BC $= x$ (say) and hypotenuse AC $= y$ $\qquad\qquad$ (say)
Given, $\qquad\qquad x + y = k$ $\qquad\qquad$ (constant)
$\Rightarrow \qquad\qquad y = k - x$

Now, the area of $\triangle$ABC is given by

$$A = \frac{1}{2} \cdot BC \cdot AB = \frac{1}{2} x \sqrt{(y^2 - x^2)}$$

$$= \frac{1}{2} x \sqrt{[(k-x)^2 - x^2]}$$

Let $\qquad\qquad u = A^2 = \frac{1}{4} x^2 (k^2 - 2kx)$

$\Rightarrow \qquad\qquad \dfrac{du}{dx} = \dfrac{1}{2} k(kx - 3x^2)$ and $\dfrac{d^2u}{dx^2} = \dfrac{1}{2} k(k - 6x)$

For maximum or minimum of u, put $\dfrac{du}{dx} = 0$.

$$\Rightarrow \qquad x = \dfrac{k}{3} \qquad\qquad [\because x \neq 0]$$

When $\qquad x = \dfrac{k}{3}, \dfrac{d^2u}{dx^2} = \dfrac{1}{2}k\left(k - 6 \times \dfrac{1}{3}k\right) = -\dfrac{1}{2}k^2 \ (\text{-ve})$

$\Rightarrow u$, i.e., A is maximum when $x = \dfrac{k}{3}$

and when $\qquad y = k - x = \dfrac{2k}{3}$

Now, $\qquad \cos\theta = \dfrac{BC}{AC} = \dfrac{x}{y} = \dfrac{1}{2} \Rightarrow \theta = \dfrac{\pi}{3}$

Hence, the requried angle is $\dfrac{\pi}{3}$.

33. (d) All of the above

Explanation: The graphical method of LP problem uses objective function equations, constraint equations and linear equations.

34. (c) $\operatorname{cosec}^2 (\cos^{-1} x)/\sqrt{1-x^2}$

Explanation: Let $\qquad y = \cot(\cos^{-1} x)$

Differentiate both sides w.r.t. x,

$$\dfrac{dy}{dx} = -\operatorname{cosec}^2(\cos^{-1} x)\, \dfrac{d}{dx}(\cos^{-1} x)$$

$$= -\operatorname{cosec}^2(\cos^{-1} x) \times \dfrac{-1}{\sqrt{1-x^2}}$$

$$= \dfrac{\operatorname{cosec}^2(\cos^{-1} x)}{\sqrt{1-x^2}}$$

35. (a) $\begin{bmatrix} 4 & 3 \\ -3 & 0 \\ -1 & -2 \end{bmatrix}$

Explanation: $\qquad B^T = \begin{bmatrix} -1 & 1 \\ 2 & 2 \\ 1 & 3 \end{bmatrix}$

So, $\qquad A^T - B^T = \begin{bmatrix} 3 & 4 \\ -1 & 2 \\ 0 & 1 \end{bmatrix} - \begin{bmatrix} -1 & 1 \\ 2 & 2 \\ 1 & 3 \end{bmatrix} = \begin{bmatrix} 4 & 3 \\ -3 & 0 \\ -1 & -2 \end{bmatrix}$

36. (a) $a_1 b_2 = a_2 b_1$

Explanation: The given points are collinear.

$\therefore \quad \dfrac{1}{2}\begin{vmatrix} a_1 & b_1 & 1 \\ a_2 & b_2 & 1 \\ a_1 + a_2 & b_1 + b_2 & 1 \end{vmatrix} = 0$

Applying $R_2 \to R_2 - R_1$, $R_3 \to R_3 - R_1$, we get

$\begin{vmatrix} a_1 & b_1 & 1 \\ a_2 - a_1 & b_2 - b_1 & 0 \\ a_2 & b_2 & 0 \end{vmatrix} = 0$

Expanding along C_3, we get

$$b_2(a_2 - a_1) - a_2(b_2 - b_1) = 0 \Rightarrow -a_1 b_2 + a_2 b_1 = 0$$
$$\Rightarrow \qquad a_1 b_2 = a_2 b_1$$

37. (a) f is bijective

Explanation: Let x and y be two arbitary elements in A.

Then, $\qquad\qquad f(x) = f(y)$

$\Rightarrow \qquad\qquad \dfrac{x-2}{x-3} = \dfrac{y-2}{y-3}$

$\Rightarrow \qquad xy - 3x - 2y + 6 = xy - 3y - 2x + 6 \Rightarrow x = y, \ \forall\, x, y \in A$

So, f is an injective mapping.

Again, let y be an arbitrary element in B, then

$$f(x) = y$$

$\Rightarrow \qquad\qquad \dfrac{x-2}{x-3} = y \Rightarrow x = \dfrac{3y-2}{y-1}$

Clearly, $\forall\, y \in B$, $x = \dfrac{3y-2}{y-1} \in A$, thus of all $y \in B$, there exists.

$x \in A$ such that $f(x) = f\left(\dfrac{3y-2}{y-1}\right) = \dfrac{\dfrac{3y-2}{y-1} - 2}{\dfrac{3y-2}{y-1} - 3} = y$

Thus, every element in the co-domain B has its pre-image in A, so f is a surjective. Hence, $f : A \to B$ is bijective.

38. (b) $\begin{bmatrix} 15 & 6 & -15 \\ 0 & -3 & 0 \\ -10 & 0 & 5 \end{bmatrix}$

Explanation: We have, $\qquad A = \begin{bmatrix} 1 & 2 & 3 \\ 0 & 5 & 0 \\ 2 & 4 & 3 \end{bmatrix}$

$\therefore \qquad\qquad \text{adj } A = \begin{bmatrix} 15 & 6 & -15 \\ 0 & -3 & 0 \\ -10 & 0 & 5 \end{bmatrix}$

39. (a) 0

Explanation: Given, curve $y = 2 \cos^2 3x$
Differentiating w.r.t. 'x' on both sides, we get

$$\frac{dy}{dx} = 2 \times 2 \cos 3x \, \frac{d}{dx} \cos 3x = 4 \cos 3x \cdot \{- \sin 3x\} \cdot \frac{d}{dx}(3x)$$

$$= -4 \cos 3x \cdot \sin 3x \cdot (3 \times 1) = -12 \sin 3x \cdot \cos 3x$$

$$= -6(2 \sin 3x \cdot \sin 3x) = -6 \sin 6x$$

Now, slope of tangent to the given curve $= \dfrac{dy}{dx} = -6 \sin 6x$

$\therefore$ At $x = \dfrac{\pi}{6}$, slope of tangent to the given curve

$$= -6 \sin\left(6 \times \frac{\pi}{6}\right) = -6 \sin \pi = -6 \times 0 = 0$$

40. (d) $4x - 2y \geq -3$

Explanation: The shaded region given in the figure is by represented $4x - 2y \geq -3$.

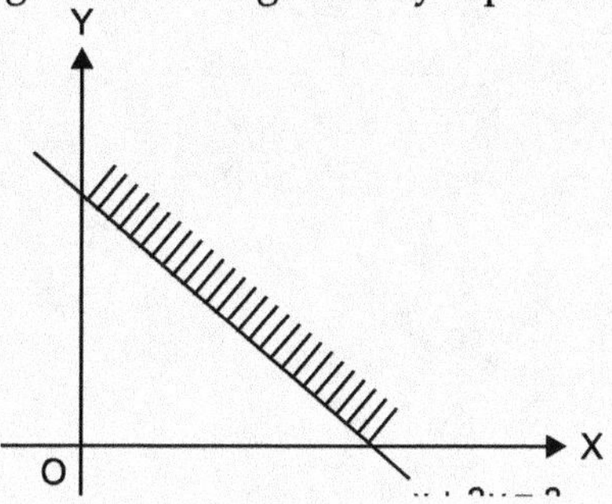

41. (c) $\tan^{-1}\left(\dfrac{3}{4}\right)$

Explanation: Solving the given equations, we have

$$y^2 = x \text{ and } x^2 = y \Rightarrow x^4 = x \text{ or } x^4 - x = 0$$

$\Rightarrow \qquad\qquad x(x^3 - 1) = 0 \Rightarrow x = 0, \, x = 1$

Therefore, $\qquad\qquad y = 0, \, y = 1$

i.e., points of intersection are $(0, 0)$ and $(1, 1)$

Further $\qquad\qquad y^2 = x \Rightarrow 2y\dfrac{dy}{dx} = 1 \Rightarrow \dfrac{dy}{dx} = \dfrac{1}{2y}$

and $\qquad\qquad x^2 = y \Rightarrow \dfrac{dy}{dx} = 2x$

At $(0, 0)$, the slope of the tangent to the curve $y^2 = x$ is parallel to Y-axis and the tangent to the curve $x^2 = y$ is parallel to X-axis.

$\Rightarrow$ Angle of intersection $= \dfrac{\pi}{2}$

At $(1, 1)$, slope of the tangent to the curve $y^2 = x$ is equal to $\dfrac{1}{2}$ and that of $x^2 = y$ is 2.

$$\tan \theta = \left|\frac{2 - \dfrac{1}{2}}{1 + 1}\right| = \frac{3}{4} \Rightarrow \theta = \tan^{-1}\left(\frac{3}{4}\right)$$

42. (c) $x^x (1 + \log x)$

Explanation: We have, $y = e^{x \log x}$
Taking log on both sides,

$$\log y = x \log x \log e = x \log x$$

Differentiating boths sides w.r.t. x, we get

$$\frac{1}{y} \frac{dy}{dx} = x \times \frac{1}{x} + \log x \times 1$$

$$\frac{dy}{dx} = y(1 + \log x) = e^{x \log x}(1 + \log x)$$

$$= e^{\log x^x}(1 + \log x) = x^x(1 + \log x)$$

43. (c) $\left(\dfrac{7}{2}, \dfrac{9}{4}\right)$

Explanation: We have, minimise $Z = 20x_1 + 20x_2$
Subject to $x_1 + 2x_2 \geq 8$, $3x_1 + 2x_2 \geq 15$, $5x_1 + 2x_2 \geq 20$, $x_1, x_2 \geq 0$
Let

$$l_1 : x_1 + 2x_2 = 8$$
$$l_2 : 3x_1 + 2x_2 = 15$$
$$l_3 : 5x_1 + 2x_2 = 20$$
$$l_4 : x_1 = 0 \text{ and } l_5 : x_2 = 0$$

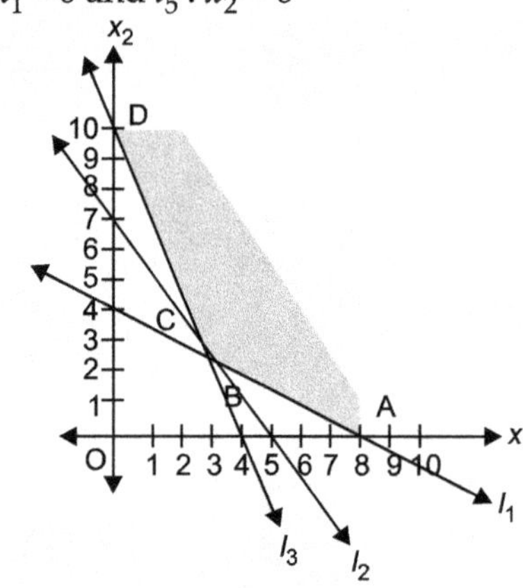

For B : Solving l_1 and l_2, we get $B\left(\dfrac{7}{2}, \dfrac{9}{4}\right)$

For C : Solving l_2 and l_3, we get $C\left(\dfrac{5}{2}, \dfrac{15}{4}\right)$

Shaded portion is the feasible region, where A(8, 0), $B\left(\dfrac{7}{2}, \dfrac{9}{4}\right)$, $C\left(\dfrac{5}{2}, \dfrac{15}{4}\right)$, D(0, 10)

Now   Minimise $Z = 20x_1 + 20x_2$

$$Z \text{ at } A(8, 0) = 20(8) + 20(0) = 160$$

$$Z \text{ at } B\left(\frac{7}{2}, \frac{9}{4}\right) = 20\left(\frac{7}{2}\right) + 20\left(\frac{9}{4}\right) = 115$$

$$Z \text{ at } C\left(\frac{5}{2}, \frac{15}{4}\right) = 20\left(\frac{5}{2}\right) + 20\left(\frac{15}{4}\right) = 125$$

$$Z \text{ at } D(0, 10) = 20(0) + 20(10) = 200$$

Thus, Z is minimised at $B\left(\dfrac{7}{2}, \dfrac{9}{4}\right)$ and its minimum value is 115.

44. (a) -2

> **Explanation:** It is given that A is a singular matrix.
>
> $\therefore$ $\qquad\qquad\qquad |A| = 0$
>
> $\Rightarrow$ $\qquad\qquad \begin{vmatrix} 2(x+1) & 2x \\ x & x-2 \end{vmatrix} = 0$
>
> $\Rightarrow$ $\qquad 2(x+1)(x-2) - 2x^2 = 0$
>
> $\Rightarrow$ $\qquad\quad 2x^2 - 2x - 4 - 2x^2 = 0$
>
> $\Rightarrow$ $\qquad\qquad\qquad 2x + 4 = 0$
>
> $\Rightarrow$ $\qquad\qquad\qquad\quad x = -2$

45. (c) $f(x)$ has maximum at $x = 1$

> **Explanation:** We have, $\qquad f(x) = 2x^3 - 21x^2 + 36x - 30$
>
> $\Rightarrow$ $\qquad f'(x) = 6x^2 - 42x + 36$ and $f''(x) = 12x - 42$
>
> At points of local maximum or minimum, we must have
>
> $\qquad\qquad\qquad\qquad f'(x) = 0$
>
> $\Rightarrow$ $\qquad\qquad 6(x^2 - 7x + 6) = 0$
>
> $\Rightarrow$ $\qquad\qquad\qquad\qquad x = 16$
>
> Clearly, $\qquad\qquad f''(1) = 12 - 42 = -30 < 0$
>
> and $\qquad\qquad\quad f''(6) = 72 - 42 = 30 > 0$
>
> So, $f(x)$ has local maximum at $x = 1$ and local minimum at $x = 6$.

46. (b) $2x + \pi y = 200$

> **Explanation:** $\qquad\qquad$ Perimeter $= 200$ m
>
> $\Rightarrow$ $\qquad\qquad 2x + 2\pi\left(\dfrac{y}{2}\right) = 200$
>
> $\Rightarrow$ $\qquad\qquad\quad 2x + \pi y = 200.$

47. (a) $\dfrac{2}{\pi}(100x - x^2)$

> **Explanation:** $\quad$ Area of rectangular region $= l \times b$
>
> $\Rightarrow$ $\qquad\qquad A = xy = x\left(\dfrac{200 - 2x}{\pi}\right)$ $\qquad\qquad$ [From (i)]
>
> $\therefore$ $\qquad\qquad A = \dfrac{2}{\pi}(100x - x^2)$

48. (c) $\dfrac{5000}{\pi}$ m^2

> **Explanation:** $\qquad\qquad \dfrac{dA}{dx} = \dfrac{2}{\pi}(100 - 2x)$
>
> Put $\qquad\qquad\qquad \dfrac{dA}{dx} = 0$

$$\Rightarrow \qquad x = 50$$

$$\frac{d^2A}{dx^2} = \frac{2}{\pi}(-2) < 0$$

$$\therefore \qquad \text{A is maximum when } x = 50$$

$$\therefore \qquad \text{Maximum area} = \frac{2}{\pi}(5000 - 2500)$$

$$= \frac{5000}{\pi} \text{ m}^2$$

49. (a) 0 m

Explanation:
$$\text{Area of whole floor} = xy + \pi\left(\frac{y}{2}\right)^2$$

$$= \frac{(200 - \pi y)y}{2} + \frac{\pi y^2}{4}$$

$$= 100y - \frac{\pi y^2}{2} + \frac{\pi y^2}{4}$$

$$A_1 = 100y - \frac{\pi y^2}{4}$$

$$\Rightarrow \qquad \frac{dA_1}{dy} = 100 - \frac{2\pi y}{4}$$

$$\Rightarrow \qquad \frac{dA_1}{dy} = 0$$

$$\Rightarrow \qquad 200 = \pi y$$

$$\Rightarrow \qquad y = \frac{200}{\pi}$$

$$\Rightarrow \qquad \frac{d^2A_1}{dy^2} = -\frac{\pi}{2} < 0$$

$$\therefore \; A_1 \text{ is maximum when} \qquad y = \frac{200}{\pi} \text{ and } x = \left[\frac{200 - \pi\left(\dfrac{200}{\pi}\right)}{2}\right] = 0$$

$$\Rightarrow \qquad x = 0.$$

50. (d) No change both areas are equal

Explanation: When the whole area is maximized, there will be no further increase in area.

❑❑

Name of Exam : _________________________

2021-22

OMR Response Sheet

Roll No.

1 ○ ○ ○ ○ ○ ○ ○
2 ○ ○ ○ ○ ○ ○ ○
3 ○ ○ ○ ○ ○ ○ ○
4 ○ ○ ○ ○ ○ ○ ○
5 ○ ○ ○ ○ ○ ○ ○
6 ○ ○ ○ ○ ○ ○ ○
7 ○ ○ ○ ○ ○ ○ ○
8 ○ ○ ○ ○ ○ ○ ○
9 ○ ○ ○ ○ ○ ○ ○
0 ○ ○ ○ ○ ○ ○ ○

Name ____

Class & Section _______________________________

Subject _____________________________________

Subject Code :

Date of Exam : D D M M YYYY

Candidate's Sign.

Invigilator's Sign.

Instructions for filling the OMR sheet :

1. Use only black blue ballpoint pen to fill the circle
2. Use of pencil is strictly prohibited
3. Circle should be designed completely and properly
4. Cutting and erasing on this sheet is not allowed

Q. No.	A	B	C	D
1.	○	○	○	○
2.	○	○	○	○
3.	○	○	○	○
4.	○	○	○	○
5.	○	○	○	○
6.	○	○	○	○
7.	○	○	○	○
8.	○	○	○	○
9.	○	○	○	○
10.	○	○	○	○
11.	○	○	○	○
12.	○	○	○	○
13.	○	○	○	○
14.	○	○	○	○
15.	○	○	○	○
16.	○	○	○	○
17.	○	○	○	○
18.	○	○	○	○
19.	○	○	○	○
20.	○	○	○	○

Q. No.	A	B	C	D
21.	○	○	○	○
22.	○	○	○	○
23.	○	○	○	○
24.	○	○	○	○
25.	○	○	○	○
26.	○	○	○	○
27.	○	○	○	○
28.	○	○	○	○
29.	○	○	○	○
30.	○	○	○	○
31.	○	○	○	○
32.	○	○	○	○
33.	○	○	○	○
34.	○	○	○	○
35.	○	○	○	○
36.	○	○	○	○
37.	○	○	○	○
38.	○	○	○	○
39.	○	○	○	○
40.	○	○	○	○

Q. No.	A	B	C	D
41.	○	○	○	○
42.	○	○	○	○
43.	○	○	○	○
44.	○	○	○	○
45.	○	○	○	○
46.	○	○	○	○
47.	○	○	○	○
48.	○	○	○	○
49.	○	○	○	○
50.	○	○	○	○
51.	○	○	○	○
52.	○	○	○	○
53.	○	○	○	○
54.	○	○	○	○
55.	○	○	○	○
56.	○	○	○	○
57.	○	○	○	○
58.	○	○	○	○
59.	○	○	○	○
60.	○	○	○	○

Name of Exam : ___________________________

2021-22

OMR Response Sheet

Roll No.						

1 ○ ○ ○ ○ ○ ○ ○
2 ○ ○ ○ ○ ○ ○ ○
3 ○ ○ ○ ○ ○ ○ ○
4 ○ ○ ○ ○ ○ ○ ○
5 ○ ○ ○ ○ ○ ○ ○
6 ○ ○ ○ ○ ○ ○ ○
7 ○ ○ ○ ○ ○ ○ ○
8 ○ ○ ○ ○ ○ ○ ○
9 ○ ○ ○ ○ ○ ○ ○
0 ○ ○ ○ ○ ○ ○ ○

Name ____

Class & Section _______________________________________

Subject ____

Subject Code : ☐ ☐ ☐

Date of Exam : D D M M   YYYY
☐☐ / ☐☐ / ☐☐ ☐☐

Candidate's Sign.

Invigilator's Sign.

Instructions for filling the OMR sheet :

1. Use only black blue ballpoint pen to fill the circle
2. Use of pencil is strictly prohibited
3. Circle should be designed completely and properly
4. Cutting and erasing on this sheet is not allowed

Q. No.	A	B	C	D
1.	○	○	○	○
2.	○	○	○	○
3.	○	○	○	○
4.	○	○	○	○
5.	○	○	○	○
6.	○	○	○	○
7.	○	○	○	○
8.	○	○	○	○
9.	○	○	○	○
10.	○	○	○	○
11.	○	○	○	○
12.	○	○	○	○
13.	○	○	○	○
14.	○	○	○	○
15.	○	○	○	○
16.	○	○	○	○
17.	○	○	○	○
18.	○	○	○	○
19.	○	○	○	○
20.	○	○	○	○

Q. No.	A	B	C	D
21.	○	○	○	○
22.	○	○	○	○
23.	○	○	○	○
24.	○	○	○	○
25.	○	○	○	○
26.	○	○	○	○
27.	○	○	○	○
28.	○	○	○	○
29.	○	○	○	○
30.	○	○	○	○
31.	○	○	○	○
32.	○	○	○	○
33.	○	○	○	○
34.	○	○	○	○
35.	○	○	○	○
36.	○	○	○	○
37.	○	○	○	○
38.	○	○	○	○
39.	○	○	○	○
40.	○	○	○	○

Q. No.	A	B	C	D
41.	○	○	○	○
42.	○	○	○	○
43.	○	○	○	○
44.	○	○	○	○
45.	○	○	○	○
46.	○	○	○	○
47.	○	○	○	○
48.	○	○	○	○
49.	○	○	○	○
50.	○	○	○	○
51.	○	○	○	○
52.	○	○	○	○
53.	○	○	○	○
54.	○	○	○	○
55.	○	○	○	○
56.	○	○	○	○
57.	○	○	○	○
58.	○	○	○	○
59.	○	○	○	○
60.	○	○	○	○

Name of Exam : _______________________

2021-22

OMR Response Sheet

Roll No.

1 ○ ○ ○ ○ ○ ○ ○
2 ○ ○ ○ ○ ○ ○ ○
3 ○ ○ ○ ○ ○ ○ ○
4 ○ ○ ○ ○ ○ ○ ○
5 ○ ○ ○ ○ ○ ○ ○
6 ○ ○ ○ ○ ○ ○ ○
7 ○ ○ ○ ○ ○ ○ ○
8 ○ ○ ○ ○ ○ ○ ○
9 ○ ○ ○ ○ ○ ○ ○
0 ○ ○ ○ ○ ○ ○ ○

Name _______________________

Class & Section _______________________

Subject _______________________

Subject Code : ☐ ☐ ☐

Date of Exam : D D   M M   YYYY
☐☐ / ☐☐ / ☐☐☐☐

Candidate's Sign.

Invigilator's Sign.

Instructions for filling the OMR sheet :

1. Use only black blue ballpoint pen to fill the circle
2. Use of pencil is strictly prohibited
3. Circle should be designed completely and properly
4. Cutting and erasing on this sheet is not allowed

Q. No.	A	B	C	D
1.	○	○	○	○
2.	○	○	○	○
3.	○	○	○	○
4.	○	○	○	○
5.	○	○	○	○
6.	○	○	○	○
7.	○	○	○	○
8.	○	○	○	○
9.	○	○	○	○
10.	○	○	○	○
11.	○	○	○	○
12.	○	○	○	○
13.	○	○	○	○
14.	○	○	○	○
15.	○	○	○	○
16.	○	○	○	○
17.	○	○	○	○
18.	○	○	○	○
19.	○	○	○	○
20.	○	○	○	○

Q. No.	A	B	C	D
21.	○	○	○	○
22.	○	○	○	○
23.	○	○	○	○
24.	○	○	○	○
25.	○	○	○	○
26.	○	○	○	○
27.	○	○	○	○
28.	○	○	○	○
29.	○	○	○	○
30.	○	○	○	○
31.	○	○	○	○
32.	○	○	○	○
33.	○	○	○	○
34.	○	○	○	○
35.	○	○	○	○
36.	○	○	○	○
37.	○	○	○	○
38.	○	○	○	○
39.	○	○	○	○
40.	○	○	○	○

Q. No.	A	B	C	D
41.	○	○	○	○
42.	○	○	○	○
43.	○	○	○	○
44.	○	○	○	○
45.	○	○	○	○
46.	○	○	○	○
47.	○	○	○	○
48.	○	○	○	○
49.	○	○	○	○
50.	○	○	○	○
51.	○	○	○	○
52.	○	○	○	○
53.	○	○	○	○
54.	○	○	○	○
55.	○	○	○	○
56.	○	○	○	○
57.	○	○	○	○
58.	○	○	○	○
59.	○	○	○	○
60.	○	○	○	○

Name of Exam : ________________________________

2021-22

OMR Response Sheet

Roll No.

1 ○ ○ ○ ○ ○ ○ ○
2 ○ ○ ○ ○ ○ ○ ○
3 ○ ○ ○ ○ ○ ○ ○
4 ○ ○ ○ ○ ○ ○ ○
5 ○ ○ ○ ○ ○ ○ ○
6 ○ ○ ○ ○ ○ ○ ○
7 ○ ○ ○ ○ ○ ○ ○
8 ○ ○ ○ ○ ○ ○ ○
9 ○ ○ ○ ○ ○ ○ ○
0 ○ ○ ○ ○ ○ ○ ○

Name ____

Class & Section ________________________________

Subject ____

Subject Code : ☐ ☐ ☐

Date of Exam :   D D   M M   YYYY

☐☐ / ☐☐ / ☐☐ ☐☐

Candidate's Sign.

Invigilator's Sign.

Instructions for filling the OMR sheet :

1. Use only black blue ballpoint pen to fill the circle
2. Use of pencil is strictly prohibited
3. Circle should be designed completely and properly
4. Cutting and erasing on this sheet is not allowed

Q. No.	A	B	C	D
1.	○	○	○	○
2.	○	○	○	○
3.	○	○	○	○
4.	○	○	○	○
5.	○	○	○	○
6.	○	○	○	○
7.	○	○	○	○
8.	○	○	○	○
9.	○	○	○	○
10.	○	○	○	○
11.	○	○	○	○
12.	○	○	○	○
13.	○	○	○	○
14.	○	○	○	○
15.	○	○	○	○
16.	○	○	○	○
17.	○	○	○	○
18.	○	○	○	○
19.	○	○	○	○
20.	○	○	○	○

Q. No.	A	B	C	D
21.	○	○	○	○
22.	○	○	○	○
23.	○	○	○	○
24.	○	○	○	○
25.	○	○	○	○
26.	○	○	○	○
27.	○	○	○	○
28.	○	○	○	○
29.	○	○	○	○
30.	○	○	○	○
31.	○	○	○	○
32.	○	○	○	○
33.	○	○	○	○
34.	○	○	○	○
35.	○	○	○	○
36.	○	○	○	○
37.	○	○	○	○
38.	○	○	○	○
39.	○	○	○	○
40.	○	○	○	○

Q. No.	A	B	C	D
41.	○	○	○	○
42.	○	○	○	○
43.	○	○	○	○
44.	○	○	○	○
45.	○	○	○	○
46.	○	○	○	○
47.	○	○	○	○
48.	○	○	○	○
49.	○	○	○	○
50.	○	○	○	○
51.	○	○	○	○
52.	○	○	○	○
53.	○	○	○	○
54.	○	○	○	○
55.	○	○	○	○
56.	○	○	○	○
57.	○	○	○	○
58.	○	○	○	○
59.	○	○	○	○
60.	○	○	○	○